Slatehead

New Welsh Rarebyte is the book imprint of New Welsh Review Ltd,
PO Box 170, Aberystwyth, Wales, SY23 1WZ,
www.newwelshreview.com, @newwelshreview,
Facebook.com/newelshreview
© Peter Goulding & New Welsh Review Ltd, 2020
ISBN: 978-1-9161501-3-3

This work is available in ebook format: ISBN: 978-1-9161501-4-0

Editor: Gwen Davies
Design & typesetting: Ingleby Davies Design
Printed in the EU by pulsioprint.com

New Welsh Review Ltd works with the financial support of the
Welsh Books Council

Thanks to the kind support of RS Powell, sponsor of the New
Welsh Writing Awards 2019: Rheidol Prize for Writing with a
Welsh Theme or Setting, and partners in the prize, Curtis Brown,
Literature Wales, Tŷ Newydd Writing Centre and
Gladstone's Library.

Slatehead

The Ascent of Britain's Slate-climbing Scene

Peter Goulding

NEW WELSH WRITING AWARDS 2019:
RHEIDOL PRIZE FOR WRITING WITH A WELSH THEME OR SETTING
WINNER

In memory of
Steve Gaines, Colin Goodey and RP Goulding

Contents

CHAPTER 1

You Are Now Leaving the Future

May 2018, Norfolk to Snowdonia

Why did I fall so hard for climbing on slate? Maybe I thought it liked me. It was letting me move in a beautiful way, it felt good, and we looked good together. I got compliments the first time I went into the quarries – new friends who were hard climbers called me 'nails'.

'So you're a slatehead now then?' someone asked. I didn't know the word, but I thought I was.

Last night I was at the climbing wall, taking it easy, careful not to pop a tendon just before I climb on the real rock. No one could commit to coming to Wales this weekend. Doesn't matter. I'll meet up with Lee and Becky when they come from Sheffield.

I'd have liked to have left hours ago, but it's after nine before I kick my van into life and drive out. All being well, I'll be in Llanberis by half-past two.

I can't do this as often as I like. I've got a son, a house, a partner and a dog. I live in the wrong part of the country for climbing – Norfolk, where sand lies over chalk, dumped by the last melting glacier.

I've got a cheap sports bag with clothes. Nothing special or technical. Just jeans, cotton T-shirts and checked shirts, sling it in the back. On top goes a very expensive climbing rucksack, and a fluorescent yellow duffel bag. My rope, my rack, my climbing shoes – a hundred quid a pop, and pink. I get a new pair every year, and last year's gets relegated to warm-up, all-day, or indoor; their soles soft and worn, sliced by slate's sharp edges.

I drive out, flick the stereo on, listening to music I liked ten years ago. I've got a shopping bag of snacks on the passenger seat. I've tried to be healthy and most of it is dried fruit and nuts, but the plastic packets are a nightmare to open doing sixty westbound. I wouldn't have this problem with a bacon roll.

Past Cambridge is my favourite piece of graffiti. The full side of a small brick building, in the middle of a farmer's field, on the westbound side where the traffic follows the path of the sun. It reads:

> *You Are Now Leaving*
> THE FUTURE

in big bubble letters sprayed to look like chrome. It makes me laugh every time.

* * *

Motorway through Britain's countryside. Past Naseby, the site of the Civil War battle. Cup of coffee at Corley, then through Birmingham's red-brick factory land, railways and car show-rooms. All these cars going past me, doing day-to-day things like taking people to work, going round in circles, to jobs, to earn other people money. I feel like I am the only person really alive, that everyone else is just wasting their days, thoughtless repetition and unintentional life.

Quick piss in a lay-by at Oswestry. I have a walk around to loosen up my back, keep the old injuries from swelling. Then on the road and the first sight of real hills, the switchbacking road into Wales.

Through Betws-y-coed – call it Betsy, and I slip a little 'u' sound before the 's', which is my attempt at proper Welsh pronunciation, though it's not quite right. This is the gateway to Snowdonia. The tourists walk on the High Street, wearing bright mountain jackets spun out of petrol silk. I keep going. Up and out towards Capel Curig, the start of climbing territory.

On the left is Plas y Brenin, an old hotel, now a training centre. I did a few courses there, learned some basics about ropes and building anchors, how not to automatically die by knowing nothing. On the other side of the road are the RAC boulders, good low-grade bouldering with grippy rock and good holds, then a long road past the lake, good for overtaking.

At the head of the lake, below Snowdon, is Pen-y-Gwryd, stone walls and dark green holly trees. It is built on the site of an old roman fort, you can still see the earthworks, from Caesar's chase of the Druids back to Anglesey. Maybe there's been a pub on the spot all that time. From dice and tired women for the legionaries, to today's mountain rescue post and souvenirs of Hillary's Everest expedition.

Then up the steep road up to Pen-y-pass, the carpark for getting up onto Snowdon. There is a youth hostel across the road, called Mallory's after the famous mountaineer. I've seen a picture of him and Siegfried Herford standing against that very wall – black-and-white, both of them looking moody like they belong in an arty band. Herford was killed in the trenches: grenade. Mallory disappeared on Everest in 1924; they found his body a few years ago.

Down the pass, narrow lanes barely wide enough, tight corners. On either side, the mountain crags, Dinas Cromlech, the open book corner with the climbs *Cenotaph Corner, Cemetery Gates* and *Lord of the Flies*. Good climbs; great climbs, even, total classics. There are eight different types of climbable rock in north Wales. I look at them from the road, but I am only curious. I have only really got eyes for climbs on the slate.

Down the road, through Nant Peris, this is the first place I see the quarries. The waste slate scree cascades down the hill, in stepped levels. When it is wet, it is a dark blue purple like a juicy sloe berry. It is dry now – it hasn't rained for days – and so it is a pale fag-ash grey. The pits, sunk into the mountain, dug out roof tiles that got shipped around the world for two hundred years. In 1969, the quarries were closed down, and work stopped. Nothing happened in there, until the eighties, when a load of climbers moved in. All these climbs have stories, and as I've climbed, I've learned some of them; tales of obsessive vertical movement and funny, awful climb names.

Below all the levels, opening onto the lake of Llyn Padarn, is the concreted entry dock to the hydroelectric power station. It tunnels under the quarries and within the mountain, and looks like the floodlit entrance dock of the Death Star. The vibrations from the turbines deep in the hill loosen cracks and fissures in the rock. With big rain storms, whole cliff faces collapse, sloughing off sheets of rock.

Up there amongst the levels and galleries are hundreds of climbs. I've done a handful of them. Not the hardest ones, either; not even close. As soon as I tried it, I loved it: it didn't seem like anything else was worth doing. Part of it was the movement. Deeply satisfying to be stretching up, twisting my body to reach a thin sharp edge, pulling my body weight through half a pad of my fingertips. I liked the fear, not the anxiety of unpaid bills, but deep old fear of death. Then the fear turned to joy when I either made the impossible-looking move or fell, to bounce safely on my rope.

I drive through Llanberis, and out the other side, up through the villages Deiniolen and Dinorwig, past climbing club huts and the modest cottages of internationally renowned mountain guides. All the way, I'm looking out for a van: Lee and Becky's white long-wheel base Transporter. I know they won't be here for a while, but I still look for it. It's like when I was a kid, when I stood in the window of our house, waiting all morning for Granny and Grandad's car to appear and park up.

I park on the side of the road at the bus-stop turning circle, engine off. Now I've got the van, I'm happy to camp up here by the side of the road, rather than the campsite on the other side of the valley. I go to the back of the van and click the flat stove into life, blue gas flame boiling a cup of water for tea. I wait for my friends. We've spent a lot of time together, driving between crags, walking through the quarries, filled rained-off days with talk instead of action. It's a very tight relationship when you trust people to hold your rope, to keep you alive when you fall off the rock. Which, if you try stuff you find hard, should be often.

In the eighties, everyone was on the dole, nothing to do. This was Thatcher's lost generation. The quarries were walking distance; they'd have a smoke or a bit of a party in an abandoned hut, then try and climb something. The ones who got really obsessed with it were called slateheads by the ones who weren't. What they did is 'little history', a small culture of nutters, artists, punks and petty thieves. Crawling up abandoned rock, then heading to the disco at the Dolbadarn.

Now I'm here again, to follow up the climbs of the underdogs, climbing amongst those great works that they weren't paid for. I met a few of them and listened to what they had to say, and they weren't how I had anticipated.

No one cares whether I get up these rock faces or not. It won't repair a relationship, or bring the dead back to life, it won't heal a family argument or repair my fucked back. It definitely isn't making me any money. But I think about it, back home; I dream and plan. For whenever I can I make the drive back here again, to meet up with my friends and climb the slate.

CHAPTER 2

Mental Lentils

May 2014, Vivian Quarry, Dinorwig

The first time I climbed in the slate quarries was with the Norwich Climbing Club trip. I joined the previous winter; this was the first time I came away with them. I had been climbing for about a year, but only indoors.

I drove up to the campsite on the hill above Llanberis, it was late afternoon, and the early May sun was golden.

I rang the doorbell at the farmhouse; two border collies just looked at me, well used to visitors. A shape through the frosted glass appeared: the farmer's wife.

'Hello,' I said. 'Have Norwich Climbing Club arrived yet?'

'Are they the ones who come every year?' she said. 'That'll be them tents down there.'

'Ah; I'll go and look for them, I'll be back later.'

'Pay in the morning.'

I could see a cluster of tents, but no one was around. Fuck, I thought. Have I been stood up? I paid my money to join the club. I didn't really know anyone; I'd only spoken to a few of them at the wall. I was prepared to think they might all be wankers, not worth knowing. That was my defence in case they didn't want to like me.

I drove back down to the village. It was a bit early for the pub, so I went to the bright cafe on the corner: Pete's Eats. They might have been in there. I popped my head through

Modern-day interior of Pete's Eats. Henry and Alice Smith are sitting in the window, Lee Mitchell waits for his 'full set' (breakfast).

the different cafe rooms. No one in.

I was hungry anyway, and I'd been trapped by the cooking smells from the kitchen. I ordered a lamb burger. The chips were big and chunky; hand-cut. The tea came in a pint mug. I ate and drank with a fixed smile on my face. That said that I am eating alone because I am choosing to, no need to pity Billy No-Mates.

No one cared.

A middle-aged couple on a nearby table were wearing good quality mountaineering clothes; both looked like they were out in the weather a lot. They could have been doctors who climb, or full-time guides with enough training to act as medics. They were talking about expeditions in the Himalayas.

'Trying to get it into everyone's head. If you tie your shoe-laces you need to wet-wipe your hands, 'cause your laces will have trailed through faeces.'

'Last thing you want is an outbreak of D and V.'

I puzzled over D and V for a minute or two. Diarrhoea and Vomiting popped into my head as I finished my last chips, using them to sponge up the salt and vinegar residue left on my plate.

There were pictures of climbers on the walls. Some are framed black-and-white photos with proper captions. Others were collages of print photos, climbers waving ice-axes around, climbing in the nude, being obviously drunk, on tops of mountains with their arms around each other.

I finished my food and took my plate and cup up to the counter: 'Cheers, mate.'

I drove up the hill again. By now, the flaps of the tents were open. A few people were sitting on bouldering mats, and walking between the tents with cups or stoves. I recognised one, walking up the hill carrying a plate. I knew his name was Lee, because I'd talked to him at the wall. He recognised me and waved.

'Alright, Pete. Everyone's in the big tent.'

I stuck my head in and said hello.

They'd pitched a huge family-size tent over a picnic table so it was like a purple fabric canteen, with walls that flexed and rippled in the breeze. In the run-up to the trip I'd been practising on the ropes at the local indoor climbing wall; it being Norfolk, local for me meant an hour's drive. I was generally alright on the big bright colours of the plastic holds, but everything I'd read says that climbing outdoors is a different story, and I wanted someone to show me what is what.

They were discussing what they wanted to do in the coming week. I said I'll throw myself at anything; it's my first time outside. Probably bouldering, because I like indoor bouldering, or some of the big, easy mountain routes, long and high and scenic. That's what I reckoned I'd like.

'I'll be in the slate quarries all week,' said Lee. He's tall, blond from working outside: Tree surgeon? I'd been watching him move across the holds at the climbing wall, precise footwork, strong and slow, then a sudden flick of movement.

The slate quarries? I'd seen them on the road into Llanberis: vast piles of purple-grey rubble, pouring down the mountainside, big square chunks chopped out of one of the smallest of Snowdonia's mountains. Industrial waste, compared to the shattered stone of the pass, with its roaring white streams and slopes of brown-green-orange grass.

Fuck that, I thought. Slate quarries? That doesn't sound very good.

* * *

Next morning, we headed down the hill from the campsite. The morning so far had been a mind-numbing faff of people sorting kit, getting dressed, then brushing teeth. Then sorting more kit, having a fag, then someone else went to the toilet, while I paced up and down.

A stop at the Spar – everyone dithered buying sandwiches. I'd made mine last night, which I now realised had saved me no time at all. Through the village and down on the path along the railway lines. There was a bridge over the river, not quaint and wooden, but concrete utility with ugly 1970s municipal railings on either side. On the far side, there was a little hut, advertising scuba-diving lessons: what the fuck? We were miles from the sea.

A path led through a man-made archway like a railway viaduct, stacked with slate. On the other side, the shelves of Vivian Quarry opened out above. The bottom of it was filled with a cold green pool of water – huge. The colour gave it away: deep; frighteningly deep. The steep rock walls slid straight in, sheer into the green. Of course. This was where the scuba diving happened.

Across the water was a prow of rock sticking straight up, twenty metres into the air. Around the edge of the pool were small unstable terraces, covered in loose scree and rock fragments, above a six foot drop into the water. Bushes and heather were growing out of the fragments, birch and rowan trees shaded the path.

Feeling safe in our group, we walked confidently in. The first part of the path was obviously safe: well fenced in wood. Two sightseers were strolling up and down: a man and a woman. He had an enormous and expensive-looking camera, a whole lot of lens. They were both wearing beige and pastel colours, but their faces were carefully neutral. They hadn't paid an entrance fee, and were worrying that they had passed a No Entry sign. They cautiously nodded hello to us in case we were about to shout at them for being there.

At the end of the path was a cluster of signs beyond the wooden viewing platform of the lake. The big stile was only for the use of the scuba-divers and anyone else was Not Allowed. The scuba-divers had put in steps into the water and a semi-submerged cage platform. It was made of modern galvanised steel, like a deck on an oil-rig. On the far side of the pool, buoys floated in the lake; two were yellow plastic barrels just like in *Jaws*. Another barrel was welded stainless steel. We threw rocks and skimmed flat pieces of slate to try and hit it. Most of our shots didn't get close.

Our first climb was amongst the trees, not too near the edge of the water: *Mental Lentils*. One of the club, Land Rover James, wanted to lead it. Calm and precise indoors; out here, he was nervous. We lounged around, watching as he moved slowly and carefully up.

The atmosphere was not of an adrenalin-soaked macho expedition. It was more like a rolling picnic, with people who just happened to be sitting on coils of rope.

Land Rover James left the rope in so other people could try it in safety. One by one, we all trailed up *Mental Lentils,* the rope hanging from above, as safe as it could be. When it was my go, the moves seemed easy at first – up from big ledge to big ledge – but as I got higher, the holds got smaller. I didn't really have anything else to compare it to. It was way better than being on the big plastic resin holds indoors; the rock was smooth and cool, pleasant to touch. Right at the top, the holds got smaller, but still not tiny. Just before the chains at the top, I couldn't see what to grab on to. I needed to grab the edge of the rock slab rather than the holds – apparently, this is called the arête – and I didn't know whether this was allowed or not: no one told me. I did it, moved up and touched the chains, then lowered down to the ground.

'Was that okay to do that?' I asked.

'Sure,' shrugged Lee. 'If you can reach it, it's in.'

We ate sandwiches and snacked on nuts and sweets. After a while, Lee and his mate Garry walked off on the thin paths round the edge of the water. I followed nervously, tagging along. Amongst the slate scree were pieces of brown-orange metal, wire rope frayed like the nylon lines tied to lobster pots in fishing villages.

There was some discussion about a climb that had apparently fallen down, called something like *Bobby's Groove*, a route 'by' someone called Johnny Dawes. This seemed important to Lee and Garry. Shattered fridge-sized blocks were perched in one of the bays; there were brown muddy streaks above: rockfall. Rainwater had swollen behind the cracks and widened them until the blocks leaned out of balance and fell. Surely this couldn't happen easily? Surely this needed a lot of time or an intensity of storm?

There was a shot hole in the corner of the bay, water gushed out of it like a fountain; it was inherently funny and we took turns to squat over it and pretend to be pissing. It didn't make sense, really, but it was a bonding humour: everyone spending a bit of their dignity on being accepted.

In the next bay was another climb, this one had a more menacing name: *Psychotherapy*. Lee and Garry looked up at it. I could see a shiny bolt fairly low down. I couldn't really understand how it would be climbed so I headed back round the paths.

The path – without railings between me and the water – gave me a powerful sense of vertigo. The water had a height of its own. Depth. Whatever. I looked at one of the cliffs in the water and realised that what I thought was a reflection of the cliff on the water was actually the continuing line of the rock down to the bottom. I felt sick, like I couldn't trust my balance. Walking normally required no care; what if my legs wobbled and I started to slide? There was an excitement to it, too. It was like walking over a bridge and having the urge to climb over the railings and jump, or take your wallet out and hurl it into the flow. Compelling and against reason, frightening and exciting.

Sandwiches. Crisps. A drink of tropical fruit.

I skimmed fragments of slate into the water. I looked up to see Garry, first here, and then there on *Psychotherapy*. He is small and skinny, but very muscly too. He was a bit annoying when you first met him, quite fast talking with a Norwich accent that almost sounds like London. I thought that he was probably quite good. I couldn't tell if it was easy or not, but he moved quickly enough. His girlfriend Alice was nice; she had straight brown hair and looked athletic. She was wearing purple trousers only a climber would wear.

'We've left the rope in. If anyone wants a go they can.' I would try anything they offered, but I felt nervous about it; I didn't want to be embarrassed if it turned out I couldn't do it. In some ways, I would rather not have tried at all, so no one could find out if I wasn't any good.

Big rugby-playing Rob tried, and couldn't make a tricky move quite low down. He wasn't embarrassed: it was his first time climbing outdoors, too. Fuck it, I thought. If I fall there, I won't be any worse than him. Next was a Polish woman called Violeta, who managed the move nicely: a graceful reach over with her toe.

Now me. Easy up to the bolt, clip it. Grip desperately on to a ledge and reach across with my right. I could just reach the next ledge. Even though it was not a good hold, it was enough to balance me out, and I could then – slightly wildly – reach my left leg across to a goodish step to bring the rest of my body over.

Then it was up the slanting crackline. The crack was as thin as the gap between paving slabs, but at places the rock had fractured, making useful little fins that were nice and sharp to grip with your hands. Here and there a complete triangle of rock – like a small pyramid – had popped off, leaving a ledge the size of a Coke can, easy to stand on.

At the top was a stainless-steel chain bolted into the rock, so you could safely lower down. At the climbing wall, you would have to touch them to say you had completed the climb. I got near them, but Garry, who was belaying, said, 'That's alright. You've done enough.' I touched them anyway, superstitiously.

Back on the ground, Lee said, 'Everyone had a different way of trying that. Some hung low. You, Pete, got really high on the move and reached across. Same as with *Mental Lentils*. Out of the people who tried it, everyone did it differently.'

That was it. Two climbs.

Just before we went, I skimmed one more stone at the metal float. As soon as it left my hand, I knew the line was good. The flat slate plate, the size of a beer mat whirled through the air – hit, skip, hit, skip, hit skip, hit skip hit skip hitskip. It smacked squarely into the side of the metal float: BONNNNNNGGGGGGG!!!

CHAPTER 3

Comes the Dervish

Mid nineties, Durham

Watching a TV show about climbing with my dad – I must have been about thirteen – it was something to do with an Everest expedition. Dad was in his chair, reciting an increasingly angry litany. 'He's dead. He's dead. Yes, and he's dead, too: he skied into a crevasse.' Triumphant, like he'd just won an argument. He had been a climber himself at university, but didn't do it any more.

Another time: a documentary about a top climber in the Alps; British, with curly black hair. There was footage of him doing pull-ups from a bar in his house. Pull-up, pull-up, pull-up: he looked like an actual machine, a steel factory component repeating a manufacturing task. The voice-over was telling us that Stevie Haston does one thousand pull-ups every morning. The man looked at the camera and slagged everyone else into the ground. 'British Alpinists do their training in the pub. They don't train at all. That's why they don't climb anything.'

An attractive severe-looking woman belayed him on something impossibly hard: a traverse underneath an overhang of rock. That was his girlfriend Laurence. She shouted encouragement with a strong French accent: 'Yeah, cool. Cool. Yeah.'

Stevie grunted back, 'You're pulling me off the cliff!'

Dad watched avidly. 'What's the point of all this? It's just silly. Could they not just stay in their house and enjoy shagging?'

Eighties, Vivian Quarry

The deep green pool at the bottom of Vivian Quarry was a magical place. It was great for a swim in hot weather, just walking distance from Llanberis along a footpath between the lake and the castle. The very top layer of the water might get warmed where the sun hit it, but just below the surface it was cold. Best just to jump in, hold your breath against the gasp and the shock, and swim some powerful strokes for your muscles to create a little heat until your body acclimatised.

Stevie Haston was a climber, originally from London. One hot day, he brought a girl here, 'a happy hippy chick, we were not burdened by clothes, we were floating, resting on the surface tension of a secret spell, between the blue of the lake and the turquoise of the sky.'[1]

Floating on his back, looking up, he could see the quarried tiers like giant steps going up the hill. They hadn't been blasted out evenly. Ridges of rock had been left where the quality of slate had not been good enough to use, or where the blasted rock would have been hard to extract. One ridge looked to him like an alpine spur, leading up to a clean-looking climbable slab three levels above. Looking up, he also realised that slate wasn't just grey. This slab had tinges of purple, which most people wouldn't have noticed.

In 1980, slate was not a popular rock type to climb on. Millions of years ago it was mud, that got squeezed and baked into geological pottery. A few people had ventured on to slate, but their routes weren't popular. The quarries were fascinating: creepy pools, broken stone buildings, steps and rusty ladders between terraced levels. But anyone wanting to climb there would sensibly view the rock with distrust. Their faces were cracked, loose and uncertain, fickle. Lethal-looking piles of scree – left over quarry waste that seemed about as unstable as skateboards – were ramped over sheer drops.

At the time, no one was really climbing on slate; climbers vaguely knew that a few routes had been done here and there. Al Harris had started by climbing *Gideon,* and the famous Joe Brown had explored a deep pit in the main Dinorwig quarries, but these climbs were not thought of as important. The stories of them were out of sight, in climbing journals and the memories of the men who did them. The real action was elsewhere.

Stevie Haston first got the idea, that slate could be good, from some early black-and-white photographs in a book by Tony Smythe: *Rock Climbers in Action in Snowdonia.* It was a minor classic, written in 1966, just when climbing was coming to the attention of the mass public.

Deep in the book he would have seen a picture of a climber, lonely, coming up an easy-angled slab, ropes trailing down to him from the viewpoint of the photographer, John Cleare. Far below him is the bleak and shattered quarry of Cefn Du (pronounced roughly, to my ear, as Kevin Dee), and a black pool of water deep at the bottom. In the background is Llanberis, and the lakes of Llyn Padarn and Llyn Peris. The much more extensive quarry workings of Dinorwig are visible; the vast mounds of slate waste and clean faces looking pale in the photo. Behind that is the Llanberis pass. A low layer of cloud hung over it, and hid the tops of the Glyderau mountains.

Haston toyed with the idea of calling a route *Seventy Thousand Assyrians.* It sounded cool, the title of a short story

An early ascent of Gideon. This photo gave Stevie Haston the idea that slate could be climbed.

by William Saroyan. In the short story, the narrator is a rootless Armenian immigrant in Depression-era America, in need of a haircut.

But, if you've got the idea that Stevie Haston was a pretty sensitive chap, reading obscure American Beat fiction and poring over black-and-white photographs, you'd be dead wrong.

'The first time I saw Stevie, he had come up from London and had his shirt off doing stretches in the car park,' said Paul Trower, a climber originally from Keighley in Yorkshire, who had settled in Wales. 'We were there, smoking a joint in our car, thinking, "Who the fuck is this?"'[2]

Haston was macho, abrasive and unafraid of letting people know what he thought about them. He liked women and he liked partying, which meant horrendous levels of alcohol intake and blaring out rock and roll, the Stones, the Clash. So he fell in with Al Harris, the one-man party planet which the Llanberis social life then orbited around. He and fellow-Londoner Harris quickly became friends, and Harris found him work in his cafe, which left plenty of time to go partying, recover from partying or – in fact – go climbing.

As a child in London in the late sixties and early seventies, Haston had been constantly wandering, running around with a Dickensian gang of friends. Tellings off, beatings and canings from school had no effect: he rapidly realised he could take the physical punishment, switch the pain off. With some desperation, his parents packed him off to the Maltese island of Gozo to live with his pappy: his Maltese grandfather. This was ideal for a freedom-loving child: a morning start of a bowl of bitter black coffee before going fishing with Pappy. To get to the sea, they needed to climb down the cliffs, following centuries of fishermen who had chipped holds in the perfect place for their hands. No streetlights, plenty of cousins, all of whom were either fishermen or priests.

How could he have settled in London after that? Not possible, despite a scholarship to an elite London grammar school. Haston's Scottish side of the family were solidly working class; staunch union men, communists, seamen and steel-fixers who utterly distrusted the bosses and toffs. At this school, he was disgusted to find the middle-class pupils had been privately coached through the entrance exam. His contempt showed, and he was caned repeatedly, but didn't care. The primitive aversion therapy of corporal punishment just showed the weakness of the teachers. Despite being one of the brightest pupils, he just switched off and thought about getting away.

By his mid teens, Haston was sticking his thumb out and hitchhiking to anywhere he could get to. He made it as far as the Alps, climbing the north face of the Eiger in winter at the age of just sixteen.

Shortly after that, he jacked his job and hitchhiked north to Llanberis.

The ridge running up the middle of Vivian Quarry looked no worse than any alpine ridge. Having nothing to do one day in 1981, Haston grabbed one of his mates and they climbed it alpine style, fast and light, a fast fun day out with ropes. They called this route *Wendy Doll*. At the top level of it, Haston climbed up the edge of the purple slab that he had seen from below. It looked clean, and solid. It also had a thin crack running up its face.

The slab had been crafted out by a quarryman looking to get paid, blasting clean sheets of slate off to reveal this last layer, for some reason not worthy of roof-tiles. But for a climber the crack offered possibilities of sharp handholds and footholds, narrow breaks that might take pieces of protection. Only small gear: number 1 and 2 stoppers: little wedges of metal the size of a smartie, with a loop of wire to clip in a carabiner and the rope.

Haston had to clean it, and perhaps check a few handholds, before it could be climbed. He nicked a knife from Pete's Eats, the climber's cafe in Llanberis. Abseiling up and down, removing dirt and loose chunks of slate, he revealed a route: climbable, but at the top level of difficulty and danger.

Once it was all cleaned, it was time to climb.

Haston still knew it would be hard to move up these tiny footholds. He needed more information, so he took a risk and gave the honour of the lead away to Tommy Jones, who was a delicate expert on a slab. Haston reasoned that he would learn how to do the route by watching Tommy climb. Tommy set off. The climbing was thin and difficult, needing precise footwork, balancing the mere side of the big toe of a climbing shoe onto tiny sharp edges, with the rest of the foot hanging in space. Meanwhile, the fingers would need to find holds barely big enough for the fingertips.

Tommy gave it 'a really good go, getting high but then ran out of strength, and psyche, but not technique.'[3]

Haston knew he was stronger than Tommy (he exercised so obsessively that he later developed major tendon damage); if he failed on the route it would be because he ran out of mental energy. 'I knew I just had to access more psyche, and so I did, I just pulled the switch and I became the Whirling Dervish.'[4]

He detached himself from the danger, switching off the short-term immediate fear and worry. Without the brain anxiously worrying about consequence and looking for escape strategies, it is free to concentrate all its energy into successfully executing the required moves. By ignoring the danger, things – paradoxically – got safer.

'I woke up above the overlap my last gear miles below, and with twenty-foot of uncleaned rock to the belay. I made it to the sound of Chipper [Tommy Jones] swearing at me for succeeding on "his" route.'[5]

Haston ditched the name *Seventy Thousand Assyrians* and went for *Comes the Dervish*. For Stevie, it marked the end of shirking the big stuff. In the following year, he started to get noticed with a series of hard climbs, accessing a fearless flow of movement. For other climbers, it became a desirable checkmark, something to brag about doing, and proof that slate could be worthwhile.

Comes the Dervish proved to be so good it was worth some hassle. As they climbed, a ranger, employed by Gwynedd council, approached the group and asked them what they thought they were doing, threatening them with the police. Tommy Jones looked at him and drawled, 'It's alright, man. We're highly experienced rock-cats.'

CHAPTER 4

Turn of the Century

May 2014, Dinorwig; 1990, Durham

Later in that first week with the climbing club, I was gingerly padding along a rusty iron tube, like an old gas-pipe. It was balanced on the edge of a cliff which shoots off down into rubble below. It was a relief when I stepped off it and onto the holds of the rock. My toes were squeezed into my rubber covered slippers, which flexed on my foot. I stood on little ledges. These ledges were small, some as wide as a thin book, or a CD case. My hands gripped on to smaller holds, thin wafers of sharp rock. Some of them were ridged, like a splayed deck of playing cards, some you could grab like a broken piece of crockery.

I stepped along sideways across the face of the cliff. The drop opened out below me, and it should have felt scary – I never like to walk close to the edge of a drop, used to feel funny walking over bridges – but I was not worried at all. I felt in control. A red-purple rope reached above me, keeping me safe should I fall, but it wasn't remotely likely. I shuffled to my right, step through – nice movement – handhold following handhold.

Kept going, easily. The line of holds followed a bulge, a ripple in the slab. At the end of that was a chain, orange-brown links. I curled my hand around it; it felt cool compared to the slate warmed by the sun. This chain used to hold the pipe that I had just tiptoed across, before it had been smashed off, vandalised by trundled blocks from above.

At the chain, the climb changed. I stepped into a slanting diagonal crack. Chunky triangles of slate had fallen out of this, leaving little shelves big enough for the toes and ball of a foot, huge for slate. I couldn't fall off. Moving from foothold to foothold, sometimes hauling on a sandwich of wafers, sometimes pulling on a flat smooth shelf, I felt like I was climbing a ladder up scaffolding, or up to the loft of a house. Completely safe, rung followed rung, hold followed hold, the climb had a logic to it.

As I topped out, Lee was sat there, pulling the rope through his belay-plate.

'You're taking to this like a duck to water, Pete.'

I grinned; I had never had a compliment like it. 'I love it. What is it called, *Tubing the* – what?'

'*Looning the Tube*. Just think what you could do if you get some shoes that fit.'

Another climb. No. This is too much. I'd fiddled a nut behind a flake. The rock flexed as I pulled it down. I'd got a cam in, lower down in the same crack. Those won't hold if I fell on them.

This route is a 'trad' route, though: short for traditional. You have to place your own gear. Neither piece could be trusted. It's not that I felt scared; I didn't, I was not very high up. I felt – correctly – that I didn't know what I was doing, that I was very slowly getting myself into trouble.

'I'm coming down.'

'Just climb down the holds. Just climb down the holds,' said Lee, patient and clear, but I tried to hold the rope, flustered. I slipped, and Lee locked the rope to hold the fall, pulled me tight.

I'd got my leg crossed over the rope as I slipped and the rope ran like a saw across the back of my leg. It stung, hot and sharp, real teeth-sucking pain. I untangled myself, and looked at the friction burn curling across the back of my knee. A red weal, skin gone; and, as I watched, beads of clear, straw-coloured fluid welling up.

That was it, anyway. Even without the injury, the end of the week.

As I walked down from the climb, heading to my car in the early evening, there was a group of six or seven lads roaming through the quarries. They weren't climbers, they were wearing tracksuits and T-shirts. I was walking down alone, spread out from the rest of my mates. The boys saw me and walked across. I had the feeling that one of them had a joint on the go; I could smell the weed fumes on the air.

'Alright mate, been for a climb?' one asked, and they cluster around me. 'What you been up to?'

Could this turn nasty? It didn't feel like it. I was in my thirties, well off the fight radar for packs of idiots looking for status and man-points. When I was fifteen, I would have been shitting myself and smiling, trying to make friends. When I was eighteen I would have been planning which one to hit first.

'Getting this,' I said, and show them the wound. They all took turns to look, pulling faces like sucking lemons.

'Ooh, fucking hell, mate.'

''Ere, what's that climb called up there – *Gadaffi Duck?*' asked one, his mates laughing at the funny name. It was not mocking laughter; if I had been a bit of a cunt with them, it would have been unfair. They were just having a wander through the quarries, and didn't mind a chat.

'That's what I got this on,' I told them. Actually, it was a different climb but I didn't feel like explaining it, and they wouldn't have cared.

As I was talking to them, my mate Rob walked up behind me and tapped me on the arm as he walked off down the hill. He couldn't tell whether they were being aggressive or not, and it would give me the excuse to break contact if I needed to. But they were friendly, there was no threat to them. A moment later, I said, 'See you later,' and started to walk off.

'See you later, mate, see you later,' they all said, and walked on to enjoy their evening.

On the drive home, I stayed in my shorts. I wasn't sure that 'letting the air get to it' would really help heal my rope-burn, but that idea is so engrained: every cut, every grazed knee since childhood, then hurts from work – cuts from chef's knives, a cut from a saw or a chisel or a slipped hatchet across a knuckle. I distractedly let it touch the fuzzy fabric of my car seat; it stuck on and I needed to peel it off. Which was not painful, but felt weird.

That could not touch my happiness after a great week. It felt like a long drive home from north Wales: five and a half or six hours. Up through the pass, past Plas y Brenin and Capel Curig, then Betws-y-coed. Oswestry. Shrewsbury. Telford. The Midlands.

* * *

When I was twelve, we left Liverpool: where my grandad lived, where all my mates were, where I rode my bike around the streets and local park. We moved to Durham, which I'd never heard of. We were warned that there were two schools in the city you didn't want to go to. One was Gilesgate, one was Framwellgate Moor, called Fram.

It was late in the summer holidays. There were no places left at Durham Johnson, which was the 'good' comprehensive. My heart sank – it would be Fram. Sixties buildings dropped in a drained marsh, between tight terrace houses, outlying pit villages and the biggest housing estate in Europe: modern detached and semis, bought by police, passport office workers and staff from the National Savings.

Actually, it was alright. No better nor worse than anywhere else. The accent was like nothing I'd ever heard, similar to but not quite Geordie – 'hellish' meant 'good' and no one said 'yes' or 'yeah'. It was always 'aye', and when I visited Liverpool at weekends my old mates skitted me for it.

PE was a nightmare of 'training runs', presided over by a sadistic dickhead who drove an army-type Land Rover to school, and disappeared for the duration of the first Gulf War. Rumour was he had been recalled by the army. Fuck knows what for – as a target, I hoped. I hated and feared the training runs: a stream of lads sprinting, running out of energy, and then walking through the driving rain and freezing wind across the Carrs, through stunted alder, willow and birch. Those who'd gone through puberty at twelve came first, using man-sized muscles. I was nowhere.

When I was in the third year, for some reason, the school got a climbing wall, built into the enormous gym; it stood in the middle of the all-weather pitch which always flooded.

I already thought I would like climbing, and I did. I went along to the Climbing Club. Mr Mawson, a maths teacher I didn't know, ran it. He came out of the changing room wearing what looked like tights, but thicker. It should have been embarrassing, but he clearly didn't care, so everyone ignored it. He showed us all how to put harnesses on; they were boldly coloured purple, and about ten of us went up and down the walls, top-roping.

I was not bad. I could do some things that others couldn't. Mr Mawson set a problem, a traverse, with a tricky section needing to swap hands and match feet. I was the first one to get past this crux, but then dropped the easier move afterwards. The next lad, Robert Dean, did it all. A mate of mine said, 'You did it really,' but no, it was Robert's and fairly done. I didn't care. I liked it for its own sake.

There was danger too: badly belayed, a lad called Alistair fell off the wall, arse first, and screamed, twitching like a fish, unable to stand. I ran out of the hall, still in my climbing harness, a moment of glory telling the secretaries that we needed an ambulance. Alistair was back to school a week later, with a carrier bag. Humiliation of humiliations, this held a rubber ring he had to sit on to protect his coccyx as it healed.

Mr Mawson took us all up to a new bouldering wall in Newcastle one evening; it was great, I loved it, but it was the last time I went. There was something uncool about it. None of the rougher, sportier lads – who were discussed by the newly sexy girls in my year – did it. I was changing, now self-conscious and not wanting to be a weak dog at the bottom of the school pack. And at home, my dad didn't like it; didn't really approve. Climbing, to him, was a dangerous waste of time.

Fast-forward to 2014, during that first week on the slate, Alice from the club said that I was 'nails'. Her boyfriend Garry said, 'Just think: if you'd taken this up earlier, we'd be watching videos of you by now.'

CHAPTER 5

Gideon

July 1964, Glynrhonwy Quarry; Vivian Quarry

Al Harris (correctly pronounced 'Arris) had been climbing hard for three weeks, and needed something different. There is only so much harrowing exposure the mind and the adrenal gland can take, piling the stress of staying alive on top of the slog of carrying heavy ropes and army-surplus gear up to the crag, often in the pissing wet.

Harris had curly hair, and a pleasant soft London accent. He had talent as a climber; he had started as a teenager, and was drawn up to north Wales from London in the early sixties. He was friendly and fun in the pub or boozy parties, and quickly became mates with Pete Crew and Baz Ingle, two of the top climbers of the time. He often stayed at their rented cottage Bryn Bigil, in the hillside village of Dinorwig, towards the coast end of the Llanberis Pass.

Harris' three weeks' hard climbing had been with Eric Penman, whose nickname was Spider. This was an excellent nickname for a climber, and Spider was all long limbs and a cool head on the Welsh rock. Of which there were plenty of different types: limestone, rhyolite, granite. These rock types burst out from under the grass in haggard cliffs in the Llanberis and Ogwen valleys. Cliffs like Clogwyn Du'r Arddu or Dinas Cromlech were the great arenas of British climbing, as 'Hard Men' climbers like Joe Brown, Don Whillans, Crew and Ingle put up routes of great difficulty and technical beauty. Slate, however, was unregarded, unclimbed, only visible when quarried.

Across the valley from Bryn Bigil was the disused quarry called Glynrhonwy. Unlike the Dinorwig slate quarries, still busy through the sixties, Glynrhonwy had not been seriously worked for years. The atmosphere there was different to the natural cliffs of the valley. Glynrhonwy was lower than the climbs in Llanberis Pass, so drier and less likely to be green with slime and moss. Rather than the tracks of sheep, there were old rusted fences, inclines and cart tracks. There were sheer cliffs and mighty exposed drops, but the scale was different; the feeling was of wild dereliction rather than wild nature.

An enormous slab of slate had plunged into the scree-lined pool at the bottom of the quarry. It was visible from the far side of the valley, from the back garden of the cottage of Bryn Bigil. The beams of sunlight roamed across the hillside, through the gaps in the cloud. One beam lit up the slab, glowing pinkish grey, an unbroken ramp of rock amongst bracken, heather and scrubby trees.

'It was never meant to be a real climb, it was just Al and I messing round in a quarry. Al was in one of his manic periods, blowing a trumpet and trundling boulders and making one hell of a racket,' recalled Spider.[6] They wandered around and found an easy scramble down the side of the slab.

The gear they had brought was limited even by the standards of the day. 'We had only an old 120ft [40 metre] rope with us and a couple of slings with nuts on.'[7] They had no pitons (pegs that could be driven into cracks in the rock to hold a fall). You weren't meant to use too many, that would be 'unethical', but it was still alright to hammer one in here and there to protect a hard move. Spider and Harris weren't making an ethical stance, they just hadn't brought any.

Harris had lost interest, his mood waning as quickly as it waxed, so Spider set out up the slab.

The slab was broken by a ledge just below half height. There were cracks there, an obvious place to fiddle a nut in for protection. Spider climbed carefully up a stack of balanced slate blocks before reaching a groove. No protection. As he reached the ledge, the way was blocked by an arête of scree – a loose stack of slate rubbish – somehow balancing on the rock. No way was this anywhere strong or stable enough to climb, and you couldn't get past it on either side.

So he headed left along the ledge. This had been colonised by moss and ferns growing in cracks. Spider could place a nut here in a cracked slot, but the traverse was exposed and uncertain, 'long and lonely',[8] until Spider reached the right-hand edge of the slab, where he could lasso a sling around a block and bring Al up to join him.

Rather than return to the main sweep of the slab they then climbed up the short boulder field, delicately trusting the stack of boulders not to slide and shoot them off. They headed up a smaller slab above and to the left. This was still a 'fairly mind-bending trip',[9] and with little gear until you reached the upright metal rod anchored deep in the rock at the top.

'I led it and named it Gideon after a quote from the Bible, "The men blew their trumpets with a mighty noise"... I don't really remember it other than it wasn't up to much,'[10] said Spider, fifty years later.

Harris wanted to make a name for himself, and new climbs had currency. Spider might not think it was up to much, but Harris was talking about it in the pub, cracking it up over pints of bitter in the Padarn.

'We understood that Al Harris had climbed the slab,' said John Cleare, a climber and photographer, 'but as it had disintegrated beneath him, he'd got to his feet and managed to outrun the avalanching slate and merely sprained his ankle. That at least was the story.... Anyway, he'd called the slab Gideon... "cos the walls come a-tumblin' down".'[11]

Glynrhonwhy is nearer the coast than Llanberis Pass, and at a much lower level. As wet air comes across the Irish Sea, it is raised when it hits the Snowdon Massif. The air cools. Cold air has less capacity to hold water-vapour, so the water condenses out and it rains: usually in buckets across anything high level. Local climbers know about this, so if it is raining in the pass you might still be able to head over to Holyhead Mountain for a day's climbing in the dry.

John Cleare was collecting photographs for a book. He and his friends headed out to check out Harris' climb, led by Peter Crew, to see whether it was worthwhile. Getting there was an adventure, crawling through tunnels, and abseiling off a decaying pit prop to get to the start of the climb. At the bottom of the quarry was a pool of water, surrounded by 'rust and moss-covered rounded shapes'. These round and tubular forms looked very like discarded RAF bombs.

The Glynrhonwy quarries had been used by the MOD during World War II as an ammunition dump. An underground set of tunnels had been served by a railway line further down the hill, and there were local memories of an explosion or cave-in which had led to the death of many men. The use of the quarries as an ammo dump was a part of local legend, and added to the fun of poking around a disused area.

'We all roped up in one long caravan, and Crew led us up the slab. Although easy-angled, the surface slates were frequently sliding off, but Crewy slotted in an odd ace of spades peg as psychological runner,' recalled Cleare. Even these pegs, with a stubby eye and flattened metal head in the shape of the ace of spades, didn't really add a great deal of safety to the climb.

'One certainly got the impression that once something really slipped there'd be no stopping – the whole surface would slide down into the bombs and you with it.' Double jeopardy, not just a surely fatal fall, but detonating old dumped army-surplus explosive to boot.

Cleare got one good photo that found its way into his book, *Rock Climbers in Action in Snowdonia*, though the climb itself wasn't mentioned in the text. This was the same photo that Stevie Haston saw in the book, that first gave him the idea that slate might be good for climbing on.

According to John Cleare, 'No one was very keen on slate.' Despite the picture, there was no mention of *Gideon* in the text.

'Al Harris was a complex guy. He had his demons, and he had a really wonderful streak. He was one of those crazy diamonds really,' said Paul Trower. 'Al could unleash the inner wildness in other people, he could make things happen.'[12]

Harris bought Bryn Bigil when the Vaynol [Y Faenol] estate was flogging off all its houses for cheap, and also bought the cafe in Llanberis called Wendy's. When he was full of the demonic spirit of life, anyone around him would be swept up by his energy. People from London or Manchester came to Bryn

Bigil, happy to buy booze just to be part of the rolling party. Harris would carry the jukebox from Wendy's up the hill, and hit the FreePlay button a hundred times to blast the music out. He loved music, and had hundreds of LPs on a shelf across the wall. Only he was allowed to handle them as he acted DJ. The drunken parties would end with shagging, or pissed-up car races – Harris loved cars as much as climbing, drink or women.

It is not an exaggeration to say that Harris was the centre of the climbing scene in Llanberis. Great boundary-pushing ascents happened at Cloggy or Tremadog, Gogarth or Pen Trwyn. Excellent climbers came and went. Americans visited, like the famous Henry Barber who brought climbing chalk to the UK for the first time ever. Al Harris continued to throw parties through the seventies, anchoring the climbing scene to debauchery.

Harris had a beautiful generous streak. Paul Trower was on his way home to Keighley, 'With my tail between my legs. I had left home, gone out to see the world, and it was all over. I was in the pub with my girlfriend, and her friend was going out with Al Harris. We were talking and I told him I had no money, no job and nowhere to stay. He said, "I'll give you all three." At the drop of a hat, he had solved my problems.'

Harris put Paul up at Bryn Bigil and gave him a job at Wendy's. Climbers like Stevie Haston found jobs at Wendy's to tide them over and keep them climbing; Harris welcomed each new generation, fresh blood to party with. As a climber, he was a brilliant employer, happy to tell someone to go off climbing while still paying them as if they were at the tea-urn.

While this attitude was great for climbers, it was bad for business. Harris partied more and more frantically, organising small-scale insurance frauds – another 'nicked motor' pushed into the water at Bus Stop Quarry – to keep the cash coming in. The police were starting to ask questions about a series of pointless robberies and break-ins near his home. By the late seventies, his black moods grew, money got tight, but still he raced cars down the narrow roads, laughing and swearing.

One night in October 1981, eight months after Stevie Haston had climbed *Comes the Dervish*, Harris' luck ran out. So pissed even his close friends wouldn't get into the car with him, he drove off with a young couple in the back, also drunk. Round a tight corner at Capel Curig, Harris lost control and collided with a stone wall. The couple were lucky to survive with injuries. Harris was killed instantly.

CHAPTER 6

Flat

May 2014, Thetford Forest

Heading home past the Midlands, past the Civil War battlefield of Naseby, everything becomes more familiar, heading for Norfolk. Kettering, then Cambridge and past the RAF airbases flown by the USAF, miles of chainlink fences and F15 jets taking off over the road. I am into the heaths of Breckland and the conifers of Thetford Forest where I have been living these last few years.

I open the front door, and my son runs at me, jumps for a hug. I swing him round, he has blond curls, but some kind of graze on his nose.

'I tripped over and landed on my nose, Dad.' He looks sad and angry, a five-year-old unable to separate his emotions from the event, even though it has passed. 'I slipped on the gravel.' He mimes the fall to show me exactly how he landed. From behind my back I pull out a small box that rattles. Lego. A guilt-at-going-away present. He beams.

'How was it?' asks my partner, Tanya. 'Were the people nice?'

The steam rises from my cup of tea; I hold my face over it, and my nose feels clammy. I used to do this when I was a kid, not sure if the wetness was sweat or condensation. My son builds the Lego truck; it is a sort of four-wheel-drive sports car. He doesn't need my help; the pictures are simple and easy to follow.

I tell her what I've climbed, the names are funny: *Orangutang Overhang, Gadaffi Duck.*

She can see I'm happy, and I think she's pleased. I can tell anecdotes, describe the people I like, but I can't touch that sensation of finding something special. It feels like I was looking for it, something I could have been doing my whole life.

* * *

The week after my first Wales trip I go back to the climbing wall, normal Thursday night climbing. Everyone is there. As we lace our shoes, we talk about last week's highlights. The skimmed stone that hit the metal buoy, *Mental Lentils* and *Psychotherapy*. Rob singing 'Circle of Life' in his mighty rugby player's voice across the cwm of Australia (Pen Garret), the sound waves of his voice triggering a rockfall. Everyone climbing Tryfan. Me climbing *Gadaffi Duck*.

Everyone wants to see my rope burn, and I peel off the colloidal dressing, a jelly layer of some kind of healing gloop. It's used for burns and skin grafts, but I bought it from Boots. The skin is knitted and pink. It won't leave a scar, which a younger me would have considered cool.

Later, I'm sitting next to Lee, a mug of tea leaking heat into my hands.

'It was great, I loved it. I want to do more, but I don't know what there is.'

'The club only ever goes to the same places,' he says. 'We went to Vivian, bottom level, and then up to two different levels in Australia. Everyone goes there. There's dozens of other places to go in the quarries. Hundreds of climbs. All the stuff from the eighties. Johnny Dawes.'

'How should I choose what to do?'

Shattered landscape viewed from *Solitude Standing*. The ruined building guards the col that leads into Australia (Garret). The pit at the top left is California (Sinc Galed). Dali's Hole (Sinc Harriet) is bottom left.

He thinks. 'I don't know. I can't tell you really. You just have to look around and see what inspires you. Listen, I've got to get climbing, I've got training to do.' He laces his shoes, break over, but turns back to me as he steps onto the mats. 'But really, you need some shoes that fit. I could see them rolling on your foot when you stood on the edges. They're at least a size too big. Probably why you fell, slipping off those footholds.'

This sounds like an easy win. Guide book and shoes, spend a little bit of money.

Summer 2014, Thetford Forest

At the end of the working day, I roll out of my car seat, the engine plinks as it cools. Driving home across the county on autopilot, same old radio, same old songs. Same old shit driving from everyone else on the road.

My tools are in bags in the back. They are muddled and mixed from the day's work. I've duplicates of some things, loads of pairs of pliers taking up weight and space. My mole-grips are missing: easily left, easily lost, easily nicked. Boxes of screws, odd sizes, no order so I never find what I need. I need to sort it out. I don't. My Astra sags on its springs, excess weight burning up a little more petrol than I need to.

I've been on my own all day. Small work, short jobs. The time has gone slow.

I am covered in dust and insulation, itchy glass fibre that crunches in your teeth. A large part of the job is crawling around in the roof space, head torch lighting up a cone of dusty void, running cables from one end of the building to another. I balance on the beams of the roof-trusses so I don't put my foot through the plasterboard, squeeze through awkward gaps in the timber, buzz screws in while I'm bent double, mounting brackets for basket, trunk, mini-trunk and cable-tray.

There is a sense of adventure, taking your kit into an unknown space, traversing the overhead tunnel above offices and waiting rooms. You could be a caver, or exploring a mine. But when you get down, your back hurts and your knees hurt; among the funny pains, some disappear within a minute, and some are with you all day.

No radio is allowed on this site: there are strict rules at some, and other factors in play, such as the extent to which the public or management might see you. This job is for the NHS, refitting a health centre, so it's strict. I'm learning bits of electrical work. Pulling cables, running them through dusty crawlspaces, fibreglass particles floating, itching and clinging to my clothes. Cutting conduit and screwing it to the walls. This isn't my trade, but when there's not much work about, you do whatever you can.

My mate Barry got me this gig. He's been an electrician his whole working life. Electricians are called 'sparks', carpenters are 'chippies', plasterers are 'skims'. Painters are 'brush brothers'. Barry's tool bag is set up perfectly; everything has its place. He can see straight away if anything is missing. Everything he needs, he can carry in one hand, his other kept free for his drill-case or testing kit.

Another of the sparks isn't like that at all. One big bag of everything, no side-pockets. To find a tool, he tipped his whole bag upside down, wire, pliers, hacksaws and screwdrivers. Amongst it all, shrapnel from Digestive biscuits, an old packet he left there weeks ago. The site agent went mad, he's been on about keeping the site tidier – not tidy, that's impossible, just tidier – for the last week. 'It's taking the piss! It's taking the piss!' he shouted.

Still, I'm not so tired that I can't go and eat dinner, then head to the climbing wall. My son waves goodbye from the window.

At the climbing wall, Lee walks in. Since the Wales trip I've climbed with him a bit, he is much better than me, and we've talked. I like the lad, and I hope he likes me too. I wave hello, 'How's it going?'

'Not bad. Look at these.'

New climbing shoes, Five Tens, snug on my feet, C4 stealth rubber and pink suede. Properly they're called Anasazi lace-ups, everyone calls them 'Pinks'.

Lee cannot hide his satisfaction.

'Spot on. No bunching at the toes. They'll be good on the slate too; Pinks are really good for edging.'

'I tried everything on. These are exactly my foot shape.' Lee nods. 'What about you?'

'I've got news: I'm going to move to Sheffield, I think. Garry's selling his house, so I've got to move, anyway. I know a few people over there, so get some work sorted, find a place. It's what I need, close to the grit.'

'Nice one. I'm pleased,' I say, but I'm not. Fucking hell. I make a friend and he moves away.

'I'm heading up,' I say to Tanya.

'I'll be in after a bath.'

I sit in bed with the book and look at what I did. Every time I go climbing to the wall, I seem to get stronger and better. Indoor bouldering problems that were hard six months ago are now easy. My new shoes fit, strong rubber platforms that can-tilever from small holds, rather than a squashy tire which slips. I start to do some of the problems on the hardest set of blocs. I am going to be a lot better next time I get on the slate. Just think what I can do with shoes that fit.

CHAPTER 7

Opening Gambit

Easter 1970, Twll Mawr

Claude Davies and a mate walked down from the small mountain of Elidir Fawr, on the westernmost end of the Glyderau ridge. The weather was bad, and they were looking to get out of the muck as rapidly as possible.

The two men walked down through the quarry workings, down a steep incline that runs from below Elidir Fawr's summit, 150 metres down until it meets the quarry road. The incline had been built out of stacked drystone slabs of slate. Along it, huge wooden and cast-iron drums, powered by big Ingersoll steam engines, had winched carts of slate down, and workers up.

Alongside the incline ran slate steps for the quarrymen, but no one was walking them now. In 1969, the quarries had closed. At a stroke, the area's main source of employment had gone, taking with it the men's livelihoods and status.

The pair wandered along the quarry road towards Dinorwig – and, as they rounded a corner – they found Twll Mawr (Big Hole).

'I looked into the "big hole" and immediately thought "Heavens!"' said Claude.[13] He had a close friend called Joe Brown, and couldn't wait to tell him.

2014, Gateshead

One weekend I am up at my mum's. After Dad died, she moved

up to Gateshead, away from the villages where we grew up in County Durham. She has been here a few years now; the furniture from our old house no longer surprises me in its new places. Mum has taken my son into Newcastle: it is the height of exploration for him to sit at the top of a double-decker, best of all when he can sit in the front window. Then be bought cakes or sausage rolls and a book or a toy. This time he comes back with a cross between Airfix and Lego, and clicks together a Messerschmitt at the kitchen table, concentrating hard on the instructions.

I like just staying in the house. The bookcases have the same books I remember, sometimes in the same order they used to be in, others in new sequences with new mates, a bit like kids moving up into big school.

I pull a book out of my mum's shelves, no dustcover. The cover's cloth is a faded purple-blue, like denim. Embossed on the spine is JOE BROWN – THE HARD YEARS. The letters used to be gold, but are now faded to a burnished brass. Inside is my dad's name. RP Goulding, 1968, in blue biro. My signature and his are related. The 'G' has big loops. We both run the 'i' and the 'n' together to make a wavy line, and the last 'g' is reversed so it looks like a cross between a 'p' and an 's'.

'Do you mind if I take this, Mum?'

'No. Go ahead. There's some others of Dad's, if you want.'

Inside the book, the first picture is of Joe Brown. He's climbing, it's captioned, 'On Clogwyn Du'r Arddu'. His fingers are crimping hard on to some marginal-looking hold, one foot is free in space, the other is standing on something tiny with a hill-boot, the kind you'd use to go for an easy walk in the Lakes.

He's wearing woolly socks pulled up to his knees and an

anorak. There is an old-style rope, twisted strands rather than modern tightly woven kernmantle, tied around his waist – no harness. The rope hangs straight below him; it probably isn't clipped into anything yet and he looks like he's hundreds of feet up – which might just be the camera angle. Around his shoulder are a few rope slings – simple loops of rope to hang around spikes of rock, or trap in cracks with chockstones – with heavy steel oval carabiners. These are probably ex-army issue, prone to straightening out like a paperclip when fallen on.

Topping it all off is a daft hat. It has a turned up brim, with a fuzz of woolly felt topped with a pom-pom. It looks like the kind of hat a Mongolian tribesman might wear. Joe used to tuck a selection of sizes of stones into the brim, jamming them into cracks to wrap a sling around, a skill later superseded by kit, when metal nuts came along.

Joe Brown, I thought. I half remember Dad telling me about him at the kitchen table. Hard as nails – poor family, big family, in Manchester, bombed out during the war: nothing like the posh, public school type climbers that went before him. And because of the war, he didn't give a fuck; any of them could have been killed by bombs at any time. He had been a builder before there were proper rules; walking around on rooves – Valkyrie Club, Rock and Ice – he broke his leg and his mates just drove him home in a van, that's how hard he was.

As I dip into *The Hard Years*, its account of him didn't seem like the same man as the rumours. Here he was a nice bloke; steady, who loved the outdoors and camping, and, as it happens, climbing. Even a bit on the boring side: he wasn't milking his adventures for drama. A talented bloke, surrounded by talented friends....

Joe Brown coincidentally put up the hardest and greatest routes in Britain. Loads of them. Across the Peak District, and then onto the cliffs at 'Cloggy', Clogwyn Du'r Arddu. Routes like *Llithrig, Diglyph, Vember* and *November*.

Legends arose. Joe Brown invented hand-jamming (a technique of clenching your fist into a crack to wedge it against the side walls of the rock); Joe Brown worked out how to use an old nut from his motorbike with a sling through the middle, thus inventing modern protection (the ubiquitous factory-made 'nuts' that every climber today has on their harness); the first man to climb an E-grade. All bollocks.

Joe hadn't started to climb with any thought of fame, and when he started there was no expectation that any kind of money might be made from it. He went climbing with his mates, and work, it seemed, would be part of life. But the ascent of the Old Man of Hoy, filmed by the BBC in 1967 as *The Great Climb*, was broadcast over three nights in July as a TV spectacular that was watched by fifteen million people.

This new fame did not suit Joe. He'd be at the crag, and other climbers would be talking about the Great Joe Brown without knowing he was eating his sandwiches behind them. This embarrassed him, and he became shy and withdrawn. The climbing press started to manufacture competition with up-and-coming climbers whose stated ambition was to 'burn off Joe Brown'. He liked to climb with the same mates he'd had had throughout the fifties and sixties, people who wanted nothing from him other than friendship and company. He wanted the same adventures that had been a bus ride away from Manchester, the same sort of fun to be had on bomb sites. And anyway, he was still an incredible climber.

Joe's hard years had ended when he moved to Llanberis in 1969, with his wife and baby daughter, and set up a climbing shop. Joe Brown's, trading firmly on the name, was one of the first dozen climbing shops in the UK, and sold a lot of jackets, boots and rucksacks. Plus a branded Joe Brown climbing helmet. There was enough of a climber's ghetto developing near the cliffs of Cloggy to just about support this, but additional, booming weekend trade began to offer Joe a solid sense of security on which to risk planning further adventures.

1970–1971, north wall of Twll Mawr

What Claude Davies had come across – Twll Mawr – was perfect for an adventure, but Joe didn't like the look of it. To get into the base of the hole would require three abseils, but Joe didn't believe that the rock would be stable enough. It looked loose and dangerous. Abseiling at this time did not mean using shiny gadgets and webbing harnesses, but wrapping the rope around the body, via armpit and crotch. You didn't do that unless you had to.

There were other crags, within walking distance of carparks, or a pleasant ramble up a hillside. So they left it for a year. No one else was interested.

Joe and Claude liked the challenge of finding new places to climb, away from the crowds. It was about the day out, not the glory of setting new routes. Joe had done tons of that. If Joe and Claude could find another way in, that could be an adventure in itself. And no bloody abseils.

When Twll Mawr had stopped being worked, the last slate blocks would have had to be removed from the very bottom of the pit. How had the quarrymen got the slate out? There were no steel wire ropes that could have hoisted out blocks, although there were plenty in other parts of the quarries. The most likely way to get the slate out was by narrow-gauge train tracks, pulled by small steam trains. These ran through tunnels, so they had to look for a tunnel.

Claude saw that in the south wall was the mouth of a tunnel emerging at a terrace, about one hundred-and-fifty feet above the lowest terrace and two hundred from the very bottom. Finding that mouth, scrambling around the slopes of unstable scree, would be fun. Joe and Claude found the mouth of a possible tunnel, but in general they never seemed to come out at the point where you would expect them to. This one was pitch dark with no visible light at the end, and water dripped from its roof. The railway track was still there, laid across sleepers, so they followed it by touch, crawling on all fours. As they walked further from the entrance, they passed into the uncertain, real deep darkness you only get underground. Would it even go anywhere?

But then they saw a chink of light. The end of the tunnel had been blocked by a wood and corrugated tin door, with rock beyond it blocking the vertical shaft. 'Fortunately, there was a way, though dangerous, through the piled-up boulders above our heads, and after some debate we gingerly threaded our way through to arrive standing on the debris below the towering walls. The scene was staggering…. Our immediate impression, when standing beneath the north-side wall, was that we were looking up an alpine face, this impression being added to by a fairly constant clatter of stone fall....'[14]

Joe and Claude looked around the bottom of Twll Mawr for about an hour, seeking potentially climbable lines. Then they turned their attention to getting out. With no gear, they climbed a smooth corner and reached the terrace that led to the tunnels at the top of the rusty ladder.

With some relief, they went in to the tunnel, and it proved to be only a hundred yards long, its exit leading to clear daylight and a terrace level overlooking Llyn Padarn. The tracks were still there, the simple route for the narrow-gauge railway carts to remove the slate from the days of the working quarry.

Joe and Claude came back with some of their mates, and started to seriously look at climbing the North Wall of Twll Mawr. The 'yellow wall' to the west just looked impossible. But the North Wall looked like a satisfyingly adventurous place to be.[15]

Joe had already seen a potential route up: a line. Nearly straight up the north face of Twll Mawr was a fault-line, a huge fissure from top to bottom of the cliff. Where the rock separates, it rarely does so evenly, and cracks and fissures provide opportunities for holds, rest-ledges and places to lodge gear.

He set out, but rapidly hit a dead end at an overhanging section of rock: horrendous. If the rock had been solid and stable, Joe could probably have climbed it, but the lumps of rick were loose, stacked rather than embedded. When they were tapped with a fist they made a hollow sound, and some could even be wobbled like a rotten tooth. He could neither trust it, nor get past it, so he came down.

After beer and sandwiches on their sunny ledge at the bottom of the pit, they looked at another line, less dramatic looking: a better prospect. Not too hard either, pitch after pitch of Severe grade climbing, topped off with a seventy-foot crack, the perfect width for hand-jamming. They called this route *Opening Gambit,* altogether six hundred feet of good climbing. It was fun, authentically enjoyable, but Joe still wanted to climb the big fault-line.

More trips in: the next day Joe and his friends brought a cardboard box that clinked. Joe tried a different start to the fault-line, trying to get around the side of the overhanging loose section. When he got to the overhang, he hammered in pitons: wedges of steel that stuck in the rock. He clipped in a foot-loop – a simple sling made of tape – and he stood in those stirrups putting footholds in. This is called aid climbing: using metal protection to hang directly from, rather than as a safety backup.

Three pitons weren't enough. The contents of Joe's box came into play: it was a bolting kit. This was a hammer and a sort of rock drill: basically a handle with a round chisel that has three grooves cut down its shaft. As he hammered the chisel, he twisted it around between strikes and it gradually cut a hole. Before electric drills, this was how all builders drilled holes, and it is a skill that no one misses. It is laborious in the extreme, taking a large amount of effort and time to sink a relatively shallow hole, into which you can hammer a small bolt. They hammered in two, to protect the overhanging crack, then climbed on up. Time was ticking on: they had taken so long over the bolting that there was no prospect of completing the climb as a team of three or four. Their mates headed down while Joe and Claude continued.

From here 'two further long difficult pitches gave exhilarating climbing in what was a most exposed position',[16] high on the wall. By now it was well into evening, the sun having dropped below the wall of Twll Mawr, throwing the base of the hole into deep shadow. The section above the crack system was still lit with sunshine, but it looked difficult and unpleasant, blocked by horribly spiky gorse bushes growing improbably out of the side of the cliff.

Joe fought his way through the first bush, but even he was put off by seeing another three more blocking the line of the crack. Instead, he headed out on to a more open area: one difficult move, then the route opened up. The way to the top was now clear, through short, steep, easy-enough walls, moving from good ledge to good ledge, resting easily in between bursts of movement.

Seven hours after they had started, they were at the top. They called this route *Hamadryad*, after the large poisonous snake. They gave it the grade E3/E4, appropriately fierce, and far tougher than *Opening Gambit*.

Not enough. More adventure was to be had. There was another line of continuous cracks which could maybe be climbed: a whole separate route. Although it was not true that Joe invented the hand-jam, the method was useful in those pioneering days on slate. To the postwar working-class climbers, it was as necessary a skill as lacing up your boots. To have learned it on gritstone – where many of Joe's early hard routes were put up – must have been an excruciating experience. That rock grazes and bites your skin, leaving scabs climbers call 'gritstone kisses'. It feels tenuous, and requires a lot of technique, to clench your hand just so, and to lean your body to improve the way it locks into place. On slate, the experience is less painful, but more uncertain. Slate is too smooth grained – usually – to break your skin, but it also has much less friction. Grit bites while slate slides, but with skill you *can* make it work.

So the cracks were an opportunity. Joe's third route took a lot more visits and more of his varied group of friends. He could find individual pitches (rope lengths) which were climbable, but the challenge was to link them together. The difficulty wasn't in doing hard moves, but finding a way through the complex rock structures to where climbing was possible. Not on blank, over-hanging, lethally loose or shattered rock.

At the weekend, Joe and Claude were back. Joe raced off up the rock face, quick due to his familiarity with the route: this was the fourth time he had climbed these pitches. He was also quick because, as leader, he wasn't carrying much.

Behind him came Claude, carrying the rucksack with a spare 150 feet of rope, spare slings and gear, together with cans of beer. This added to Claude's difficulty and he considered sack-hauling, pulling up the rucksack behind him on a rope. But that was a frustrating and tiring process. Rucksacks have a habit of catching on a complex rock face. Trying to drag it free might tear the canvass, dumping your cans of beer down the rock face to explode like foamy fireworks. Luckily for Claude, the climbing got easier after the second stance and he could continue up with it still on his back.

The weather was deteriorating, with a heavy rainstorm brewing. They were running out of time. 'It was obvious that if Joe could not now solve the problem of the next section in the next half an hour, retreat would again be necessary.'

This was the critical fifth pitch, for which Claude was carrying the spare rope. Joe climbed up into the steep section above, fixed a thread runner – a piece of rope or tape through a gap in the rock like the eye of a needle – and dangled the rope down. By keeping his weight on the rope, he became a human pendulum who could swing over to a shallow groove: this was the last pitch, which led more easily to the top.

Making this move pulled the rope tight against the sharp edge of the arête. Slate can produce incredibly sharp corners and fins, sometimes so fine they can slice fine paper-cuts into skin. When under tension, a rope is much easier to cut or damage, and it was a scary moment, committing to a move that would rub this rope across such a sharp piece of rock. Joe called this climb *The Razor's Edge*.

Joe climbed up, and Claude followed, just as the thunderstorm broke. It rained down hard. In the wet, slate has the same friction as polished glass. Claude could only squirm his way up, using his knees where he could. He found Joe on a ledge above, 'saturated but now content'.

Britain's greatest iconic climber (and his mates) had climbed a handful of routes. These were successfully repeated, and gained a reputation as being serious, hard, exploratory routes, within the capability of the top climbers of the day and in a stunning location. What followed next was....

Nothing. No one was interested.

CHAPTER 8

Twll Mawr

Mid nineties, Durham; Newcastle

In my teens, I started to notice how autumn drew in, and that slide into November. I started to hate November.

Like any teenager, I started to go out to parties and pubs. As the November nights drew in, I would feel grilled under the orange of the sodium streetlights. Stuck at home in a village six miles from where my school and mates were, desperate to go out. The Rugby Club party, with its notoriously lax age-checks, was never as good as I'd promised myself it would be. Someone else would be talking to the girl I fancied, and I never noticed her mate who kept looking at me. No one would come up to talk to me. I'd drink harder, then quickly be too drunk, never knowing my limit, never accepting that my light frame couldn't soak up the pints like heavier-built kids. Then red vomit, and the jeering and shame.

I recognised the feeling at sixth form. September and October still had the light and heat of summer days. You had the novelty of choosing school subjects and finding out your timetable, working out who was in your classes and if you fancied them; if you had a chance. November was shit. I was stuck, committed to courses that I didn't want to do. I didn't know what I did want to do, but I knew it wasn't those. It was worse that month; I would argue with my dad. His fixed ideas, based on what had worked for him, of the worth of qualifications, which could lead to being a teacher. I didn't even want to go to university. My mates weren't going. They were staying around Durham. Tuesday was the Punk and Indie night at Britain's worst nightclub, then lunchtime playing pool in the Angel every Wednesday.

I applied for and got into Newcastle Uni. It was only a train ride away, not even a new city. University was the same as sixth form, except you had to cook for yourself. I thought it might be a new life, a room of my own where I could smoke without an argument. Where there would be worthwhile women, who would be both beautiful, interesting, and interested in me. It didn't seem like I was asking too much, but by November it was clear that I was.

Orange sodium lights and drinking – triple vodka and coke, price-fixed at one pound at every nightclub for students – while I worked in a pub near the railway station. I worked and studied half-heartedly, I drank with commitment. What I was missing wasn't being filled by being there, and the hole was at its deepest in November.

Autumn 2014, Twll Mawr; Thetford Forest

I now have some tactics to fight November's gloom. Book a trip, make a plan. One weekend, I bring a multinational gang of mates for a second trip up to north Wales. We had been up on the Glyderau on Saturday in the snow, easy winter walking. This morning it is pissing down hard, low cloud hovering over the tops, coating them like a soggy duvet. Nothing for it, we have a lie-in, coffee and a leisurely breakfast, and then drive to the quarries for a moody stroll.

The slate quarries in the rain are dark and gloomy. The wet slate is a deep black-grey, like the skin of an orca. We walk along the quarry road, towards Watford Gap, where two pillars of slate pinch the path. Through it on the left is Twll Mawr.

'What is this place? Twill Mower?' asks Hasier. He is a Basque, from Saint Sebastian. 'What does it mean?'

'"Tuff Mour",' I say, playing the expert, although I'm not really sure I've got the pronunciation right. 'The Big Hole.'

The barbed wire fence doesn't quite meet up to the slate edge of the pillar, so we all squeeze carefully past it. We walk around the pit, nervously, the drop straight to the bottom, seventy-five metres, longer than most ropes. It provokes a specific type of fear, the kind where you think you should throw yourself off the edge just to get it over with.

We walk further around the rim, near to the huge rubble-glacier which flows down one edge, brought down by big rainstorms in the eighties. The rain has soaked the slate scree. Water is running down it, making the plates of slate move against each other, a creepy sound like rats' claws: *scritter-scritter-scritter*.

I lean on a big flat block at the end of the pit's rim. I feel alright when I'm still. I don't like to see my friends walking around the edge. I can see the drop below Santi – a Catalan-speaker from Valencia – as he inches nearer to peer over into the pit. He leans back, repelled by sensible levels of fear. I want to shout warnings, tell everyone to watch out. I settle on, 'There's a good view from here!' I don't want to sound bossy.

The others come over. Hasier looks over with me into the bottom. Far below, we can see a tunnel emerge out of the rock, way below the quarry road. I point. 'Look, down from there. Can you see the ladder?'

Dangling out of the tunnel mouth and down the side of the cliff was a minute ladder, orange with rust. Twisted by rockfall, it was now too short to reach the bottom. Hasier couldn't see it at first, then groaned. 'Oh my God. It's so tiny.'

Seeing the ladder puts the cliff faces into proportion, making them scarier, more real, the drop more automatically fatal.

'Pete, are there routes in here?' Hasier asks, but my expertise has run out. I can't answer because I don't know.

The guide book comes through the post a week or so later. It is the Rockfax guide, *North Wales Climbs*. It is beautifully photographed apparently, but the pictures of climbers don't mean much to me: I can't see myself in those poses. I like the pictures of the cliffs with the little red dotted lines showing the course of the route, the 'line' of the climb. These are the 'topos' (topographs). They have the same appeal as looking at a map and wondering what it is like to walk the foreign ground.

'I'm heading up,' I say to Tanya. Our son is asleep in his bed with his light on, curled up amongst his duvet printed with friendly looking dinosaurs. His cuddly toys – we call them his 'chaps' – sit around him on watch against nightmares and the loneliness of the night.

I flick through the pages. There is so much here; some of it I've heard of. All those cliffs, crags and venues. Dinas Cromlech with its classic Joe Brown lines, *Cenotaph Corner* and *Cemetery Gates*. I have an idea my dad climbed one of these in the sixties, I will have to ask my mum. Then Clogwyn Du'r Arddu, another famous cliff with *Llithrig* and *Vember*, more Joe Brown classics. More and more; the multi-pitch routes in Ogwen valley, training for the Alps. The sea cliffs at Gogarth, lashed by spray.

A Dream of White Horses, Britomartis. Anarchist. Alien. Positron. Mousetrap. Mantrap. I love the names, micro-poems which are even better in a list when they're next to their mates.

There is a lifetime's climbing on every type of rock – volcanic igneous, veins of quartz boiled out by superheated steam, limestone from the shells of dead creatures squashed into rock, sandstone pressed out of a million days' flow of brown rivers you couldn't have seen the bottom of. All those potential days out: the atmosphere of the cliffs crashing against a boiling sea, a heathery slog up for a light and fast alpine day, views of the hills looking out over Anglesey, picking out Liverpool from the top of the Glyderau.

Except, I just keep reading about climbing on slate. These cliffs are more relatable. The climbs I've done, I pick out and cross off. It felt like a lot, but here it equates to nothing. Nothing! Not compared to everything else in the book. There is so much more to do.

Twll Mawr has its own section. The photograph spreads across both pages: it must have been taken from very high up on the back wall. It captures the depth of the place, but not the fear you feel looking in. There are routes, marked on with red and yellow candy-striped lines, like a specific type of road on an OS map. One is called *Black Holes and Revelations*; with a thrill, I realise it doesn't just run next to that tiny rust ladder, it actually uses it. The one next to it is *Supermassive Black Hole*. That sounds good I think. It is given 7a as a grade. The route description calls it 'a stellar line up this wall – something of a safe adventure.'[17] On the other side of that is *Black Hole Sun*. This gets the grade 7a+, which means it has passed the Rockfax threshold of a 'hard' climb. I don't consider that one. Too hard.

Thursday night, and the climbing wall is closing, the staff shouting 'Last climb, please!' just like I used to shout 'Time-at-the-bar, thank-you'. I pull off my shoes and pack my rucksack.

Land Rover James wanders across. 'Beer pub shop?' he asks, which he considers to be humorous.

He and Darryl are going. So are a few of the others from my first Wales trip back in May. If I go to the pub, then I'll be back at midnight. I calculate my chances of being home in time to have sex if I don't go, but they are already low to non-existent. Fuck it, I think.

It's a chain pub up near the airport, dark wood tables, green upholstered chunky furniture, gleaming brass and quiet before the Christmas drinking starts. You could assemble it out of a kit. I know what the chips would look like without having to order them, rectangular in section, pale yellow, fried in corn oil and bought in one kilo bags, frozen, from Brakes Brothers.

Around a table in the empty lounge, Land Rover James imparts facts.

'Once you have done that grade of climb, you can't just go on to the next grade of climb. When you've done a Severe, you need to do some more before you go up to Very Severe. Look at Darryl, here. Darryl gets out there and gets the mileage.'

Darryl agrees enthusiastically. Land Rover James has taken Darryl under his wing. Darryl started climbing at the same time as me, and so obviously loves it just as much. It seems like he is off to the Peak every other weekend to get some more mileage in.

'How many had I done that time?' Darryl asks James. 'Must have been up twenty routes by ten o'clock.' It's a high number, and we all fall silent for a moment.

'Anyway,' says Land Rover James, 'look at Tryfan. Great day. I led you and Rob, and Darryl here led his first multi-pitch with Viola. Great way to get mileage. Loads of climbing, not too hard, lots of gear placements and learn the skills.

'Climbers who immediately start well and fly through the grades can find themselves in very dangerous territory, without necessarily having the experience to handle the situation they themselves have landed themselves in.'

My mind wanders slightly. I liked the mountain-day up Tryfan, it was great – really great – but it wasn't the slate quarries. The climbing was easy: too easy? I take a sip of my drink, lime and soda because I'm driving, feel the bubbles over my tongue.

'Good thing about a multi-pitch up Tryfan is the length of the routes. After all, Tryfan is 999 metres high; one more metre and it would be a thousand.'

I snap back to the conversation. 'Tryfan isn't 999. It's nine-one-five. Glyder Fawr is nine-nine-nine,' I say without thinking. Fuck, I think. That came across as rude. I'm not even sure I'm right, though I often remember numbers: there is a lump in my brain that they just stick in.

'Tryfan is nine-nine-nine,' Land Rover James repeats. 'One short of a thousand.'

'Anyway,' I say, 'you'll hate what I'm planning to do. Next trip, I'm going to have a look at *Supermassive Black Hole*. 7a multi-pitch,' I say. To me, that feels like a worthwhile ambition, amongst the working landscape of the quarries and the history. Land Rover James likes climbing the slate too, but he also wants to try more obvious climbs on the mountains of

Snowdonia, stuff that people have heard of, a Good Day Out, then tea and cake, or a pint at Pen-y-Gwryd. I want to slink off where I'm not allowed and go and do something without success guaranteed.

This does not go down well. Land Rover James looks at me carefully, his eyes narrow.

'Can I make a suggestion?' he asks. 'You need to get more mileage. A 7a multi-pitch is very hard.'

'Only the first pitch is 7a. The next ones are easier. 6b, 6c, 6a,' I say. 'I've thought about it. It's good value.'

'A 7a multipitch is very hard,' he repeats at me. 'Even Lee would struggle with that. I think you should do *A Grand Day Out*. That's a good multi-pitch.'

'Yeah. You need to get more mileage,' chips in Darryl.

I am fuming, angry. My glass sticks to the mucky varnish of the table.

* * *

Conservative and risk-averse. I've suspected this for a while, actually. For fuck's sake. Why couldn't they just have been happy for me? This is typical, I think, as I take the roundabout on the Norwich Outer Ring too fast, squeezing the accelerator to pull the back end back into balance. Knockers and naysayers.

I already know I've got talent; after all, I could do stuff that other people in the club couldn't. They gave me compliments, didn't they? Indoors, at the bouldering wall, I can do stuff that other people can't. After all, I have been climbing some of the problems on the second hardest circuits in a very short space of time. Yeah. I can do it.

This is not going to happen by accident, though. I need to

plan. I need to split this big impossible task into bits, really murder it, lump by lump.

First. I haven't done a multi-pitch, not led one, anyway... so I need to do one. A multi-pitch is a climb where you don't just go to the bottom once you get to the top, because you can't. You have to build a stance (position for belayer), bring your second up so they can climb above you to reach another stance, bringing the rope and all the clips you put in with them. Leapfrogging up a cliff-face of theoretically infinite height. There must be some skills and knots and shit you have to learn.

Next. I haven't climbed 7a. The best I've climbed, in my very limited experience, that is one outdoors trip, has been 6b. This means a jump of 4 whole grades: 6b+, 6c, 6c+, 7a, the pluses being a whole grade in themselves. So I'd better fill in the gaps. 6b wasn't that hard by the end of the first week, so maybe I can start by warming up on a few of them.

Which is of course what Tweedledum and Tweedledee mean about mileage. Except in my case, I'm going to get all that fucking mileage in a week, before triumphantly ascending out of Twll Mawr, and dragging the rest of the club kicking and screaming into a revolutionary era in which they have to confront their own lack of achievement. Fuck them.

Meanwhile I'm going to keep climbing twice a week at the local climbing wall – one hour away – just like I'm always doing. If I can't get the time on the rock, then there have to be small ways, little hacks I can use to make myself move more efficiently. I'll hang off the door frames while I'm waiting for the kettle to boil. I go up the stairs in huge moves of four steps at a time in order to practise rockovers. At odd moments, I wonder what the fuck am I doing?

I keep reading the guide book, make lists of all the climbs that will lead up to what I want to do. A structured plan, highly concentrated, whisky not beer. Now I'm into my mid thirties, I won't improve the same way younger climbers can, and with a family I haven't got the same commitment or free time. But if I tick off what's on the list, I'll be ready for it.

May 2015, rim of Twll Mawr

Lee unfolds himself out of the driver's seat; I wave and bound forward, handshakes and clapped backs. We're at the same campsite, same tent pitched over the picnic tables. Some new people with the club, some of last year's. I put him a tea on.

'How's Sheffield?'

'Yeah. Yeah. Amazing. Should have done it years ago. Really good load of people, if you aren't at the crag and the weather's nice, they're asking you "Why not?" Climb when I like, can get two hours' bouldering in after work.'

'You getting better, then?'

'Oh yeah. Grade's gone right up. Put enough water in for two; Becky'll be here in a minute, she's driving down herself,' he says.

Becky parks up in her car, a small blue Clio. There is a pink-lettered sticker on the back bumper: You Just Got Passed By A GIRL. I've met her before, earlier in the year in a National Trust car park in the Lakes. When she met us all in the car park in Langdale, she was obviously trying hard to be friendly, making an effort, but I didn't have much of a chance to talk to her, only enough to know that she grew up near me in the north-east of England, not much else.

She still carries the accent. 'Hey, Pete, how's it going?'

She is a sharp contrast to Lee: she's short, he's tall; she's dark haired and light skinned, freckly, whereas he is blond and tanned from working outdoors. She is chatty and outgoing to his quiet presence.

'Ah, not bad, not bad. What are you wanting to get on this week, Becky?'

'I'm up for anything. I've only done a bit of outdoors before, nothing much more than VS. I'm hoping he's going to take me up some of the hard stuff.'

'Plenty of time,' says Lee. 'Plenty of time.'

I like her. I like how direct she is. She looks like she fits well with Lee. If they last as a couple, it will be because she wants to climb as much as he does. Most other people don't.

Equality in climbing has come on a long way since the seventies or eighties. Back then, very few women were new-routing or doing significant early repeats of new climbs. That's not to say there weren't strong women climbers but the quarries didn't attract them, really, for whatever reasons (odd climbing, serious routes, lack of aesthetics in the quarry?). I don't think it was intentionally macho, at least not in an unpleasant way, it just happened to be guys who were bonkers enough to go delving into the quarries in the main.'[18] Whatever it was, it doesn't apply to Becky, or women in our club like Violeta, today. Nor to Hazel Findlay, one of Britain's best trad climbers, who likes sea cliffs and slate.

I wonder what it would be like if Tanya and my son would come climbing, like Becky. They like it well enough when we go to the climbing wall, neither of them are bad at it. But I think it would be frustrating for all of us. I've been bitten badly by the need to do well at this, and I don't want to make the concessions that a parent or a partner needs to make, to keep everyone happy. It is selfish. And I need that, just in this one thing, so that when I go home, I can do the rest of it.

The next day, Lee and Becky march ahead of me. Rob and Sam are behind; they've teamed up because they're mates and work together. Land Rover James looks like he's climbing with Darryl: they'll be getting some mileage in, no doubt.

It dawns. I've fucked up. I'd assumed I could just climb with Lee. Within the club, we are the two slateheads – though I don't have the credentials yet – and well matched for single-mindedness. Neither of us would be tempted off by some boring ramble, a ledge-shuffle up the side of a hill.

But Becky and him look like a unit. They tramp decisively up to Australia, drop rope bags, straight into harnesses, and – while I watch – they lead straight up the first route. At the chains, then down, then straight on to the next route. Right, someone else will have to do. By the time that Nick the Policeman, a long-standing club member, has caught up, and I've cornered him into belaying me, someone else is already on one of my chosen warm-up routes.

It is late afternoon that same day. I'm in a camp chair, Darryl has outfitted his tent from Go Outdoors, like a Himalayan expedition. I've got a mug of tea, and my feet are up on a rope swing, a stick of wood threaded in between the loop of hairy blue polypropylene rope, the kind every builder has. My head is back. The sun is starting its three-hour descent towards Anglesey.

Lee walks over, he's just got back. 'You alright, Pete?' He

isn't just asking as a pleasantry, he can see I don't feel happy. 'How did it go?'

'Ah,' I say. 'Not great. Everything I got on was just so much harder than I thought it would be.'

'You haven't been here for a year, though.'

'Nah. But it shouldn't feel that hard. I did next to fuck all, really. Went the wrong way on *Peter Pan*, couldn't be fucked on *Sans Chisel Variation*. Had a go on *Whizz-Bang*, fell off that on the crux.'

'Shit,' he says. 'Are you alright?'

'Fed up a bit, really. Doesn't matter, though.'

He knows what I want to do, and knows I've been training for it, insomuch as I know how to train at all. I'm starting to suspect that just going to the climbing centre twice a week, and doing what I feel like, might not be enough. I've carried a back-injury for the last eight years. Even though I can still work, still do a tough manual job, there is a level in me that knows I am not how I was when I was twenty-four. I see others around me who climb harder at the wall in Norwich, who are stronger and more skillful. If they don't climb this kind of stuff – 7a on slate – then why would I think that I can?

Lee says, 'Later in the week, if you want, we can abseil into Twll Mawr. Have a look at *Supermassive Black Hole*.'

'That'd be good. See how we go.' I doubt it.

Sunday night, Becky heads back to Sheffield in her Clio: she's got work on Monday morning.

Lee and I go and look around the rim of Twll Mawr, looking down the seventy-metre drop. Right on the edge are a couple of shiny abseil bolts. To get to the bottom, we would clip in carabiners and drop a rope. I stand back from the edge, but Lee walks right up to it, the toes of his trainers over the drop. I look at him, afraid that he could inexplicably collapse, fold, turn to jelly and slide off, into a cartwheeling fall through space until he smacked into the rocks below. No rope, no second chance. The thought of abseiling in scares me, that moment when you lurch, walking backwards over the edge. It's a long way into this pit, down the sheer cliff walls.

'What do you want to do?' Lee asks gently. 'Do I need to get my abseiling gear?'

The very fact he's asking means he already knows.

I turn away. 'No, mate. Not this year.'

CHAPTER 9

Fresh Air

May 2015 (a few days later), California, Never Never Land

I see how unrealistic my list of climbs was. My logical progression on paper doesn't mean a thing. I've said what I was going to do and then not done any of it, because I can't. I haven't enough mileage, so haven't developed the skill and the fluidity of movement. My finger tendons aren't strong enough yet.

Climbing forces honesty. Gravity doesn't give a monkey's fuck how you look in front of your friends. There are only two real crimes in climbing: deliberately damaging the rock, and lying about what you've done.

After the disappointment of the first few days, I dig in and decide to save something of the week. I'm still there, knocking round with my mates, so it's just a case of getting on stuff and climbing. I've still got my list of things to do. Most of the rest of the club decide they want to do the Welsh 3000s challenge, all fourteen fucking peaks in twenty-four hours. This idea starts with Holly and Nick saying they'll do it, and suddenly a ripple of agreement runs around.

The logistics look enormous. The twenty-four hours challenge will apparently need three days to prepare for, including dropping a car off at the end, and everyone sitting about for an entire day at the campsite just so they've got enough energy in reserve.

I look at Lee. 'Welsh 3000s?'

'Fuck that. Quarries. I went up Snowdon before. It was boring.'

I agree. I've been hillwalking before. The Lakes, the Dales, Snowdonia, the Highlands. I like it well enough, but I'm not getting younger. I need to make the most of this week before family responsibilities kick in.

The following day is bright but windy. Lee, Environment Agency Tom and I go back into the quarries. Somewhere different, California. Up and around Dali's Hole, where the spiky skeletons of drowned trees are submerged in vivid turquoise water. Dust blows along the quarry road. We wend our way along faint goat paths through the scree, underneath a big cliff wall. We trail round them, down and around as far as a tunnel.

The tunnels look black and dark until you step into them; this one has a blaze of light at the end, only fifty yards away. Immediately, we are in calm still air. The tunnel emerges at a path that skirts a long drop into a pit. A huge block has dropped out of the roof, a one-metre square dice. To get past it and onto the thin path you have to either squeeze through the gap near the tunnel wall or step over the space of the drop below and step over thin air.

A waterfall drips down the cliff, misting the rock bay with damp. Ferns hang low over the path, growing out from wherever their spores lodged. The path is a normal width, but the drop to the side is house-height, nervy. Scree blocks swirl in geological slow motion down the great plughole. I stride so confidently it becomes a nervous skip.

Past the waterfall is another tunnel, shorter, which leads out

The Guillotine Block in the double tunnel, entrance to California.

into California, another of the quarries. A blast shelter is built into the arête of the cliff. I look back. Below the level where the first tunnel emerges is the black chasm of Hades, a great split in the rock into which the scree pours down. The waterfall trickles away into the fissures and hollows of the mountain, never filling it up. I shudder, and not from the cold of the damp shadows.

I'm becoming a connoisseur of the beauty and fear of the quarries. The entrance to California comfortably makes the top five.

Up we go, around another scree staircase to find a black cliff wall, permanently in shadow, dark with a thin layer of algae, which is black but smears green when wet. Lee points out a few climbs: *Tambourine Man* is very hard, *Californian Arete* has easy moves, but nearly completely unprotected, so very scary.

We start out up *We No Speak Americano*. Nice and easy, originally climbed by a nine-year-old boy and a twelve-year-old girl, admittedly under the watchful eye of their dad. It's good practice, there's nothing in the movement to fluster me, so I can concentrate on building the skills.

I get to the ledge at half height, pull up on birch trees which grow amongst tufts of grass. On the wall behind me are two nice shiny bolts. Lee laconically shouts advice, from his reclining seat on a rock. Environment Agency Tom belays me up. I need to clip in two carabiners, one to each bolt, and tie my rope into them using clove hitches. The ledge is huge, four feet across, the size of a bus stop.

Click, the first carabiner goes in, the rope through it. I go to tie a clove hitch in the rope at the big pear-shaped carabiner in my loop. The clove hitch is an easy knot. It's standard, Boy Scouts do it. I've tied it before, dozens of times. Except, for some reason, I just can't get it right. I tie everything but a clove hitch, starting with an Italian hitch which changes sides when you put tension on it. Then a lark's foot, then an Italian hitch again. Calm down. Next attempt, I make the two loops, called bights if you're a knot boor, and confidently stack them on top of each other, and *I swear* the rope passes through the steel of the carabiner like a magician's trick. If I'd have done this in the fucking pub they'd have thought I was Merlin.

Finally, I get it right, and belay Tom up. I set off confidently up the next pitch, but I have forgotten to collect the quickdraws from Tom. I make a move, then have to climb back down to get them. Up again; this time, no more fuck ups, and up I go.

The sun is bright, and down on the ground, Lee is shaking his head.

'If we'd have had that when we were in the Big Hole, there'd have been words,' he says, but he is grinning, and Tom and I both get the giggles, creasing up halfway up the cliff. I'm not even embarrassed. As the sun climbs and the air clears, it is too nice a day. Mileage.

The next day, we head back into the quarries, along the quarry road and over the fence to Nuremberg. A few easy climbs, there's a beautiful classic slab called *Fresh Air*. It's easy enough, but the gusting wind is disconcerting. It gets in your face, whips your ropes around, makes you doubt your balance. The moves are easy, though, enough to build confidence and enjoy how your muscles flex.

Just across from it is another called *State of the Heart*. It's a lot tougher, 6c+ no less. Another one on my list plucked from the book. I look at it, log the bolts and map the moves. There's some tat hanging off the third bolt up, a collection of old rope. It's a funny-looking climb for slate: the rock is like a set of irregular blocks, big ledges but long reaches between them. Something like climbing up a collapsing brutalist tower block, balcony to balcony.

Why not? Fully bolted, so nice and safe. Off I go, stepping easily up a slab, clip, then a long reach and a haul to get up to another ledge. More of that, another ledge. From this, I've got to step up to chin height, like getting over a brick wall. And again, more of that and I'm onto the slab with the tat on the clip. The ledge now is nice and safe, and I can stand easily in the corner. The slab is blank, or blankish, bare holds. Oh fucking hell, now I see what I have to do.

I take a long time to rest. I'm afraid to commit to this next bit. Okay. I step up onto a small shattered seam on the slab – enough grip. Crimp hard on a loose piece of slate and lean up, grab a poor ledge, and I've got enough reach to clip the next bolt towards the top of the slab. It is scary, and my fear bubbles up; I must keep moving, but everything is such a strain. I step up and pull on poor, blunt, rock fins. The only way to make these work is to lean right back and lock my arms, but that makes me too far away to each anything else.

The strength in my fingers starts to fade, like a power-bar in a computer game – green to orange to red. It is not the prospect of the fall, but the way the fact of it creeps inevitably forward towards me. I can see it coming in a few seconds' time. The fear bubbles up and bursts into words, a babble of unconsidered phrases – 'I'm sorry Dad, I'm sorry Dad' – and then I'm off.

My fingers uncurl, and the rest of my body tenses, my feet slide off the slab. Instinctively, I put my hands to the knot on the rope. My chest tenses, and I start to swing in a short tight arc, off into space. Weightless, not touching anything solid, and then I whip below the rope, it stretches then goes tight, my feet skitter along the rock face, one of my elbows smacks a ledge. It seemed like it took a minute, but actually it has been less than three seconds.

I am now swinging safely on a stainless steel bolt drilled into the rock, a couple of metres below the highest I got to.

In the second I fall, I get a rush of joy. It feels amazing to be even trying this route, amazing to be daring to be up here at all. *This* is the feeling. It eclipses the ambition, the need for acknowledgement. When I feel and recognise it, I see that this is what will bring me back. It fills the hole.

Lee lowers me down to the ground so I can rest my fingers.

I'm buzzing with the fright and the complex chemicals, adrenaline and cortisol. But, just like after a good night out, part of me worries that I have done something embarrassing.

'Here,' I ask. 'Did you hear what I was on about up there?'

Lee looks at me. There's perhaps the faintest of smiles in his eyes before he pretends he can't remember.

'Oh, you were just talking nonsense mate. I don't think you knew what you were saying.'

I have some more goes on *State of the Heart*. I get a bolt further, but each time the fear of moving up the thin slab leads to inefficiency and each time I am off. I'm back to loving it though.

The compulsory rainy day later in the week, Lee and I have a stab at finding the tunnels that lead into the bottom of Twll Mawr, that would cut out the need to abseil. We go through Watford Gap, down the quarry road and find the big incline that runs from the very top of the quarries down to the scree slopes. We hop over a fence, climbing over by a straining-post, and pick our way down loose slate, dropping a level. Then we walk over a flat plain of scree, tufts of grass and heather poking through the waste. The sun breaks through the rain-clouds and the light glares off the wet slate waste. I squint against it and soon my cheeks ache.

There is some order to the blocks of slate, and we realise that we are walking over some set of structures, square voids, metal frames that once held rooves, dozens of them, too many to be blast shelters. What were they? Old cutting sheds, perhaps.

The plateau runs out and the level narrows, down to a path-wide ledge of flat slide rubble. Below us, the slope runs unbroken down the hill. If we slid, we would splash into the lake, having been shredded and tumbled around the razor-sharp blocks first.

The path narrows even more, then there is a gutter where water has drained from above, washing out the scree: we take a 'bad step' where we step over space and dozens of metres of drop to land our feet on the other side, a pile of balanced slate plates, undercut and unsupported. It is delicate. The plates hold. We step by and soon the path widens, leading to a pleasant grassy bay and the entrance to a tunnel.

This is the tunnel that Joe and Claude walked out of. If you approach it from the western edge of the quarries, the way is a lot simpler. If we had read the guide book we would have known this, but then – experience is what you get just after you needed it.

We walk through the tunnel – it's one of the eyes of the skull you can see from the valley road. The train tracks are still there, the tunnel is solid and cool in the heat of the morning. The tunnel forks, and at the left fork you find the top of the orange-rusty ladder you can see from the edge of the rim, and a sheer drop, twenty-five metres straight down.

Take the right tunnel and there is a shattered old quarry building, walls drystoned out of slate waste and huge telegraph pole timbers fallen through and rotting. Its chimney is still up, but its roof-slates have crashed into the pit of its interior, cracked and useless.

We pick our way through fallen blocks, ferns and heather; we are halfway up the glacier of scree that pours down the northern face of the big hole. With balance and care you can walk down it like a staircase, but if you step on the wrong bit of rock it can see-saw or shift. CLOCK, CLOCKY-CLOCK. There is no wind in here, and the sound is flat in the dead unmoving air.

We get to the bottom of the pit, there are plastic oil containers, bits of cars thrown in by local teenagers, and skeletons of wild goats that slipped from 200 metres up. In shadow, the rock is cold to the touch, subtly grained and satisfying on your finger tips.

I say to Lee, 'If, for any reason, I am not around when Ellis is old enough, will you bring him here to show him what it's all about?'

He kills himself laughing.

Above us is a big sheer wall. *The Quarryman* is up there, and a load of others I don't know the names of. I know they're important, and especially to Lee. He's explained some of the moves to me, though I didn't understand what a chicken-wing was. A climber called Johnny Dawes is mentioned a lot; Lee thinks he is a genius.

'Let's have a look around,' Lee says. 'Might be some crag swag; people drop bits and bobs from up there all the time.' We walk along the bottom of the cliff. There is a sludgy pile of slate fragments, muddy and turning into coarse soil. I see a bit of fabric and dig it out with my fingers. It is a sling, about an inch wide, quite thick purple webbing, with an old chunky carabiner on it.

'Hoho!' I say, 'Crag swag! What do you reckon Lee? 1990s?'

The carabiner is quite big, about the size of a jug handle. Its shape is asymmetric, but not the waspish lines and stamped steel of a modern 'biner. It has a pale, bluish metal finish, coated in zinc? Or made of aluminium?

Lee looks pleased. He would like to think it is one that

perhaps Johnny Dawes could have dropped.

'No one's looking for it. Have it as a keyring.' A keyring? It's fucking huge. I would never lose my keys, and thus my life would become that little bit easier and therefore less exciting.

We start to make our way back up the boulder slope. The old carabiner is heavy in my pocket. I don't know. The rain spots and the sky is grey, I'm tired.

Fuck it, I think. I'm not keeping it. I take it back out and flick it back into the rocks.

Lee looks at me, puzzled.

'I don't know. It felt — unlucky.'

CHAPTER 10

Bluebottle

May 2015, Joe Brown's, Llanberis

On the way out, I stop off at Joe Brown's gear shop in Capel Curig. There's a book I want, the Ground Up guide called *Llanberis Slate*. That's the one Lee has got; Garry's got a copy too. It has got every route on slate, rather than just the edited highlights that Rockfax has.

It seems like it costs a fortune: the neck end of twenty-five quid! But guide books are expensive; they only ever have a small print run. It is heavy and solid, like a birdwatching guide. The cover is heavy and grey, a picture of someone climbing something that looks impossible on the front, his yellow T-shirt a splash of colour against deep greeny-bluey-grey, white handprints of chalk up the smooth groove.

Climbing is a niche hobby – don't dare call it a sport– and climbing on slate is more specialised still. This is the second year I've been on the club trip to north Wales, and I don't want to borrow someone else's guide book any more, or read over their shoulder. I want my own book, so I can scratch biro marks against the descriptions of climbs I've done, and find the ones that wink at me and smile 'come over here'.

In the back of this guide book is a list of all the routes in the quarries, who climbed them and on what date. There are forty pages' worth. Someone must have spent hours going through the new routes books to make this list. Frankly I couldn't care less. All I care about is what I am going to climb next.

Although, saying that, there are a couple of pictures at the front, of some 1960s climbers. One of them shows about six men, standing on each other's shoulders to start a climb; they are all obviously pissing themselves laughing about it, a fun mess around with mates.

Immediately above the picture is an entry:

1969 June 10 Bluebottle *R Kane, J Brazinton.*

That's a funny name, Brazinton. And I've heard it before.

Eighties, Liverpool

In our house in Liverpool there was a heavy white helmet, which I used to take from my dad's wardrobe because I liked soldiers, and wearing it while jumping down the stairs made me feel like a paratrooper. It was Dad's climbing helmet, with hard leather straps which bit into the skin under your chin. The enamel on the top was scuffed and scratched, and there was a maker's badge stuck inside, cloth, red-purple with gold letters. I can't remember the maker's name, but Dad had written RP GOULDING across the edge of the label with biro.

Dad had only climbed for a couple of years in university ten years before I was born, then didn't bother any more. He still spoke about it, though; I knew he was – in some way – 'a climber'.

Once, he told me about a friend he had climbed with, John Brazinton, who everyone called Little Brazinton.

'He was short, very strong, but he was very afraid when he

Dad, 19, Norway, 1968. The white helmet behind him was still at our home in
Liverpool in the 1980s.

climbed. He'd get just up off the ground, then freeze. He'd stay
there for ages until he pulled himself together, then he'd go and
climb it.'

'Was he a coward, Dad?' The way a ten-year-old thinks,
raised on war stories.

'No. He could always make himself do it.'

One night at a party, someone changed the music on the
record player and Brazinton didn't like it. He broke a pint glass
over the bloke's head, who went down like a sack of coal. In the
morning, Brazinton went to the police station to hand himself
in, believing he'd killed the man. The police told him to fuck off,
no one was dead that they knew of.

Dad and I watched films together. My first memory was seeing *Duel* – Spielberg's first film – with him. I'd not been able to sleep and went downstairs, and he let me stay up to watch it: I liked the truck in it. One night we watched the famous climber Catherine Destivelle soloing: climbing without ropes, hundreds and hundreds of metres from the ground, on African sandstone the colour of honey in the evening sun. She wore green Lycra shorts, and she was beautiful. Long tanned limbs, curly hair, brown streaked with blonde from the sun. The movement across the rock, totally fearless and graceful. No hanging around, arguing with herself about whether to go for it, she just moved up the rock as if it was a dance.

Dad shouted the first time she hung upside down from her feet and hands. I kept on shouting every time she moved. Dad said, 'Shut up will you.' I had thought he would approve; I was just copying him.

I can't ask Dad about John Brazinton. For one thing, in June 1969, when *Bluebottle* was climbed, Dad was nowhere near north Wales: that summer, he and his mate Neil drove a knackered van from Europe through Iran and into Afghanistan, just for the crack of it. Dad had stopped climbing by then.

For another thing, Dad is dead: bowel cancer at age 53, when I was twenty-five, in 2003. Killed by his diet, everything out of a tin and never a lettuce in sight. He thought the stomach pains were because onions gave him indigestion, or maybe he was drinking tea too strong. For fuck's sake.

I saw a photo of him from the spring before he was diagnosed, and can't believe I didn't notice. I was just back from Australia, so I had a tan, but he was white. White skin, white hair. Maybe I just thought he was getting old: actually, he was bleeding into his guts, becoming anaemic, while little clumps of endlessly replicating cells swam around his bloodstream, lodging where they could and setting up house in his lungs, his stomach, his kidneys and – fatally – his liver.

Mum and Dad met at Liverpool University in the late sixties, through the climbing club. The climbing wall was in the university sports centre; we walked past it when Mum took me and my sisters swimming there when we were still living in the city in the eighties. The climbing wall frightened and fascinated me. It was made of dark grey, blue-black concrete, cast pillars and buttresses, ruined fortifications from the castle of Llŷr. They hung out of the wall above the badminton courts.

You got to the changing rooms for the pool by walking along a raised walkway, so we were level with the top third of these columns. I looked over the railing, and it added to the fear. Sometimes there were climbers there, often on the middle column, hanging from their red ropes as they belayed their partners up to meet them. Rarely, there was someone trying the right-hand third of the wall, with much smaller blocks and featureless gargoyles sticking out, but I never saw anyone on the left-hand line, which was no more than dents and sharp shallow bulges in the concrete.

That was the hardest one, Mum told me.

'Can I go on it one day?'

'Ask your dad. He might take you.'

He never would. He hated it. To him it was a waste of time, and dangerous. I overheard him once at the kitchen table, counting

Dad belaying John Brazinton, who is leading on *The Sickle* – graded XS or Extremely Severe at the time – at Llanberis Pass.

up: eight dead. He showed me a photograph of him, with another man, climbing something in Wales called *The Sickle*, Dad

belaying, sitting on a rock with a hook nose and curly hair from under his climbing helmet.

Dad pointed at the lead climber and said, 'That lad is dead now. He got hit by a rock in the Alps.' It didn't mean anything to me. The picture was in black and white. I could tell the belayer was my dad, though. It was the way he had his sleeves rolled. He always had them rolled into a flat rectangle a bit above the elbow. He had gingery-gold hairs running up his arm, and freckles that faded and stopped where his shirt blocked the sun. When I looked at the ash we got back from the crematorium, I couldn't believe that the freckles were gone.

The climber, it turned out, when I checked with my mum, was John Brazinton.

Summer 2015, Thetford Forest

Mum comes to ours to visit. She sits in the front room, we've been for a walk in Thetford Forest and eaten cheese on toast. Mum has picked up a climbing book I've borrowed from a mate, which is, of course, the only book I want to read: *One Day as a Tiger,* about Alex MacIntyre (Dirty Alex), who was killed in the mid eighties by a single stone which fell from Annapurna's south face. It's a new book, recently written by John Porter, twenty-five odd years after his mate died.

I start to plan how I can get the book off her – divert her with a gardening book perhaps – when she speaks up.

'Ooh. Al Rouse. I knew him.'

I look at her. Al Rouse was a serious climber, one of the best ever, who died on K2 after being the first Brit to summit it. He had been in the Piranha Club along with Al Harris: the club motto being 'That Which Is Sufficient Is Not Enough'.

'What are you on about now, Mother?'

'Al Rouse. Your dad and me climbed with him in Liverpool. He was very good looking, girls liked him.'

'Not possible I am afraid, Mother. Al Rouse went to Cambridge. Famously. Your wits are addled.'

'It says that here, but he was from Liverpool; he must have been in Merseyside Climbing Club. We didn't know him well, just to say hello to.'

I quickly check on Wikipedia and am furious to find out she's right.

'Ooh, look, Mike Hammill. I knew him too. He was hard, one of the hard climbers. He had a face like a sledgehammer. I've told you about him. He was from Sheffield, he was always on about Stanage. Stanage, Stanage, Stanage.'

I sit and consider. She turns a page in the book.

'Any other famous climbers you know, Mother? Chris Bonington perhaps?'

'Who's he?'

I give up. I sit and think for a while.

'What was Dad like as a climber, Mum?'

She drops the book and looks up into the air.

'Well. Quite good I think. I remember him doing *Cemetery Gates*, everyone seemed quite impressed. He got bored of course. A lot of the men were very macho; macho types who couldn't make it with women. Then in his third year he knuckled down to work a bit, and of course he was going out with me, so we spent all our time together.'

I pick up my slate guide book and point to the name of a first ascensionist of one of the early routes.

'Is this someone he climbed with, Mum? "J Brazinton"?'

'Yes: John. He went out with your Auntie Nica. She worked at Plas y Brenin one summer. John was one of the macho types, he couldn't believe his luck with Nica, and they weren't together long.' Auntie Nica was glam.

'Well who's with him? R Kane?'

'Yes. Rick Kane. He was lovely. Very quiet, lovely lad. Always wore nice jumpers. It was terrible when he died.'

She looks at the book.

'Funny. They never really climbed together, they weren't much like each other. Maybe it's not the same ones.'

'Brazinton and Kane? Look at the names. It'd be a bit of co-incidence, don't you think?'

I give up again.

Dad didn't like climbing because of the mortality rate at the time. Climbers in the late sixties could and did die. The gear was only starting the long journey to standardised high quality and rigorous testing. At the top level, many of that generation climbed themselves into extinction. So in Dad's head, climbing was lethal, made more so by car crashes, on the fast roads and blind corners of the roads heading into north Wales.

I can't find out much about Rick Kane and John Brazinton. The route they did – *Bluebottle* – was a direct start to Al Harris' *Gideon*. The description in the guide says it is a 'bold alternative start to Gideon'. A later guide book will call it an inferior variation. For Rick and John, it was a day out in the early seventies, spent doing something; then they would have gone and written it up in the 'new routes' book, at the time kept in Al Harris' cafe. Maybe they went back to Deiniolen – the Liverpool University

Club hut was there – and maybe they went to one of Harris' infamous parties afterwards, but I can't find out.

John Brazinton was hit by rockfall in the Alps, apparently retrieving a rucksack from high up on a climb. Rick Kane was killed in an electrical storm in the Alps, struck by lightning. Few people, if any, climbed *Bluebottle*.

To my dad, it must have seemed such a waste of life. 'Couldn't they just be sensible?' he shouted at the telly, frustrated at people suffering the consequences of their actions, the death or injury from risks they just didn't have to take.

Most mornings I walk my son to school. There is a busy road to cross with a pelican crossing. When the red light shows, I look at the lorries and cars approaching and decide whether I think they are slowing down at all before we start to cross with the bleeping green man. My son is riding his bike, and every time he lurches up to the edge of the road my heart hops, and I spring into my step, leaning forward on my toes like a boxer. Ready to sprint and grab him from danger. I look at his curls escaping from under his bike-helmet – we call it his 'lid' because it keeps his jam in.

I won't imagine him being hit by a car. I can't imagine him dead in a car crash as a teenager killed by the bravado of one of his mates. Or overdose, or suicide. I can't imagine him hit by rockfall, or zapped by lightning. I get it, Dad, I do. I understand why you didn't like the risks I took when I was a teenager. You wouldn't like what I'm doing now, not the climbing. But it was never really your choice.

On the way back from school, my son asks if he can ride back on the road, just the little street that we live on, quiet. The pavements aren't very wide and he occasionally falls off them.

'Okay,' I say. 'But if a car comes you have to move to the side of the road.' I speak sternly, as if I am cross with him, but I'm not. I watch him go, and hope that he listened, hope that the next person coming around that corner isn't a dickhead. Someone who thinks their 'skill' means they can drive fast. For whom the laws of physics don't apply. Someone who thinks that because there isn't usually a child on a bike, then there never will be. Someone not tired, not careless, not fiddling with the CD player. Everything that everyone does.

CHAPTER 11

Never Never Land

May 2015, Thetford Forest

When I come back from the trip this time, it's nice to sit down and have a cup of tea without brewing it on a camp stove. On the settee, telly on, chips for tea.

The nice feeling of everything being easy lasts for about an hour. The blare of the telly, a dance competition, with celebrities I've never heard of, that is: no climbers. I watch the routines, I can't tell what's good or bad, instead I think about which of the dancers I'd like to fuck. All of them, I decide. The chips weigh heavy in my stomach, I feel sleepy from the insulin coursing round my blood dealing with all the carbohydrates. The third cup of tea, overbrewed and over-sweetened, furs up my mouth.

There's so much to do. Plans for the garden, plans for the upstairs bedroom. Hedges to cut. Work to sort out because this current job is nearly done, the rooms in the health centre looking more recognisably like consulting rooms and X-ray suites. I don't have anything else in the pipeline.

'I'm heading up,' I say to Tanya. 'Come on, son. Time to brush our teeth.'

I climb up to my son's bunk with him. He doesn't like to go to sleep on his own. The light is on, so I read my new guide book while he turns into his duvet. He is holding on to his toy badger called Stripes. Tanya's dad, who died a few years ago, got it for him when he was a few days old. His breathing slows, but I know it will be a while before I can sneak out, climbing down the steps of his bunk-bed with delicate footwork and good control of my core muscles.

While I wait for this chance; wait for him to be properly asleep, I read the book. It turns out that the cure for an obsession is not more information. There are a lot of routes in this book, nine hundred in total. It is not just the photos and route description either, there's other bits and pieces. Some pieces of writing called 'Diary of a Slatehead', made to look as if they're type-written. I dip into them; apparently, they're the story of someone called Martin Crook who climbed in the eighties. The sentences are long, complicated and run forever.

* * *

Early eighties, Liverpool; Caernarfon; Dinorwig

Unemployment had started to rise from the already high levels of the 1970s, eventually doubling to around 3 million people.

There were different names for the same thing. The dole. Unemployment benefit. The Rock and Roll. Government Sponsored Art Scheme. (Art? Because you were drawing it.) 'The sixties, it was a party time wasn't it? Full employment. The people who came here could afford to drop out. But with us – we squeezed things pretty hard,'[19] said Martin Crook, who everyone called Crooky.

Crooky, short and light, boyish proportions, had learned to climb on the crags around Liverpool: on the good red sandstone of Helsby, and the tough ten-metre climbs of Pex Hill. Pex Hill had more graffiti than gear placements. It made your fingers tough and technique perfect, or scared the shit out of you then broke your ankles. For Crooky, all of this was just training, he liked to climb in the Alps on high mountain routes with ice-axes and crampons.

But there was nothing to do in Liverpool. Not just a temporary situation of no work, but absolutely no prospect of it. And dozens of others, everyone you'd been to school with, for a start, were in the same boat. Across Britain, teenagers with no money but infinite time formed bands or spent all their spare time dressing outrageously: Punks, Goths and New Romantics.

To sign on, you had to go to your local dole office, fill in a form, declare that you were looking for work, and a fortnight later you would receive a cheque through the post – the giro. So you could wait for the giro, which came fortnightly, in your home town, likely in the house you had grown up in, with nothing to do. If your mates started to get birds but you didn't have one, or the girlfriend you'd had from school chucked you for a lad with a gold Cortina, what were you staying for?

It was just as easy to sign on in a different town, the same rules for unemployment benefit applied across the country. If you did not like being in Liverpool, or London, or Bolton because there was nothing to do, you could hitchhike, or save the money for the bus or the train and get out of town. For those who had found climbing, perhaps through a sympathetic teacher at school, the answer was to head to somewhere with a large amount of rock. North Wales was ideal.

Once in north Wales, the first stop would be Caernarfon dole office to sign on, queuing on hard plastic chairs in a cloud of cigarette smoke. It was atmospheric, the hum of Welsh and English being spoken, glares from the indigenous unemployed, and the dead eyes of the clerks assembled from the parts of once-decent human beings. The best bit of the brief interrogation was the discovery that if your address was in Llanberis, Clwt-y-bont, Deiniolen or Nant Peris, then you were in a golden territory, which meant, according to the rigid rules of social security, that you could sign on by post. You would only have to send in a form every fortnight declaring that Yes, you were still looking for work, and No, you hadn't found any.

Then every Thursday the Post Office van, jolly in clothes of red and gold, would make the rounds of the villages and drop the giro cheque through your door. £18.50 per week in 1980, so £37 for the fortnight. Happy spending. While it lasted.

The climbing community followed crazes. In 1981, everyone was at Tremadog, where Ron Fawcett put up *Strawberries,* and Johnny Redhead put up *Sexual Salami* and *Hitler's Buttock.* The climbing press, led by *High* and rival *Crags*, picked up on this, and Tremadog was where it was at.

Then in the summer of 1982, round about the time when Argentinian troops surrendered to British forces in the Falklands, everyone went to climb limestone at Pen Trwyn. Mel Griffiths put up *Axle Attack,* Johnny Redhead put up *Disillusioned Screw Machine* with Andy Pollitt, and Jerry Moffat put up *Masterclass*. There were sixty-seven new routes that year, and more than a hundred the year after[20] – that is a lot. But these crazes could fade fast.

When you couldn't get a lift out of Llanberis valley, the quarries were only a walk away, up the steep path, to have a poke around. Climbers and locals would wander up and take a few roofing slates or the beam from a roof. These might become part of someone's building project and be sold for a few quid. Some of the huts still had quarrymen's stools or a forgotten tool, but these disappeared as souvenirs. 'We'd do a lot of exploring, wandering around and the rest of it. Sometimes we'd go there to smoke dope or just have a wander around. It sounds a bit daft. We'd go and have a bit of a fire in one of the huts, or a bit of a party,' said Martin Crook.[21]

Crooky had a natural eye for rock. He had a database brain of 'every bit of rock he'd ever seen'.[22] By just hanging around in the quarries, Crooky saw the quarried faces as none different to a natural cliff face. Black powder had operated just like freeze-thaw, the fast expansion of hot gas rather than the slow expansion of ice levering off blocks and slabs, exposing bare rock underneath: slabs, arêtes and corners.

In February 1984, all hope was at an end, just as it was every February. The days were short and heavy, long nights of electric lights and drinking boredom. Christmas cheer fades quickly, signs of spring would be a month away – may as well be never. It rained.

The quarries fit the mood, unlike the surrounding sheep-grazed hills, or the elemental anvils of the sea cliffs. The sheds and blast shelters were empty, doors and windows off. It was like a battle had passed by, clearing the inhabitants from a once busy landscape.

There was a strange sound through the quarries, a mono-tone buzz on the edge of hearing, weirdly electrical. At first it was spooky; almost imaginary: was it the start of some devastating brain illness? But no, the noise was real. It was the vibration of all the millions of gallons of water running through the shaft right through the middle of the mountain, powering the turbines for the hydroelectric power station. From being spooky and eerie, familiarity made it reassuring, the snore of a friendly giant.

There were odd buildings and structures left behind from the quarries or newly built for the power station. Around one corner from the quarry road was a concrete plinth with scaffolding handrails. It looked like the podium from which Hitler made speeches, so the climbers called this area Nuremberg. A climber could stand up there, back straight, and, with much hand waving, deliver a speech in silly accented mock-German – 'Kartoffelkopf verboten nicht!'[23] – while his mates cried with laughter.

'People like us, in the early days, quick as we can, brush a load of stuff off, sweep stuff off ledges, quick test of a handhold, and then just go and try it. Usually taking several attempts,' said Crooky.[24]

Crooky's first climb on slate was called *Never Never Land*. It was a groove up a tall slabby cliff, round the corner from Nuremberg. Halfway up was an old metal spike, about two inches thick and maybe a foot long, some long-lost use for supporting quarry pulleys or a skyline. Looping a sling around this spike was important for protection, and it was just before the hardest bit of the climb. The thing was, it was also bent upwards, so if you fluffed the hard moves you would be rectally impaled on it.

'That was bit hard for me, had to push myself a bit on that. I didn't particularly like slabs that much. But we did have fun climbing it and – retrospectively – walk past it and think, you know, it was a good line.'[25]

This was the start of the boom in routes on slate. Really, it was just clumps of mates going off into a weird bit of wasteland, trying to kill some time and have a laugh.

The climbing itself was strange compared to rhyolite in the mountains around, or limestone on the coast. Slate had little friction, it was smooth, even glass-like. To climb it, you had to use the little cracks and fissures, you couldn't paste a toe on to a slight change in angle and expect it to stick like on gritstone in the Peak District. But slate dried really quickly, water flowing straight off it.

On the ground, walking around and laughing with your mates would be good fun, sometimes they wouldn't even actually climb anything because something else funny had turned up, or everyone got too high, or it rained. Or you would all be there laughing and get out on a climb and – it would change. 'You'd be on a climb and it's all a good laugh, and then suddenly you're in a different world'.[26]

Crooky's mates would be at the bottom of the cliff, looking up, oblivious, no sign of trouble apart from the immobility of the leader. 'There'd be a load of people at the bottom just standing, rolling joints, thinking "get on with it".'[27]

High above your mates, far above your last piece of gear, life looks fragile. 'I've come a bit far out now, and I can't get back down.'[28] The holds might run out, or the next visible one would be out of reach. A quick check, looking down. Too far from gear, likely to hit the deck and make a crater when you landed. No choice but to get yourself together and try and move upwards into the better holds or to the next piece of gear.

Looking back, Crooky is reflective. 'We couldn't have stayed like that. We'd all just have died. Fairly early.'[29] These young dole climbers didn't die. They hung around with each other and went climbing, and got better and better at it.

CHAPTER 12

Llanber'

August 2015, Llanberis

A weekend here, a weekend there. Tanya is off to London for a few days to show my son what an actual city looks like. I've been before and I don't want to go again. Last time, as we threaded our way through the crowd of people milling up to the escalators on the Tube, some twat cut in front of us and pushed my son out of the way, not realising he was even there. I shouted 'Thanks, mate!' after him, trapped by the crowd heading up to the daylight, but I didn't want to just shout. I wanted to grip him by his throat, push him down off the platform and press his face onto the third rail. Best I don't go.

Last night's rain sounded heavy in the tent, crackling as the drops hit the waterproof outer. This morning the sky is light and, although it's still raining, it looks like it will be on its way soon enough. Anyway, I've driven a long way to be here and I still want to go climbing.

Lee is already sitting in his car. He's got his Astra parked on the gravel at the farm campsite above Llanberis, so it faces the slate quarries across the valley. When you know the quarries well enough, you can pick out the features, the different pits that the quarrymen named after women and places: Matilda, Garret, California. The big crater of Garret has been misnamed Australia by climbers; actually Australia was only one small part of it, which climbers now call the Far Out Level. I only know the levels and little areas by the climber-given names: Nuremberg, Watford Gap, the back wall of Twll Mawr. I can cover with a sliver of fingernail the climb I fell off yesterday. I know the shape of that piece of rock, its slabs and overlaps and lack of holds.

I open the passenger-side door: 'Do you want company, mate?'

'Get in. I'm not wanting to sit around the campsite all day. What do you want to do?'

'I'm not fucked about shiny-shopping. I've no money and I don't need owt.'

Shiny-shopping means going to the gear-shops down in Llanberis and buying gear for climbing. There are many kinds of carabiners, and metal wedges threaded onto wire called nuts. Cams expand and lock into a crack when you release a spring-loaded trigger. Everything is anodised in happy colours or polished bright chrome.

Going shiny-shopping feels like it is climbing. You look at the gear, thinking of those ambitious climbs you could use it for. You handle something immaculately polished, a piece of metal the size of a wine gum that could hold the weight of a Land Rover.

Then you are sixty quid lighter, adding value to your rack of five hundred quid's worth, and no nearer the top of anything.

'We could head out in a bit? It might clear up?' I ask.

'I was thinking that. If it stops raining, the slate is going to dry pretty quick, especially if there's a bit of breeze on it.'

Across the valley is the zig-zag of a path. It's like a cartoon lightning flash: drystone slate walls through the small-oak woodlands. The trees are greener in the rain, and the stone of the walls looks black and shiny.

Lee and I walk out of the campsite and down the hill, past small sheepfields towards the village; a row of terrace houses reaches up from the village. The slope of the road is hard on our shins. My boots go *clump-clump-clump*; it sounds like a marching soldier.

The rain taps on our hoods, but it's not enough to trouble our alpine-grade waterproofs. Lee's jacket can scrunch down to the size of a wizened apple, and mine is made of some siliconised space-age hydrocarbon which looks strangely crispy. The right colours too, grey of slate with orange zips like rusty machinery.

We walk down Ceunant Street, a terrace of quarrymen's cottages. There is a tall well-built chapel on the right, with high narrow windows and grey stone: as severe as Methodism but with none of the humility. This chapel was built by the Welsh-speaking villagers, some of them the quarrymen. It sits higher on the hill than the Anglican church in Llanberis: St Padarn's was built by the Assheton-Smiths, the English-speaking quarry owners, who made sure the tower was higher than the chapel's.

The road flattens out, Ceunant Street turns into Capel Coch Road and this comes out onto High Street just next to Joe Brown's. He still lives somewhere on the hill behind us, and he likes to be left alone.

Lee and I walk over to the Spar and buy our lunches for the day. For me a bag of bread rolls, pack of bananas, cheese slices, salami. We both get pork pies, factory made with a purple and pink label on their cellophane wrapper. These ones are pretty good. Lee rates them as 'the best factory-made pork pie ever'.

He trained to be a butcher years ago, straight out of college.

In the queue, the girl behind the counter speaks in Welsh to the old man before me. I love to hear the flow of the language, the trickle of the sounds. It's a nice feeling to see people talking to each other and enjoying hearing them chat, without knowing what they are saying. When I step up, she doesn't even try to speak Welsh with me; straight away says, 'Hello. Do you need a carrier bag?' I don't know how she knows I don't speak Welsh. It's probably obvious.

High Street is wet, the pavements shiny, water drips off the scaffolding up around the chipshop that burned down last year. The houses and shops are built in narrow tall terraces, three storeys high, big clusters of chimneys for multiple Victorian fireplaces against the chill damp. The houses are built of slate or rubblestone, but they have been rendered and then painted. Towards the middle of the village they are white, pale yellow or mint green, but at the far end of the High Street is Pete's Eats, the climbers' cafe, painted in daring Mediterranean shades of indigo and terracotta.

There are quite a few people up and down the street, despite the rain. Grannies wear Marks & Spencer macs which are such good quality that they have lasted long enough to become old-fashioned looking. Builders are in jeans and branded hooded tops which will end their days covered in cement dust and silicon. Climbers are obvious because they wear bright waterproofs in the same shade as Pete's Eats' paintwork. They'll be wandering between the five or six different gear shops, before dropping money into the local economy for tea, cake and all-day breakfasts.

Lee and I aren't going into the village for the cafe and gear-shops. We head down the other way, towards Dolbadarn Castle, built as a prison eight hundred years ago. As we walk down the street, a memory surfaces, something from my childhood.

I've walked down this way before. The first time was on a week-long trip in 1989 when I was eleven, on a week's worth of tame adventure: easy rock climbing, dry-slope skiing, archery: all the normal shit Liverpool schoolchildren needed to broaden their horizons. The first night, the instructors took eight of us on a night walk up to Dolbadarn Castle, under the orange of the streetlights, then turned our torches off and told ghost stories.

The trip had already started badly. At Llandudno, we disembarked from the coach, which drove off. Apparently the booking forms for the dry-ski slope were on it, and the manager took one look at us and refused to honour the contract without the paperwork to prove they *had* to teach us. Instead, the teachers bravely took us on a walk up Great Orme in the freezing wind, then allowed us to mess about on the beach. I fell into the water from a pier, soaking wet tracksuit bottoms clung to my legs.

That evening at the youth hostel, we were shown around by a female instructor in her early twenties, who had blonde permed hair and looked athletic. The dorm-rooms were given geographical names. I was in Abyssinia, which I vaguely knew was the old name for Ethiopia, famous for its famines. My friends were in a dorm named Virginia, which unbelievably had *triple* bunk beds.

'Now,' the blonde instructor said, 'can you remember what dorm you are in?'

'Vagina,' said my mate Rick, utterly straight faced.

She barked a laugh in surprise, then strangled it in her

throat with an odd gulping sound. Her facial muscles locked. Was she going to crack? No, she was not. She went to the door. 'Tracy, can you come in here a minute?' Tracy appeared, with dark permed hair.

'Now, tell me again, what room are you in?' she asked Rick, with barely a flicker of amusement.

Now, Rick knew he had gone too far the first time. But his only chance now – not to have this reported to our teacher, the feared Mr MacCausland – was to play his hand to the bitter end.

'Vagina,' he said again, as if he was a doctor telling them they had cancer.

The two women looked at each other and dissolved laughing. Twenty minutes later, our group of mates was dragged off into the night to see Dolbadarn Castle.

We spent a rainy week being driven in minibuses between the various outdoor activity centres in the valley. We shot arrows at targets and predictably lost one in the bracken and spent an hour looking for it like a police forensic sweep wearing tracksuits instead of white overalls. We shot playing cards with air-rifles in a barn. We were top-roped up a slab of rock, with our climbing instructor shouting, 'Don't grab the heather. The heather. There. That bush you're holding. Let go of it. Let go.'

We started on a march up Snowdon, and our instructors binned it off after ten minutes walking, turned around and took us to a river. They threw a rope across and made us all get soaked crossing the flood-swollen river, upside down, commando-style. 'Freezing!' we shouted, as the instructors relaxed their grip on the rope enough to dip us into the river, icy water flooding up our backs under our cagoules.

The instructor told us he couldn't believe our language. In

the minibus back we all sang '*Fuck* fuck fuck-fuck, *Fuck* fuck fuck-fuck, *Fuck* fuck fuck-fuck....' I think the instructors liked us, but they were also pleased to see us go.

Whatever it was that inspired me did not happen on that school trip. No one could have known that what the dropouts and students were doing up there right then would be important to me so much later in life. I had to find it myself, or more accurately, be shown it by friends like Lee.

When it rained, the unemployed climbers could not sit around their manky houses all day. Few had televisions, maybe an old black-and-white Philips, or a huge Hitachi wooden box with bulbous screen. Anyway, telly used electricity, and using electricity meant feeding the meter with fifty pence pieces.

Sitting around the house meant sitting in the wreck of last night's drinking, or confronting the growing pile of washing up left by housemates: invariably other dole climbers. Sooner or later, the unemployed climber would have to leave the house in search of conversation.

That meant going to Pete's Eats, the cafe on the corner of High Street and Goodman Street. When it rained, you could just see, through the condensation, people sitting inside. You would try and work out who was there before you walked in. Usually there would be the kindred spirits of the climbing unemployed, killing time.

There were still relatively few people new-routing, maybe a dozen climbers. 'Llanberis was grey. The village was grey, the slate was grey. The people were grey. Even the climbers were grey,' said Mike Raine, years later. 'What we did was: get our dole cheques, sit in Pete's Eats 'til it stopped raining. When it did you would go up to your patch and start cleaning your line from a top-rope. Then when you were ready, you'd ask for some help belaying, and you would go and climb it.'[30]

Some of the climbers were not strictly speaking unemployed, just doing a good impression of it. Andy Newton had moved down to Llanberis from Liverpool, working as an outdoors instructor and studying for a PGCE (teaching qualification) at Bangor University. He was on teacher's pay and conditions, and got time off for working evenings, so could hang out in Pete's. 'Pete turned round to me one morning and said, "Have you got a job?" "You cheeky fucker, of course I've got a job! How do you think I spend all my time in your cafe if I haven't got a job?"'[31]

Pete and Vicky Norton had opened the cafe back in 1978 and put their hearts and backs into it. The food was basic and cheap, and there was plenty of it – massive portions of hand-cut chips, fried breakfasts, enormous amounts of cheap greasy calories. Tea came in pint mugs and cost pennies. When the dole youths were flush, that is, on giro day, they had the incredible pleasure of ordering a 'full set', the British Isles' greatest claim to civilisation: bacon, egg, beans, black pudding, fried bread, fried tomato, mushrooms. Nothing left off. This was also a pleasure for the spectators. Watching a skinny dole youth polishing off a plate of food bigger than his head would cause gasps of amazement: where did it go? Acclaim.

Unlike other cafe owners, Pete didn't ask anyone to leave. If someone could scrape up enough for a cup of tea, or if they couldn't but were sitting with someone who had, then they could stay there all day. Pete and Vicky's idea, that teenagers weren't automatically trouble to be glared at and chased away, was revolutionary and in sharp contrast to Britain's national culture. Youths in general were viewed with total distrust and exiled to kick empty drinks cans around wind-blown shopping precincts.

Climbers could chat with their mates, repetitive conversations that just filled in time. That time you climbed *this,* Stevie Haston's latest horrendous crack climb. Relief as the news was that it had fallen down. News, a fight in the pub. Kung fu and martial arts. Semi-clever attempts at finding out whether anyone had got off with the girl from the hairdresser's without giving away that you fancied her.

From time to time, the condensation would be wiped off the window and the sky looked at. The stacked levels of Vivian Quarry could be seen from the Goodman Street side window. The line of *Comes the Dervish* was visible, assuming the rain didn't blot out the far side of the valley. Were there other lines as good as that? Was the rain clearing? Was the sky brighter? Could you maybe get out that afternoon?

Climbing magazines, *Crags* and *High,* bought by Pete, were passed around and read to tatters. Every picture, every route analysed and sucked dry of clues. The Javlin adverts in *Crags* were particularly closely studied, as they featured sexy women semi-clothed under bright thick-pile thermal fleeces. Climbing books, the pornography of adventure, were passed around and lent out.

Pete's Eats was also the home of the 'new routes' book. In any climbing area, the New Routes Book is traditionally kept in the cafe or pub which is friendliest to climbers. A climber coming in from the first ascent would go straight to the book and write up what he had done, and what grade he thought it was. On a rainy day, others would flick through it, and contemplate repeating the climbs. Or adding to them.

More and more slate climbs were added to the new routes book. Each one represented someone's day out, a day of being something other than unemployed. More climbers came to the area, and added more climbs, so the scene started to build momentum.

The turning point for slate's popularity was the 'St Paul-like transformation of Paul Williams'.[32] Paul Williams was an influential climber and guide book writer; everyone loved him despite, or because of, his embarrassing sense of humour. According to Paul Williams, slate was a load of crap and a waste of time. No one knows what happened – maybe the drip-drip of the stories about the quarries in Pete's or in the Padarn hotel or photographing some of the first ascents of the Rainbow Slab by Johnny Redhead and pals – but Williams changed his mind.

He disappeared into the quarries for months. When he emerged, he had climbed an enormous route called *Colossus*, which he declared to be an instant classic. He wrote an article called 'The Slate of the Heart', then set out on tour with his 'Slate of the Heart' slideshow. He projected his pictures onto the walls of any climbing-gym, gear shop or village hall that would have him. The light shone through the celluloid, the projector clunked and clicked, the slides shuffled in and out of their mechanical magazine. The sunlit sweep of rock of the Rainbow Slab, a tiny dot of a climber on it in an unlikely shape. His belayers hanging in space from the bolt belay. The colours of the Lycra, turquoise and yellow, bright rose-red. A shirtless Stevie Haston, Maltese black curly hair and physique from the pull-up bar in the back room of Pete's Eats, squatting like a frog about to spring on *Ride the Wild Surf*. A climber teetering his way up a rusty hydraulic pipe left over from quarry days, now the basis of different climbs: *Looning the Tube*, and the less well known *Tubing to Loon*. This no longer exists, the pipe was smashed off the wall in early 1986: without the pipe, it was named – logically enough – *Pruning the Tube*.

These photos had an immediate effect: it set climbers' minds on fire. The moves and the body positions looked like something you couldn't get anywhere else; they were so much more than ladder-climbing poses. The clothes were remarkable, a fuck-you to beige, with stripy Lycra leggings and punky armless T-shirts. The falls looked barely survivable. All this was very attractive: come and be a micro-quarryman,[33] go west and seek your fortune. There's fuck-all where you are.

One of the pictures showed a local climber called Trevor Hodgson, better known as Carlos because of his Spanish-waiter moustache. The photo has been double exposed, taken from the belay on the Rainbow. On the left of the picture, he is in a typical uncomfortable-looking slate-climbing pose. One hand is up, elbow cranked, his legs are bent and toes stand on invisibly small holds. He is scraping his nose on the rock and forcing his weight through his thighs and calves, pushing up, with his body nearly sideways on, like a crab scuttling upwards. To the right of the picture, taken a second later, he is falling so fast his face is blurred. He has turned to face the camera, grabbed the knot of his rope with both hands and is looking down, a moment of total sensory clarity about what is happening and where he is going, which is down. His shadow is cast on the rock, his rope is suddenly slack, he is in for a whopper of a fall.

This kind of thing drew more climbers in.

CHAPTER 13

Red and Yellow and Pink and Green....

August 2015, Rainbow Slab

Past Dolbadarn Castle, then through the gate by the football fields. It is dead flat ground, floodplain and alluvial silt, grassed over. The footpath runs next to the tourist railway, then turns towards the huge waterwheel and workshops of the National Slate Museum. At this valley-floor level were workshops, foundries; everything they needed to get the slate out. We could go that way. At Vivian Quarry there is an old incline that leads up the hill, but I have a different way to try.

We can't go along the road toward the power station: most definitely not allowed. The company that owns the power station is First Hydro Company: the whole of the slate quarries is theirs. Officially, it doesn't allow climbing, and it's never liked it. A few years ago, the climbing got really visible, really popular, and a lawyer decided that they 'could be liable' if anyone had an accident. It took a lot of negotiating by the British Mountaineering Council (BMC) to keep the blind eye turned.

But through the scrubby oak woodland that starts to creep up the valley side, there are traces of paths, marked by posts with discreet yellow and blue paint. Steps and worn footprints through the moss and leaf litter expose the fractured flat slate fragments that make up a third of the soil. The faint trails lead up a few metres and we hit the start of the zig-zags. A track between parallel drystone walls strikes down the hill to earth in the oak trees.

A wooden gate leads in. The walls are high, so you can't see over them. It is as steep as a staircase. My legs are weak, I don't need big thigh muscles to climb well. Just for once, I regret not doing something like running. Not enough to actually take it up as a hobby. It's just a fleeting desire, to not feel like I am dying because I am out of breath.

I sweat under my waterproofs. I whip my hood down. I can barely feel the rain on my head. It's clearing up, I tell myself, but when I touch my hair, it is soaking. When it runs down my face, it is refreshing like a cold drink, then tickles. Finding something else to be annoyed about diverts my mind from aching legs and bursting lungs.

Fuck's sake! I'm meant to be in good nick!

Lee plods on in front, hood up. He trudges up just like I do, but he's got a lightness of step. He's wearing trainers, I've got heavy leather mountaineering boots on, tiring to wear. If you save a pound weight on your foot, the saying goes, it's worth saving four pounds weight in your pack. Is this because of the leverage of your leg? Could be.

Then the zig-zags straighten out and the slope flattens. We emerge underneath an iron bridge. Crude, just girders and sheet steel rusted orange, thin handrails eaten thinner by the Welsh weather. The bridge is at the top of the incline that leads down to Vivian Quarry. That's the way Lee has always walked up into the quarries; he's been coming a few more years than me.

'I've walked up across that bridge so many times. I never wondered where this path actually went,' says Lee. Just beside it there is a cluster of small cellular buildings, too far away from the action to be blast-shelters. Offices, or engine houses, or barracks for the workers who came across from Anglesey.

On one of the slate-stacked walls, someone has graffitied a life-size picture of an angel. Life-size? The same size as a human anyway. Who knows how big angels are? The artwork of the graffiti is good, in black and white, the face hooded, gothic looking. It took talent to get it like that.

Cantilevered across the top of one of the walls are huge spikes of slate, overhanging the path. Lee hops up, grabs on and does a pull-up or two. So do I. This is how traditions start.

Gentle slopes now, trails through the trees. None of the trees are very big; they have stayed small and stunted. Above us, one oak got enough light and nutrition to shoot up tall and spread like a lowland oak. But its branches are bare, a few twiggy clusters of green, the last gasps of panic as the tree realises it is starving to death. Too big to support itself on the thin soil, which is nothing more than rock fragments, really. As it has got weaker, fungal spores have lodged and spread threads through its timber. In a couple of years, it will start to drop its limbs, the insects will move in and its death will feed a million lives.

We come out across the stream, stepping carefully over stones in the white foam. On the other side are brambles and a swampy puddle which I can wade through with my heavy boots. Lee can't – he's got his trainers on – and hops across stepping stones, then dances across the top of a wall that runs along the cliff edge in front of us. We turn the corner and walk along a nice generous path, the rock on our left and the drop to our right. Views of the power station buildings below us, and that concrete curved bridge across the llyn (lake). Then turn a corner, and we are at the bottom of the Rainbow Slab.

Spring 1984, Tal-y-waenydd, Fachwen.

John Silvester saw an 'amazing piece of obvious rock'[34] from the valley road down from Nant Peris. He turned a corner and, across the valley, amongst the grey rubble of the levels was a sheet of rock, a cliff just out of vertical. It was as blank as a car windscreen, except there was a strange feature running across its face. It looked like 'there was a ghost train still running along the old tracks below the rainbow, heading towards Llanberis, with its smoke trail heading skywards, then flattening out'.[35]

This slab obsessed Silvester; he had to go looking for it to see if it could be climbed. When he found it, the ghost-train-smoke-plume feature was obvious: enormous and strange, formed by huge geological pressure, like a monster-child bending a lead pipe. It made a curving arc rippled from the slate; a thin, braided bulge that came out nearly a foot in places, rounded and smooth but with irregularities that might offer holds to a skillful climber. The rest of the slab's surface was crazed with cracks and rippled with texture. It shot up, steep for forty metres, with purples tingeing the grey-black.

It looked difficult but not impossible to climb, and so Silvester needed to drop a rope down from the top, and abseil to check if there were any holds or gear placements, knock off loose rock. The thing was, he hadn't got a rope. Well, he had – but it was a tatty abseil rope that he had retrieved from the Eiger, left behind on someone else's hasty retreat from a storm. Luckily Silvester was living in a caravan in the garden of someone who could lend him one. His 'landlord' was Johnny Redhead, otherworldly artist and north Wales' 'best' resident climber at the time. But asking was a risk. Silvester wanted to be the first to climb that route; if word got out, wouldn't other climbers race in and steal the lines?

Johnny Redhead had bought this cottage, *Tal-y-waenydd,* in Fachwen, from Paul Williams in the late seventies or early eighties. The houses around the area were cheap, no more than a few thousand pounds. No one was valuing them as assets, they were still just places to live. As the deposit, Redhead included one of his own paintings, *The Disillusioned Screw Machine,* for Paul Williams' art collection (which would only ever comprise a single painting). The painting is best described by Redhead: he wrote that it was a portrait 'of a young nurse I used to know. She is rising naked in the air, squatting atop a giant pappus cock, her legs spread to reveal a filigreed vagina of winter larch... A mushroom type growth emerges from her left knee and threatens to topple her back into dense fecund vegetation.'[36] This was a painting – outrageous sexual subject, taunting name, intricately and sophisticatedly executed – that Redhead was proud of.

But a major source of his income was churning out canvasses of landscapes for the local tourist art trade. The money was useful for bills, or for buying Paul Williams' house off Redhead, but the process revolted him.

To put some distance between him and this commercially produced shite, Redhead sold them under pseudonyms: the names of his climbing partners. Dave Towse, his second for many of his most difficult leads and a gnarly climber in his own right, became the painter of 'mist-laden, lonely Fens landscape', while Andy Newton – funny, pleasant, sociable and

Liverpudlian – became the 'seascape artist who depicted long and low, moody canvasses of the sea and sky... to match the colour of your wallpaper.'[37]

Funded by these sales, Redhead could produce art to challenge the modern consumer society he loathed. He lived in a cottage with his partner and their kids. They had goats, rabbits and the occasional pig, and Redhead liked to do manual work on the smallholding, digging cesspits, logging and poaching: a John Seymour-esque ideal life. Climbing was a part of this, and indivisible from the art. 'When he was climbing well, he was painting well,' said Andy Newton.[38]

Redhead had an outrageous sense of humour: sex and shit, genitals, the ridiculousness of modern life. He found outrage amusing, saw it as betraying a defect in people's values or repression in their thinking. He loved to feign offence at other people's criticism of whatever he had just done, whether it be putting on an art show with giant papier mâché phalluses at Liverpool's Anglican cathedral, or drilling a bolt into a piece of virgin rock.

This often came across as extremely sexist. The climbing community was still male-dominated, as was the rest of society. Even amongst the 'traditional' values held by climbers on the scene, Redhead could cause spikes of offence, particularly with route names. His friend, Paul Williams, renamed *Menopausal Discharge,* calling it *Misogynist's Discharge*, in the Llanberis guide book. Attitudes in society were changing. Redhead rejected what he considered to be political correctness as another societal construct that he personally didn't feel bound by, another way to wind people up and create a reaction.

Redhead didn't give a fuck. He was an astonishing technical

climber. He prowled up the rock like a big cat, slinking up its face with small shifts of his hips to balance his weight and release his limbs. He was bold in the extreme, capable of keeping a lid on his fear where any other climber would have 'frightened themselves off'.[39] His routes, such as *The Bells! The Bells!,* could be terrifying experiences: it took six years for anyone to dare to repeat it.

When John Silvester knocked on Johnny Redhead's door in 1984, it was obvious something was up. Silvester was an intense man, well over six feet tall and – according to Redhead – a manic persona.[40] Obsession was shining out of Silvester's eyes. He looked excited and wanted to borrow an abseil rope: Redhead *had* to know what all this was about. Sylvester swore Redhead to secrecy: the line on the slab was 'classified information' and must not be revealed.

Actually, this suited Redhead fine. He was recognised by most in the climbing community as the best climber around, but he preferred to be an outsider. He didn't like crowds, he had no time at all for the manufactured competition from *High* or *Crags* magazines adopted by other climbers. He claimed never to have competed, climbed for the authentic desire of performing the movement and taking the risk, a spiritual deal in which he negotiated with his own life. He liked to climb with a close circle of friends, people who liked a laugh as much as he did. A secret slab with the potential for incredible lines would be just right.

CHAPTER 14

The Rainbow of Recalcitrance

August 2015, Rainbow Slab

Today, the Rainbow Slab is wet, soaked by last night's rain. Water is gradually draining from the whole of the levels, through cracks that emerge on the face of the slab. The water is running down the face of the rock, leaving black wet streaks. Slate is impermeable, that's why the quarry made so much money from roofing slates. When the bloody rain stops, we could stand here and watch the rock dry, turning from deep blackish purple into a paler grey, with the purple thrown deeper within.

As it is, no chance of climbing anything on it. Wet slate has the friction of wet glass. If you were high on a climb and the clouds broke, you would have to bail out, abseil down immediately. At the moment, we wouldn't get off the ground.

Lee points towards the end of the slab. 'That's *Red and Yellow and Pink and Green...* I did that on my birthday with the *Richard of York* finish. That was good. There's not much gear on it.'

Despite the rain, the sky is bright, and the bolts and their hangers shine. They don't run up in straight lines; rather, there are clusters of single and pairs of bolts in strategic places. Tracing the routes is like working out the constellations in the night sky. Here and there is a rough line; two bolts together marks a stance someone could belay from.

'*Pull My Daisy,* that'll be good when you're sharp on placing gear. The top third is run-out, though, and the climbing is still interesting, it's no romp to glory.'

I look at it. Another for the 'Not Yet' list.

'Do you remember that picture at Pete's Eats?' Lee asks.

Johnny Redhead climbs *Raped by Affection* (the image is prominently displayed in Pete's Eats).

I do. The camera shoots diagonally down the slab, Johnny Redhead is poised crawling up it, bearded chin pressed against the rock. His jet-black hair is curly and he is looking up, the white of his eye clearly visible. His climbing shoes are on holds so small it looks as if they are magically stuck to the rock. The fingers of his near hand are boning down hard on the smallest of holds, they are white, the blood squeezed out of them. His other hand is stretched up for his next hold, hasn't reached it yet, and hard to see what it is. In this stance, he looks like a lion sneaking up on an antelope. Below him is the llyn, with the power station road and concrete slab bridge across the reflection of clouds in the water. Underneath it was captioned 'Johnny Redhead on *Raped By Affection.'*

If I ever were to climb that – and I'd have to be a lot better, a lot braver than I am now – I think I'd flinch before telling people. Today, the name feels far worse than any 'fuck' or 'cunt' could be. Despite the fact that the name would make my mum, Tanya – and basically any woman I care about – instantly furious, I would still want to climb it.

What a name, though. What a fucking horrible name.

1984, Rainbow Slab

Johnny Redhead and Dave Towse wandered down to the base of the slab, with Redhead's lurcher, Ochre, in tow. They looked like gypsies: poachers or hunters, medieval gaudy clothes, earrings and long curly hair. But they weren't looking to take a rabbit or deer from the heath, they were there to climb. Out of deference to the 'classified information' and the claim that John Silvester had made, they left the smoke-trail feature alone, but anything else was fair game, whatever they could take was theirs.

Their first route was named *Cystitis by Proxy*, deliberately juvenile. Whoever first climbs the climb gets to name it, there are no rules – you go and write it in the 'new routes' book and that's it, it's named. *Cystitis* was as hard and as dangerous as they come. Normally, the first climber might be expected to name the slab. Fortunately, a climber called Mark Lynden (another of Silvester's friends and climbing partners) had climbed an easier line on the slab a few weeks before. To Lynden's less earthy mind, the smoke trail had looked like a rainbow, so he named his climb *Red and Yellow and Pink and Green, Orange and Purple and Blue*, after the children's song. This was lucky for the slab, which now would be known as the Rainbow Slab, rather than the Cystitis Slab. Not that this would have stopped anyone climbing the lines; for many climbers, claiming to have just 'got *Cystitis*' would have been the epitome of wit. Perhaps the next climb would get a better name....

The next climb was *Raped by Affection*. It was named after another of Redhead's paintings. The name is shocking, but deliberately chosen. Nothing he did was accidental, he was always looking for outrage and shock, jolting people out of comfortable thinking.

Redhead was genuinely trying to express the way a relationship can feel claustrophobic. No one else would see a climb as a 'way to, through and out of a relationship'.[41] The moves themselves, the alternation between extreme difficulty and easier ground, the change in emotional state across the course of the climb – 'He is dragged into town on shopping trips! He contemplates the sixty-foot fall ... She writes a "miss you" letter. The bolt is just out of reach!'[42] The description, in *...and One for the*

Crow, continues into what rapidly becomes cruder territory, involving 'the protagonist' having sex with a watermelon clasped between his partner's legs, while she reads *An Unsuitable Job for a Woman* by PD James.

After that, the next climb was *Poetry Pink*, by which time no one could be convinced it didn't have gross sexual meaning. Actually, it 'does not refer to the female labia ... I give no response to this nonsense.' All along – Redhead claimed – the name had referred to the shifting colours of the slab.[43]

Finally, John Silvester emerged from his caravan to climb the smoke-trail feature. He climbed up the first part of the Rainbow, but took two 'very big falls' from the hard bit.[44] Silvester was wearing a type of climbing shoe called EBs, soled with rigid rubber. A new climbing shoe called the Firé, made by Spanish company Boreal, was just starting to appear in Wales. They had soles of butyl rubber, sticky like warm liquorice. Climbers lucky enough to have a pair would lend them to each other, in the manner of cultists of a new and secret religion making converts.

The sticky rubber made a crucial difference, allowing Silvester to use just the friction of the rubber to stand on nothing more than a slight change in angle of the rock. The route was his. He called it – altogether more sensitively than Redhead or Towse – the *Rainbow of Recalcitrance.*

August 2015, Power Station, Rainbow Slab

At the head of the gorge, there's a little trail through and between the blocks, where the slate waste has been crushed by
feet. It stays well back from the edge, which is good – the drops
make me nervous. I'm careful with my balance on the wet rock.

Directly below us must be the concrete opening to the power station within the hill, two or three levels, perhaps thirty or
forty metres. It looks like a submarine pen and opens on to the
llyn. A concrete bridge curves in a smooth S-shape across the
llyn. The power station buildings, workshops and offices are on
the dock. The offices are oblong and utilitarian, made of slate
blocks like the old cottages, but roofed in ridged steel panels.
There is a white twenty-ton gantry crane, for unloading the
massive kit – enormous oil-cooled transformers, the turbines
themselves, replacement parts and drum after drum of copper cable. Around them are white lines and chevrons marking
out parking spaces, places which must be kept clear. They look
like hopscotch patterns or playground markings for football or
basketball.

It doesn't seem far down, because everything is recognisable, cars and vans of nameable models. Occasionally a person
walks between buildings, close enough to see whether they are
wearing a smart suit or workclothes, not close enough to really
recognise faces. We can hear a radio playing over a tannoy system, music, clang of a dropped tool and a shout across the yard.

I don't like to look at the people. I feel like they would be
more likely to see me if I looked at them, shout that we weren't
welcome. But today, the last of the rain is keeping people's
heads down, and when they come outside, they walk quickly

between the buildings or to their cars.

The quarries aren't entirely closed. Way above us, halfway up the hillside, the old quarry road is open. It runs between the end of the road at Bus Stop Quarry, at the Anglesey end of the quarries, up to Nant Peris at the bottom of the pass. On either side of it are fences, waist-high and barbed-wire topped, but not formidable. They are symbolic: you are Allowed on the quarry road, and Not Allowed onto the much more interesting territory beyond.

There are warning signs, red, yellow, black and white on plastic laminate boards, or sheets of aluminium. *Perygl! Dim Mynediad* with helpful subtitles of Danger! No Access.

Hah! I think. Laughable. How can a sign stop a determined man? It's a modern-day superstition, the quarry owners legally crossing themselves against the threat of liability. Physically as much use as saluting a magpie. But signs like that, brightly coloured and everywhere, create a *drip-drip-drip* that forms stalactites in the consciousness. Day to day we feel that there are unseen risks and dangers, that those in authority are wisely protecting us from. Unseen rules for our own benefit, and without knowing why, people become less willing to cross the fences.

If you go exploring, it's not safe. There are some long drops in the quarries, and bad steps, and some of our trails go across stacked scree next to a nasty edge. I wouldn't want it to be different. I wouldn't want the quarries to be tidied up, with way-marked trails and information boards.

Better to have those fences, and cross them deliberately, accepting the consequences. There is a trespasser's code – leave no sign, walk quietly, draw no attention. When fences do get damaged, near the quarry road, someone who may or may not be a climber walks up there. They will carry wire and wood, and put a quick, neat and effective repair in. Us trespassers will wink and the quarry owners will look back blank-faced, like the poacher and the gamekeeper crossing paths in the village pub.

1984, Power Station, Rainbow Slab

Neither Redhead nor Towse were the kind of climbers that wear olive green army surplus and long to be mistaken for members of the SAS. Towse had a pork-pie hat, with a bloom of curls bursting from under it, and a worn soft brown leather jacket. He looked like he could be in Dexy's Midnight Runners, per-haps playing the fiddle. Redhead had equally curly hair, a wild beard, gold hoop earrings and bright clothes; he looked like a sexy gypsy rogue, with a glint in his eye.

Both wore stripy Lycra leggings in the colour of wine gum or Love Hearts wrappers.[45] The style was emerging out of the punk look, gradually losing the aggressive leather biker jackets but keeping the dayglo. The Lycra, skin tight over muscled buttocks, thighs and calves, gave youthful male climbers an attractive sil-houette. It would look as if the climber was naked from the waist to the ankles (assuming for some reason that the viewer could ignore the incredible patterns), but wearing a baggy Christmas jumper or stripy punk T-shirt, socks and trainers. This looked ruder and more sexual than someone just being completely naked: like one of Vivienne Westwood's Seditionaries line of punk T-shirts, with two strong-legged cowboys lighting each other's cigarettes, their dicks nearly touching but hats, jackets and boots still on.

The bright colours, shouts and laughter as the climbers explored the lines attracted attention. They were only a few hundred feet higher than the offices and workshops of the power station. The official mind could not handle punk harlequins, climbing uncontrolled above the power station. When climbers were spotted on the Rainbow Slab, officials, security guards and police started to trudge arduously up the paths between the levels: sallying forth to repel these invaders from the high ground above their concrete castle, a thigh-busting hike up the levels which guaranteed a foul mood.

The less bloody-minded might have slunk off until the fuss died down. But Redhead and Towse were actively seeking to reclaim the quarries from those who could only trivially 'own them', and Silvester was just too obsessed. More routes went up: *Naked Before the Beast* and the easier but still difficult *Pull My Daisy* (named after a 1959 film adapted and narrated by Jack Kerouac).

While Redhead belayed Towse as they climbed *Released from Treatment,* a security guard appeared. He shouted at the two climbers and threatened to pull them down by their ropes, losing his temper, his threats forcing him into a corner of aggression.

Dave Towse was high up on the climb, psyching himself up for the hard moves that he could see coming up. He needed a zone of psychological calm to be able to do these moves, and all the shouting was not helping him achieve a meditative state.

Redhead started shouting and swearing back, unintimidated, and hauling rope in so that the official couldn't reach them to carry out his threat. This further upset Towse. If he continued to climb, further away from protection, more rope would be run out. So he would fall further before the small wires he had placed caught him, and be more likely to hit the ground.

Towse had had enough. Rather than continue climbing, he jumped – a big sixty feet fall. This shocked the security guard. In that second, the official believed that this flying man was about to die. He saw the reality of his threats, knew he couldn't carry them out, and retreated. Dave Towse swung, angry but safe, on the end of his rope.

This couldn't go on. The climbers contacted the BMC, who routinely negotiated access rights with farmers and landlords, then started to negotiate for access rights to the quarries. Essentially the BMC pointed out that there was no real way to keep climbers out of the quarries, and collectively promised not to sue if anyone got hurt. In return, the power station got a voluntary ban on the levels closest to the power station, just below the Rainbow Slab. That way, none of their people would be put at risk going to help an injured climber, who after all had chosen to be there.

Redhead felt 'lucky in being deemed too irresponsible to take part in such negotiations and I carried on the anarchy of "confrontation and fun" in the battlegrounds and trench warfare of the quarries – good days!'[46]

CHAPTER 15

The Quarrymen

August 2015, below Rainbow Slab

Lee and I keep on walking around the back of the short gorge along the Rainbow Slab. At its head, there are tumbled slate blocks, some the size of cars, with smaller rubble in between. For some reason this wasn't wanted for splitting by the quarrymen; small birch trees had seeded and set themselves amongst the rubble and little tufts of heather poking out here and there. They'll be putting their nets of roots down, threads which tie it all together.

On the other side of the gorge, the heather is more established. Coarse rank grasses have moved in, and the few birch trees are bigger, throwing out millions of seeds each year. There are thin trails that run between clumps of heather. The levels are dead flat in the quarries, easy walking. There probably used to be train tracks along here but there is no sign of that now.

At the end of the level is an old winding house, like a medieval castle tower. It looks like a good place to drop stones, fire arrows or pour boiling oil down on attackers below. A set of steps lead up, but some are loose, some have been clattered by a falling block from above. We look carefully where we place our feet. Where the slate dust has collected, it has formed a crude proto-soil, enough for tiny little succulent plants with fleshy leaves to grow. None are taller than your little finger; they are green, grey and red, and sometimes with a delicate white flower, a little star.

At the top, Lee drops his pack. He looks up at the sky. The rain is very nearly spent. I look up into the bright cloud layer, just a few drops here and there.

'Let's have a pork pie,' he says. 'Another few minutes will give it a chance to dry out.'

We eat our pork pies while we look out down the winding tower. He was right about them, they are great. Plenty of jelly, nice pink meat, good pastry baked conker brown. Above our heads, the winding wheel is still here, big beams of timber taking the weight, unrotted. Inside the tower is still a smell of tallow grease, and black crusts like lumps of shoe polish near the bearings. There are cast-iron levers, black metal, pitted but unrusted.

'Look at this.'

One lever is at about chest height; the operator must have thrown it forward to engage the brake. The knob of the handle is not black and pitted; it is silver and bright. I put my hand over it and feel the smooth metal, my palm adding an unmeasurable amount of polish to the years and years of quarrymen's hands.

1962–69, *closure of Dinorwig Quarry*

In 1962, British Pathé Pictures shot a short informational film about the Dinorwig slate quarry. In the film, the quarry is dry, it is sunny weather. The little narrow-gauge trains pull wagons of slate, looking down into the vast basin of Pen Garret, which climbers know as Australia.

On film, a quarryman presses a rattly looking pneumatic drill into a face of rock, pushing it in with his thighs. He is wearing a steel hard hat shaped a bit like a bowler; he has scratched his name, 'Trevor', into the shiny black paint. Trevor wears a wool tank top over a white shirt. His clothes are dusty and worn; they might have been his Sunday best a few years before. His mate pushes an explosive charge down the hole, then they walk to their blast shelter.

The men climb over the rock faces, hanging on to ropes and levering off blocks of slate to crash down below. Trevor and his mates load the thin slabs onto the narrow-gauge railway carts. They all look strong, with wiry forearms, but they also look old. It isn't just the effort of a difficult and dangerous job: the quarry workforce is ageing, with fewer and fewer apprentices following their dads into the trade. The voice-over tells us that 'the slate they produce lasts for well over a century.'[47]

There are other British Pathé films about the quarries. In 1958, the Pathé film is of 'The Unemployed on the March'. In black and white, the quarrymen of Pen-y-groes march to Caernarfon to ask for the right to work. The men are all smartly dressed, in long, good-quality woollen coats which reach down to their knees. It is a big march, orderly, and crowds turn out to see them and show their support. The marchers have a brass band, their instruments gleaming and unpawned, despite the struggle of keeping households going on the dole.[48]

Efforts were made, support was given, new factories for making slate waste into building blocks were planned, but none of it would really work. The quarries were declining. Dinorwig had only 300 workers, down from 3,000 a hundred years before. In a few seconds of film, we see the empty pubs, the closed and empty shops, and are told the young people are leaving for work elsewhere. The quarry villages were becoming quieter and poorer places.

Unlike the coal mines or steelworks, the quarries had not

been deemed essential to war production during World War II. The Blitz demolished houses and blasts stripped slate rooves clean. But quarrying slate wasn't winning the war the way that mining coal or pouring steel was, so the slate industry wasn't nationalised or regulated in the same way. When post-war governments planned the economy, the roof-slate industry was unprotected. Ceramic and concrete roof tiles could be made cheaper, and that is what new post-war housing was built with.

Dinorwig Quarry was left dependent on the French market for roof-slates. When the franc was devalued in 1969, the ongoing order for roof-slates was first reduced and then cancelled. The quarry did not have enough orders to keep it going.

The news came when the quarrymen were on their holidays. Like many big workplaces, factories and mines, the whole complex closed for a few weeks every year. Everyone took their holidays at the same time, then got back in time for the quarries to start work again.

In August 1969, Dinorwig Quarry would not be reopening. The postman had come around the quarrying villages with sackfuls of identical letters, telling the men their services were not needed, and enclosing their final pay. At the stroke of a pen, the line of quarrymen – from father to son, back through generations – ended.

Mid eighties, neighbours

Mike Raine, one of the eighties dole climbers, had lived next door to a former quarryman. The quarryman was old, while Mike was young and helpful: he sawed wood for the old man's fire, a neighbourly gesture. Mike was from a northern mill town in Lancashire; he found the people in Llanberis very similar to those he had grown up with. Small differences in language and accent but the same down-to-earth tolerance and humour.

When the climbers moved into the community, they often had retired quarrymen as neighbours. The quarrymen had their own names for the different workings, Sinc Harriet and Ponc Morgan, Dyffryn, Sinc Galed, Matilda. Adwy Califfornia, Ponc Abyssinia, Ponciau Califfornia, Ponc Awstralia.

When they first went into the quarries, the young climbers were often unaware that these areas had names at all, so applied ones they made up. Often the names given by the youths were based on the features of the rock, like the Rainbow Slab or the Skyline Level. Other areas were referred to by the names of prominent climbs, like Looning the Tube Level, or Never Never Land. When the young climbers did talk to the quarrymen and tried to apply the proper quarry names, they often applied them to entirely the wrong area, typical of the scattiness of the dole youth. Hence, Ponc Morgan became California, while Ponciau Califfornia became the Rainbow Walls. A single small level of Garret was called Australia, but the climbers misunderstood, so called the whole giant crater Australia. Then called the bottom of it Tasmania, or another bit Alice Springs or Ayers Rock.[49]

In the splitting sheds, blocks of slate had been sawn by big circular saws into workable blocks. Years in the sheds had filled the quarrymen's lungs up with dust. For a hundred years, the quarrymen had known the dust was unhealthy, an opinion often denied by the doctors employed by the quarry owners. Anyone who worked in the sheds hacked up black phlegm every morning.

In fact, the dust was lethal. In the strongly unionised and nationalised coal mines after World War II, there was growing recognition of the damage caused by dust. Particles of coal dust would lodge in the men's lungs, healed around by a microscopic scar. Over time the accumulation of these scars would lead to breathlessness and ultimately death: when the lungs start to struggle, other organs start to collapse and fail.

South Wales coal miners were more symbolic of Welsh heavy industry. In contrast, the slate quarrymen were somewhat overlooked. But the reality was that working conditions for both sets of workers were equally unjust. The slate dust was more reactive than coal dust, and the quarrymen were affected just as badly as coal miners. It took the law until the late 1970s to recognise the various forms of pneumoconiosis as an industrial disease, worthy of compensation.

Mike felt self-conscious about going up to the quarries to climb, and asked his neighbour what he thought of it. 'He thought it was fantastic, us going up there. The quarries were alive again. In a way, the locals had saved the quarries for the climbers. When they closed and the power station moved in, they [the power company] offered to fill them in, all landscape it. The locals wouldn't have it. The pits had been dug by their sweat, and they want them to stay there, as a sort of a monument.'[50]

The locals hadn't done this for the climbers, but the community was tolerant of the young dole climbers. Lloyd George had been the Liberal MP for nearby Caernarfon (at the time known as Caernarvon Boroughs), and his reforms which laid the basis for the welfare state were influenced by bitter industrial battles – like the great Penrhyn lockout – between the quarrymen's union and 'the dukes', English-speaking aristocrats who owned the land and the quarries of Wales. The climbers, seventy years later, were beneficiaries of that too.

CHAPTER 16

The Take Over by Department C

August 2015, Rainbow Levels

The rain has stopped and the rock is already drying, starting to turn a paler fag-ash grey. We walk along the level to where there is some graffiti daubed in thick egg-yolk paint, the same colour as double yellow lines. It says:

TAKEN OVER BY DEPT C 74

This gave the climb its name: *The Take Over by Department C*. The paint is thicker where the foreman dipped his brush, you can still see the streaks of the bristles in the yellow.

I liked the name when I first read it, and it is the right grade – 7a – which for me was where 'hard' started. I have to demonstrate to myself that I can do something like this. Then I know I can do that first 7a pitch on *Supermassive Black Hole*.

Today, I am back to try again. I look at the guide book, re-read the description, though I know it off by heart:

A technical offering which weaves up the wall…. Start right of the graffiti 'Vernon and Alun' and climb the wall to a ledge and a still tricky finale. May be easier for Albatrosses? Lower off.

[N Harms, G Hughes 08.09.86][51]

The guide book has it wrong though: it's not 'Vernon and Alun',

Taken Over by Department C – the quarryman's instruction that inspired the name of the climb. The yellow paint has begun to fade from repeated impacts by climbers' rope.

it's just 'Vernon Alun'. Shame to lose the sexual tension.

I get my shoes out, put on my harness, and uncoil the rope. There is still a thin black seep of water down the rock face, but it is keeping a crucial hold wet. This would be enough to keep me off the climb, and I don't know how I feel about that.

I look up at the wall, trace thin holds and potential steps. Within a few minutes, the seep of water is nearly gone.

Lee suddenly starts laughing.

'What's up?' I say, a bit bewildered.

'The look on your face,' he says. That makes me laugh because I know he's right; my face is an open book. Part of me wishes it would stay wet, so I wouldn't have to try. This is nothing like the danger of the routes on the Rainbow Slab, and it's only fifteen metres rather than fifty. But here and now, it is scaring the shit out of me. Fifteen metres? It will never let me up it.

I plot the line of the bolts; there are five spaced up the wall. Two more than the original three the route was climbed with, added in the big rebolting campaign starting in 2006, when the rusting 8 mm bolts were replaced with stainless 12 mm you could hang a truck off.

I know this is safe, but it doesn't feel like it is. My neck hurts a little, my muscles clamping with tension. Ah, fuck it. I take a deep breath and stand up.

Lee sees this. He's been quietly getting ready to belay, nothing obtrusive.

'Ready, Pete? Give it a good go.'

'It's only climbing,' I say, an old joke between us.

I stand on a bulge of rock, like a barrel below the cliff face. I climb, get my rope through the first clip. To start with, I am on good ledges, but then on smaller and smaller crimps: narrow ledges and shelves the width of the spine of a thin book. I lock my fingertips onto them, grabbing little spikes and fins.

I put my rope through the second clip, weaving between odd zig-zag footholds. The holds are so small and I'm pulling so hard it feels barely possible but I *am* going up. It doesn't feel like I'll fall, but every time I move up I use a bit more of my strength.

Above me, just above and to the left of my forehead, is the bolt-hanger. I need to put my quickdraw through and then pull my rope through and clip it.

It takes effort to let go with my right hand and gently weave it down next to my hip. I feel the quickdraw on my harness. I gently unclip it and start to bring my hand back up to head height. Everything feels out of balance, any little wobble and I will be off. I can feel the fingers in my left hand. They are already tired, and gradually, inevitably weakening: how long? how long? Gently, I reach, just a little bit more and 'click', the quickdraw is through the bolt-hanger. I reach down and pull on the rope. Below me, Lee throws out a bit of slack, enough to clip the quickdraw. But the way I'm pulling the rope is making my body twist, and my left-hand fingers are gradually opening out: I have seconds left.

'Take!' I shout, which is the command for 'I am falling off'. Lee heil-hitlers his arm up, taking all that slack back in, incredibly quickly, and then my left hand uncurls and I am off, head and shoulders back and through the air, slamming back into the wall, turning upside down from the sudden chaos of forces and pivots.

1986, Rainbow Levels

If you hadn't got any work, and your A-levels were good enough, you could go to university. If they were slightly worse: polytechnic. Student grants still existed and gave enough money to live in cheerful poverty while pursuing higher ideals.

Nick Harms arrived in Llanberis on the back of an outdoor education degree at Liverpool Poly. Harms went to a party and got drunk, meeting another newly arrived climber, Paul Pritchard, straight out of Bolton. Pritchard needed transport, and Harms had a van, so the two teamed up out of convenience and a quick-starting friendship. To the local climbers, however, it looked like Nick and Paul were an established team, which meant they were very rapidly accepted by Johnny Dawes, Gwion Hughes, Moose and Trevor 'Carlos' Hodgson: the boys of the hard climbing scene. They didn't have to ask anyone else if they could tag along, or get a belay, and it was just assumed that they would know what they were doing.

After the climbs on the Rainbow Slab and Paul Williams' slideshow, interest in slate had exploded. Everyone wanted to climb these dangerous-looking lines, but the rest of the quarries were a blank canvas. Climbers wandered up into the quarries – often it was too wet to go anywhere else – to try and find something they could climb and get their name in the 'new routes' book. In fact, so many new climbs were going up that hardly anyone was bothering to repeat them.

Nick quite quickly got really good at climbing, but after a year or so, the style of movement on slate was starting to bore him. He felt he knew how hard slate slabs were climbed; he had done *Windows of Perception*, with slate's single hardest move on it. So he went looking for steeper rock, with interesting angles. He found a shortish wall with yellow graffiti, and so drilled in some bolts.

At the time, there was an unwritten rule that there could only be a maximum of two bolts in any climb. This was how many Johnny Redhead had put in each climb on the Rainbow Slab. Other climbers like Stevie Haston didn't like bolts at all, preferring the rock to have a 'sporting chance at repelling boarders.'[52]

Nick Harms was oblivious to the 'two-bolts-per-pitch' rule. He thought you were allowed as many bolts as you wanted, as long as you had a chance of hitting the ground at each bolt. The slate routes weren't long, so to Harms it was just coincidental that most of his early new routes had two bolts. *Watch Me Wallaby Wank, Frank* (named just to see if it would get censored in the next guide book – it was), *Moving Being* and *Fat Lad Exam Failure:* all had two bolts and some prospect of hitting the ground from each one. ('Ground' is a bit of a misnomer for *Wallaby:* you start from a ledge halfway up a cliff, and it is the ledge you would break your ankles on, if you weren't cushioned by crushing your belayer.)

But what would become *The Take Over by Department C* was a departure. Harms was good at balancey technical slabs, but actually not that strong. He was five foot nine, and only weighed eight stone and nine pounds. He always looked ill, thin and pallid; everyone called him the Stickman. His friend Pritchard wondered how he could 'do this on his diet of chip butties and Newcastle Brown?'[53]

The Take Over was nearly vertical and needed strength. Harms abseiled down and drilled three bolts in, each one with the chance of decking out – hitting the ground at the bottom.

'Over tea in Pete's or Newcy Brown in the Pad I got talking about the line. I remember there were some raised eyebrows at the three bolts in forty-five feet but I think I managed to bluff out that it had the obligatory ground fall potential and the matter rested,' remembered Nick Harms. He had stuck two fingers up at the ethics, and so far survived.[54]

Plus, interest in the slate was waning. Climbers were looking elsewhere for their kicks: Gogarth sea cliffs, limestone at Pen Trwyn, even out to France. On the continent, the French were happily drilling bolts in all over the place. 'What was evident was that [limestone sport] routes weren't being developed with a built-in ankle/pelvis/spine/skull fracture potential... if you're running it out above horrible landings and the odd 8 mm bolt or two, every day, then someday your luck is going to run out.'[55]

Harms' next routes – and there were some hard classics to come, like *Cwms the Dogfish*, *Pas De Chèvre* and *The Dark Half* – were fully bolted. 'If we carried on bolting routes in the style we had, the climbers that would come after us just wouldn't go into the quarries, we were in danger of creating a museum to eighties' excess.'[56]

August 2015, hometime

My climbing shoes come off, relief for my cramped toes and a sudden waft of sour sweat smell, mixed with rubber. I stand on the chips of slate littering the ground; they are cool and dry, not at all sharp or painful. The first spots of rain tickle my forearms and the back of my neck. Harness and quickdraws go back in my rucksack, clinking against each other and squashing the remains of my sandwiches.

I flex my knuckles, working them. They are sore, and I shake them around, trying to get some blood back into my hands, with its soothing bath of repair-hormones and nutrients. There will be microscopic tears in my tendons, which will heal and make them incrementally stronger, more able to grip harder for longer.

Lee coils the rope across his shoulders, pulling loop after loop out of the mess of spaghetti, then wrapping it in flicked coils and locking it with a solid knot. He tucks it under the lid of his rucksack.

Spots of rain hit the slate, leaving dark flat dots. The first few dry off in seconds, but as more land they start to join up. We are stopping just in time; in a few minutes the handholds up there will start to get wet and slippy, impossible to adequately grip.

'That,' says Lee, 'is a good choice of project. Good moves on it.'

'I'd have liked to have done it, though.'

'Well,' says Lee. 'It's meant to be hard. It should take you a few goes for the grade.'

'I dunno. I know its progress but I just think I need a win, you know?'

'You're winning by being here,' he says.

I can do all the moves in isolation, but I need to link all of it together, do it in one go. Climbers don't consider that they have done a climb if they fall off during it, then finish from the fall; we call it 'dogging'. I haven't practised the top of the route, so it'll be a surprise when I get to it. For some reason – I can't explain to myself – that feels like 'fairer' to the rock.

'It feels possible, though,' I say to Lee.

'Yeah. You want to get smooth going up that first bit of the wall, nice and quick, and then you'll have some energy left for the top bit. You'll have that.'

His reassurance sinks through my tired disappointment. He's right. I grin at him; it's been a great day. I didn't need to get to the top. We've been out in the weather and amongst the history, with the ghosts of the quarrymen and the routes of the old climbers. The company of my friend. High-quality pork pies. Movement that makes you feel alive.

To the west, over Anglesey, the sky is dark and heavy with the new waves of incoming rain. The light is strange over the valley, yellowish. Walking down, we can see the spread of Llanberis, the bright colours of the buildings on High Street. Pete's Eats is obvious. If we stay another night then we would probably get our tea there. I like the omelettes. But as we walk down, the rain starts to strengthen. Lee looks back over his shoulder. 'That was the right time to leave, I think.'

Back in mobile phone signal as we walk through the village, we see that more bad weather is coming in; it will be lurking over north Wales for days. Our brief window of opportunity is closing. You can't fight the weather.

So we load up and drive out. Lee is heading back to work a few days early, to conserve some of his precious holiday time. I'm going to head back home, six hours away. My young son will be surprised and pleased that I'm back early to play Lego with him. He likes making vehicles, while I always try and make a Lego rock face for his Lego men to climb. Some of them have got little printed climbing harnesses, rucksacks and ice-axes. None wears Lycra.

CHAPTER 17

Hogiau Pen Garret

May 2016, Tŷ Powdwr; Australia; Caban

Becky, Lee and I set out from Tŷ Powdwr, which is now a climbing club hut. The building used to be a gunpowder store for the Dinorwig quarries, it's just next to a much smaller structure called Tŷ Ffiws (fuse house). Tŷ Powdwr's walls are two feet thick, made of stacked layers of slate. Originally, the roof would have been wood, with no metal used in its construction – not one single nail. It's sheltered by the hill behind it, but not from the wind or the weather. If the gunpowder had ever exploded by accident, the blast would have gone straight up through the roof and travelled harmlessly across the empty valley – no iron nails to turn into bullets – although the few little cottages you can see would have had their windows blown out.

It's a stroll across to the quarries. The day is sunny and fetching out to be warm, not ideal climbing conditions. The rubber on your climbing shoes sticks less – its formulated to be at its stickiest at 5 degrees – and your hands sweat more, so we are heading over to East Braich, a horseshoe ridge that curls around the huge quarry-working called Australia. This will be in shade all day.

My back is really bad. I had to lift a load of oak the week before, for not enough money, either; building work is wrecking my body. Then, sitting still for the six-hour drive west from Norwich has thoroughly inflamed it. My thighs feel tingly and odd, and muscles in the top half of my back have been cramping as I hold my posture awkwardly, trying to take the weight off my poor burst discs. Thankfully, Lee and Becky are carrying the rope and other gear. The climbing I've done this week is helping stretch everything out, but I'm still not right.

As we walk, Becky and I chat about the stuff everyone talks about: work, family, study. She grew up near me in the north-east of England and did an animation degree at Sunderland. I've never met a climber yet who doesn't like films, but Becky explains in detail how to make an animation of a punch in the face really work, enough to make people flinch.

Lee is quiet, listening to us chat. Becky tells me about getting ready for a fancy-dress party at uni. She went as Lara Croft out of Tomb Raider, which I can see would work.

'So I was running back to my room, really late, and the taxi's waiting and I dropped my fucking pistol, I just thought, keep running, had the keys in my hand, into my room, grabbed my purse and ran back. Without even stopping, I just grabbed the pistol. Then I thought, fuck it, and did a commando roll, just for the hell of it, you know? I thought, I wish someone had seen it...'

We walk up, through the gate near Bus Stop Quarry, then follow the quarry road along the shady birch woods. Old dry-stone buildings are lost amongst sedges and reeds from pools where the water runs off the hill. Across the valley, up towards the pass, the plume of smoke from the steam train climbs Snowdon with another load of tourists. Further on is an old, long cutting shed covered in a rough cement render, its roof long gone.

Slate has a distinct set of physical characteristics. Millions of years ago, in deep geological time, layers of clay mud or volcanic ash, carried by the tides of a tropical sea, were dumped out of the water as it lost the energy needed to transport it. The mud sat there, until it was buried by the movements of tectonic plates. Then it was baked at extreme temperature, extreme pressure, for millions of years, in the Earth's kiln. It became tough, and durable, but easily cleaved into flat leaves of stone. These specific characteristics made slate very useful as a building material, when people finally thought to use it. Large chunks could be split into thin tough sheets, and then nibbled into shape to form many different things: writing-slates for children in Victorian schools, the beds for billiard tables, gravestones, whetstones for knives, but, most importantly: roofing slate.

In the 1962 Pathé film, the quarrymen work away, setting charges, driving small trains, hitting things with hammers. Orchestral music plays, and a voice in the newsreader's received pronunciation of fifty years ago describes how 'fyescinating' it all is. The voice-over starts with 'Few can resist the sight of men digging a hole, or indeed the hole itself',[57] and, frankly, it's downhill from there.

The script's closing remarks are unintentionally perfect. Despite the modern locomotives and explosives, we are told that 'time has stood still'. Slate was quarried here much the same way one hundred years ago, and there is no doubt that in one hundred years' time it will be quarried in much the same way.

In 1969, less than eight years later, the hammer fell. Dinorwig Quarry was closed by its owners, who blamed that cancelled French order. Communities that had housed and bred the men who worked the pits were, at a single stroke, gutted.

Over another gate, now we are in that part of the quarries where 'Public Access is Strictly Forbidden'. Up towards what climbers call Australia: the quarrymen called it Garrett. It is a huge crater, as if a volcano has blown off one side of the mountain, except it was gunpowder that did the blasting: ninety tons of it per year over dozens of years.

The path up to Australia runs between the buildings visible on that old Pathé film, now smashed to rubble. A few stumpy walls made of brick still stand, lined with ceramic tiles. This must have been a shower block. Coal mines, eventually by law, had shower-heads at the pit-head for the miners. It must have been the same for the quarries.

We head up wide steps in the slope between Dali's Hole and the Incline, where great lumps of slate used to be winched down. Up the slope runs a strange concrete trough, capped with paving stones. This holds heavy-duty electrical cables running up to the reservoir at the top of Elidir Fawr. This powers the sluices, gates and valves for the hydroelectric plant buried deep in the mountain's guts.

At the col halfway up the side of Australia, most climbers head to the levels on the western side, where there are low-grade sport climbs. It's often in the sun until late afternoon; that's where I started climbing here. Now, I want to push my grade and climb more challenging routes. We need the shade, so we head to the right. The East Braich is hundreds of metres high. A flight of steps runs up to its crest.

'What's these stairs called, Pete? A Welsh name, hasn't it?' asks Lee, which is a compliment in itself: he knows the guide book by heart.

'Nah. The Stairs of Cirith Ungol: from *The Lord of the Rings*. In the book, it's the back way into Mordor.' Which is spot on, because there is a quarry pit called Mordor, the hardest part of the quarry to find, and this would be a roundabout way to get to it.

The quarrymen walked these steps every day, if they had work up here, but they called them Llwybr Llwynog, which means 'Fox Path'. The steps are wide and flat, and made of waste slate. Each roof tile wasted four-fifths of what was quarried from the ground, but the waste was well used. At any size, slate could be split into dead flat slabs and lumps, so it was easy to make plank-like sections that balanced on flat-sided blocks, locked together by their own weight, no mortar needed. A load of the old houses round here use the same idea.

The steps are worn from hundreds of long-gone feet. The quarrymen wore wooden clogs, which polished the slate to a smooth shine, rather than scratching tick-marks like hobnails would have done. The steps are strewn with little chips and lumps of slate that have fallen or been carried by the water, so you have to keep an eye on where you tread. I've done enough on mountains, with endless, boring snowy slopes, to know that the trick is to keep going, steadily.

It's hot, and sunny, and my back sweats clammily beneath my rucksack. The three of us plod up as the path curves round, no longer talking. I haven't counted the steps; maybe there are just a couple of hundred, maybe five hundred.

At the top, the ground opens out onto a wide, flat plain, shaded by a wall of rock. Where the steps end is a cluster of huts. The biggest and best preserved is the Caban hut. The cast-iron stove is still there, was never stolen – it would weigh a ton, and there would be all these steps to get it down. Until a few years ago, the last quarrymen's overalls and boots hung from the pegs where they'd been left, until some fucking fool torched them.

There is still whitewashed plaster on the walls, with graffitied names carved in since the quarries closed. TREV and DARREN make their regular appearance, but I don't notice any of the normal toilet wall cocks. Amongst all the recent graffiti is a small panel that says 'Hogiau Pen Garret', which means 'the boys of Pen Garret'. There is a list of names: Jack Jones, Dafydd Esther, Arthur Owen, Robert Hughes, Wil Rees and Will Rhys, many more.

The Caban was a quarryman's institution: the hut where the men gathered to eat. On the rock face, men worked in small teams of three or four, but mealtimes were social, reinforcing the bonds of trust that were so important when your life depended on the man working next to you, rigging your ropes and setting the charges.

This was much more than just a canteen. Just as the pub or church were focal institutions in the villages surrounding the quarries, inside it, the Caban was the heart; a community centre controlled not by the owners but the workers themselves, where grievances were settled and whip-rounds, donations for the injured or bereaved, collected. The men sung and held poetry and prose competitions, debated politics and trade unionism.[58]

It sounds unbelievable. The canteens I skived in on building sites never held a poetry competition. Playing cards for money, competitive swearing, sadistic practical jokes and unending racism, football and misogyny: that was the soundtrack to our break times. In those canteens, you'd only ever find *The Sun,*

Star and *Sport*. Detailed on football, most of the lads read them from the back to the front, where they turned into a load of bitter shite: murders by illegal immigrants, single mums claiming £27,000 of benefits per year. A colour picture of a nineteen-year-old from Minehead with her tits out. Poetry competitions? No.

The quarrymen in the nineteenth century read Welsh-language newspapers: some aimed specifically at them, usually Nonconformist and Radical, although *Y Chwarelwr Cymreig* was controlled by Lord Penrhyn's Tory interest.[59] Heavy on local news, but with international affairs and politics, and usually a poets' corner and short stories. There is no mystery, really. Just the human impulse to be more than your job. If your job gave you status, some slight surplus of money, some free time in the summer evenings, then coal miners and factory hands found things to do, societies to found, sports to play, rabbits to breed and pigeons to race. Inside the Caban, quarrymen could pursue these interests during the working day and outside the control of the owners, contributing to Welsh-language culture on the quarry's time.[60]

Becky, Lee and I set up near *G'Day Arete*. Becky walks around taking a few photographs. There is a huge abandoned rusted steel bucket into which a small picnic of people could fit, and she frames the entire basin of Australia with it. There is also a thick steel rope, running diagonally down the cliff; still in place the rusted dolly that hauled slate up and down. Lee and I hang onto it and do pull-ups; it doesn't budge an inch.

To warm up, I get on *Hogiau Pen Garret*, named in tribute

The Oildrum Glacier framed by the rusted steel bucket, now collapsed.

to that piece of graffiti in the Caban. It should be straightforward and it's well within my grade, but there's a tricky move three clips up, which I drop, and I'm left swinging in space, Lee holding the rope below.

'Good effort, good fall, Pete!' shouts Becky. She isn't mocking. Lee and Becky have got the same attitude as me: it's good to fall. If you don't fall you aren't trying hard-enough climbs, and by taking fall after fall, the fear retreats and you can ignore the consequences. I get back on and finish the climb.

A little later, I get onto *G'Day Arete*, which I really want. It's graded at 6c, so it's possible for me to do this, but not without effort. It's a great-looking climb, too; right up a clean edge like the corner of a house. The slate is textured and grainy, and the holds are widely spaced. There are little ridges that require you to lay your whole weight on them, and you have to weave around both sides of the corner to find a way to go up. Tricky, and hard to adjust your mind to.

Becky is belaying me. She is a good climber; really game, bold and skilled, but she is even better as a belayer: totally attentive, and confident enough to pay out enough slack for the rope to take the shock out of a fall, absorbing it into the inherent elasticity of the rope.

Two clips up, I get into a strenuous position, all my weight pulling sideways on a hold, strength fading, and my feet not quite high enough to reach the next hold – a square ledge. Last chance, I try and throw my hand up, using the spring of my body to gain the extra centimetre I need. It works, but my feet cut loose, no longer supporting my weight, so sure enough I fall.

Becky already has the rope locked on her belay plate: my fall doesn't surprise her. I weigh more than she does, so I pull Becky right off her feet and up into the air, but she knows this is coming and jumps into the rock face, springing feet out, cushioning the blow with her legs. We balance out, both laughing.

'Thanks for the catch, Becky!' Her feet are just off the ground and I'm hanging about six feet above: I reach down with my hand and we high-five. Lee is grinning; he's taken photos of it all.

After this fall, I've had enough. It's not working for me today, I'm not climbing well and I'm tired. Lee and Becky head off down some sketchy ladders, bolted to the rock face to find *The Road to Botany Bay*. I will meet them back at the hut. I am going for a moody walk around the top levels of the quarries, where few people go.

Winning the slate out of the ground was dangerous and highly skilled work. Shot-holes were bored up to seven yards deep with pneumatic drills. These drills were heavy and rattly; the quarrymen held them braced against their thighs and forced the drill bits into the rock. The vibration damaged the capillaries in the quarrymen's hands, eventually leading to white finger, an industrial disease affecting the circulation and finger dexterity.

With the shot-hole drilled, explosives – sometimes a small paper-covered gelignite charge, more usually, gunpowder – would be dropped into the hole, a cord of fuse threaded in and then sealed with clay. On the hour, every hour, a siren sounded and, wherever they were, the men lit their fuses, all across the various workings. The fizzing flame ran along the cord and up into the rock, while the quarrymen walked, rapidly, to the slate blast shelters nearby. A thump and a puff of smoke, amongst the dozens that echoed out across the quarry. The explosives had to be very carefully worked out: too much would just blast the huge blocks of slate into splinters, which was not the point. The idea was for the explosion to force open existing cracks, or run new cracks along the bedding planes.

The quarrymen would climb down to the face from above, sliding on ropes, using their feet to brake the speed of descent. Their ropes were perhaps two or three inches thick, made of natural fibre like sisal, jute and hemp. When they had climbed to where they wanted to work, they wrapped turns around their waist or thigh to hold them there. With six-foot long iron pinch bars, they would prise the huge blocks free from the face to crash on the level below. These men on their ropes were the earliest climbers, although they didn't name their climbs. No point. Whatever they climbed down would be blasted off tomorrow, or the week after. They stopped working a face when it no longer became practical, or when a hidden flaw – a ripple or dolerite seam – meant the slate would be no good for splitting.

* * *

I walk up through the old structures. Here, high on East Braich, most things have survived pretty well, the original build solid and skilful. Towers still hold steel rope skylines, dangling carts full of slate, frozen in the act of winching them up and down. Railway tracks – there were dozens of narrow-gauge locomotives stealing in and out of the quarries – and inclines, sloped tracks, with big winding wheels, are still here, made of wood and cast iron. Nearly all this equipment was made on site, down at the bottom of the quarry, next to the lake. Joiners put wood together. Patternmakers made templates for cogs and pulley blocks, which moulders cast in molten iron or steel. All this went up the hill, installed and assembled by millwrights and engineers. The technology tended towards the simple and the massive.

Finding my way about is an adventure in itself. This is not a waste of a day. I love all this, rambling and scrambling, seeing strange things and unexpected views. Two levels up, there is a building, long – more than a hundred metres – and low, with its roof tiles missing but steel frames still in place. I enjoy the challenge of finding a way up to it, following an incline that offers an incredibly wide set of stairs with tiny treads.

I have found a splitting shed. Inside, there are dozens of circular saws. The toothed blades are still here, and the steel frames, and the big sheet metal cutting beds that the slate slabs laid on, moving smoothly on runners, to cut a dead-straight edge to the block. Everything is rusted orange. Holes have blown through the sheet metal with corrosion, and cast casings have cracked, perhaps when the roof fell in, perhaps smashed by someone bored with a lump of stone.

These sheds were where the splitters worked. These were perhaps the most skilled craftsmen of all. Given a two-inch thick piece of slate sawn into a rectangle, they would be expected to split out at least sixteen roof-slates, and nine to an inch was peak performance. Each roof-slate would be about the thickness of a pound coin. The splitter tapped in a long, wide chisel, running the split around the edge of the block, until with a last decisive strike, the complete tile would fall away. The feat was so skilled that slate splitting was one of the main competitive events at the eisteddfod; as important as the poetry and singing competitions. Reading the slate was an emblem of Welsh culture[61] that was given public status by the local eisteddfodau held throughout these strongly Welsh-speaking quarrying communities.

This splitting process converted slate from stone into saleable commodity. Splitters worked long hours, day after day, perched on a stool. One defining industrial injury of this work was a bad case of piles. Far more serious was lung disease caused by sitting daily in the shed's thick atmosphere of slate dust.

Some of the old splitters still give demonstrations of their skill at the National Slate Museum in the old quarry buildings at the level of the lake. I saw one once, a room full of tourists and teenagers on a school trip. At the end of the demonstration, applause. One of the boys carried it on much too long clap – clap, clap – the sarcasm obvious. I could have fucking strangled that lad. He wouldn't have lasted a day up there.

At the bottom of the incline, I swing my leg over the gate, which clangs on its hinges. That's it, I am back in the part of the quarries you are allowed to be in.

The road sweeps out from here back to the gate at Bus Stop Quarry. It's a lovely easy walk, a bit of up-and-down, but nothing grim. Everything fenced and safe, and big wire cages containing the rubble at points where the scree of slate waste threatens the path.

People may as well be wearing uniforms of their tribe. There are birdwatchers looking for choughs and peregrine falcons – they always dress in black and olive green, carry tripods and walk slowly because they're old. Runners stretch past in Lycra, with funny arm pockets for their iPhones seamed into hi-vis running tops: they're usually old, too. On an evening, you might see a load of teenagers walking together to a party up among the old quarry buildings. The girls dress smart and sexy in jeggings and strappy tops and the boys look casual and cool; a few years ago, every third one wore a pork-pie hat.

Climbers look like climbers. Scruffy fuckers as a rule, synthetic fibre trousers that can dry in seconds but are cut to be ugly and utilitarian. Bright jumpers and jackets in bold colours, bobble hats and beanies. There is a whole set of brands you can spot, and a sliding scale of authenticity. North Face means petty drug dealer, at the level of doing a deliberately obvious deal in a supermarket carpark; Mountain Equipment is what teachers might wear on playground duty, right the way to Organic,

Patagonia and Arcteryx at the top. If you were really cool, you wouldn't bother with any of this, would you? But we must wear the colours of our tribe. I've got my rucksack on. My helmet, I've clipped to the shoulder strap, I like to rest my elbow in it as I walk, so – yeah. No prizes for guessing I'm a climber.

I walk along the road, through Watford Gap, headed for another padlocked gate, where a family walk towards me. Middle-aged mum and dad, lad about twenty and daughter late teens, all of them smartly dressed: trainers, Adidas, jeans and sweaters. I smile and say 'hello' – I always do, and not just because I feel happy. Everyone said hello in the villages where I spent my teens. They all return my greeting, and the dad says, "Ave you been climbing then?' Nice north Wales accent, I'd listen to it all day.

'I have, aye. Too nice a day not too, eh?'

We all agree it is.

'Yeah,' I say, 'the slate suits me; I love it here in the quarries.'

The mum looks at me. 'We like walking here. But a bit sad for us, because our grand-dads all worked here, before it closed.'

'I know,' I say, 'I grew up in the coalfields. Not here, up north.' It's a gesture of understanding, the demise of the pits isn't the same as the closure of the quarries, but something passes between us, anyway.

A few minutes later, I hop over the five-bar gate and down the hill, and back into the part of the quarries where access is forbidden. I should have asked them what they thought of us climbing there.

CHAPTER 18

Avalanche

May 2016, Tŷ Powdwr; Snowdon rescue; Colwyn Bay

I am sitting reading a book about climbing in the living room in Tŷ Powdwr. Lee walks through the door. I grin up at him.

'You haven't heard, have you? Did you not have your phone on? Rob and Sam have been in an accident, they had to get choppered to Bangor.'

'They alright?' I feel cold inside. It's like when you are having a perfectly normal day, then hear enormous news of something absolutely shattering, planes into skyscrapers, bombs on buses, a tower block burning.

'Rob has smashed his arm, he's in surgery. Sam's up there with him.'

Hours later we wait for Sam to get back. As it gets later, a few people start to head for bed, as fatigue catches up. Finally we hear shuffling outside and the clang as the metal door is pulled open.

Sam looks fucked as he comes through the door; he is white and smiles wanly, his eyes flat and tired. I had been going to do some stupid joke. Instead I just tell him I am glad to see him and give him a hug. He hugs back, tightly. He is obviously exhausted, but wired, not ready just yet to crawl into his sleeping bag.

We pour whisky; Sam always brings single malt on the club trips. My mouth is furred and coated with dinner and cake. The whisky tastes medical, peat phenethylamine.

Sam tells us roughly what happened, only the bare bones of the story. Sam says Rob is a 'double-hard bastard'. Tough enough to climb to relative safety even with a shattered and bleeding elbow.

'Anyway, then the helicopter came,' says Sam, and we know there's more to it, but he is starting to stare at the table. 'I think I'd better go to bed.' We help him, all kind and slow, and he says goodnight.

As soon as he does, Land Rover James looks at me and Dentist Steve. We march out to the car and grab the bags from the hospital, special clear heavy plastic bags. Inside it is all their gear, as much as Sam managed to bring with him from the hill.

Sam's down jacket is covered in blood. When Rob had been stranded below on a ledge, Sam had passed it down to him. Rob was getting cold quickly, losing blood, not moving and stuck on a stone. Rob had screamed as he put his shattered arm through the sleeve, and Sam had shouted at him just to drape it over his shoulder. We want to get this at least rinsed before Sam gets up in the morning. There is a big Belfast sink in the toilets, for filling up mop buckets. Climbing bunkhouses often want you to clean up before you leave.

Blood swirls down the sink. I plunge my hands into the down and squeeze bloody water out.

'Ach,' says Dentist Steve in his quiet Scottish voice, 'it always looks like more than it is.' He is quiet and calm, quietly unstoppable, hard to flap – he always is. He has been mountaineering for years and prefers the trad routes in the Welsh mountains to the routes in the quarries. He's more used to blood than any of us, and his calm settles me down to detach and keep working.

The other down jacket is obviously Rob's. It's tattered to fuck, like a load of moths have swarmed on it. I turn it inside out. There's blood soaked in, and little lumps of matter – bone marrow, muscle? There are about a dozen of them, white and fatty looking. One sticks to my finger.

'Let's get this to Bangor – they can reattach it,' I say to Steve and he huffs a laugh. I flick it into the sink.

I turn to the racks, Sam's is – mainly – okay but some of Rob's gear is covered in rusty patches of blood. I go through everything, a piece at a time and wash what needs it. We bin the stuff that the medics cut off him – what would we keep that for? It is gone two before we go to bed.

We're up late. Land Rover James corners Lee and me.

'We think it would be a good gesture if someone went and got Sam and Rob's packs.'

Lee nods.

'I don't know,' I say. 'Sam said he didn't want anyone going up there. It's just stuff. I'll chip in for a new rucksack.'

'We would like to send you two because Lee is very experienced and, out of everyone, you are the most comfortable on the rock.' My lips go thin. I don't like the thought that I am being 'sent'; I am not in some fucked-up chain of command, a good little soldier.

'Come on, Pete. We'll get it done quickly then back into the quarries in the afternoon.'

Lee's silver Astra is very like my silver Astra, except mine is a sixteen-valve petrol, and his is the diesel. The back of mine is littered with tools and boxes of screws, but Lee has clean upholstery and plastic boxes to keep car-jacks and climbing gear in. I have never washed mine, and on a small seam between metal and plastic on the boot door, a lichen has started to grow, frilly green flaps that have doubled in size in the last year.

Lee drives sensibly, below the speed limit and in smooth curves down one side of the valley and then up the other, controlled and smooth gear changes.

'Are we actually going to climb up there?' I ask.

'Don't know yet. We'll take the gear. It's not my kind of thing really. Bit of a ledge-shuffle. Boring.'

We park at Pen-y-pass, there are already dozens of people heading up Snowdon. Most people are sensibly dressed, no jeans, because people have clear ideas about wearing different uniforms for different activities. Polyester trousers and technical waterproofs, some from Mountain Warehouse. Nearly everyone has walking poles. We barely look at them, a quick debate on whether we are paying for one hour or two, then up the big metalled path.

My back is tingly. We've got full packs, and I could do without it. I clench up my core and we march along then split off along the shoreline of the llyn under the Snowdon Horseshoe. I step along the rough sheep trail, and when it runs out I struggle along the hummocky grass, a missed step giving me a back-wrenching lurch and an 'ah!' of shock and pain.

This is sheep territory, grazed hard, few but the most resilient flowers surviving in the more accessible of places. The cliff of Y Lliwedd rises out of the hummocky grass and bilberry patches which will swarm with midges in the right humidity.

We'll be lucky if we don't get prickled by them.

It's hard to find the route at first, the guide book would have been another inessential half kilo to carry. Finally we get it and walk up the thigh-busting slope to the base. A stone corner rises out of the grass; there's a lot of grass up there, probably holding the whole face together, leaving bouldery stones in place until hapless climbers haul on them.

'Look,' says Lee and picks up a nut with a quickdraw. The carabiner of the quickdraw has green insulation tape marking it. Sam's. This is the place. Rob's rucksack is a few feet away, fallen from above, knocked off the ledge by the prop-wash of the helicopter.

I look above at the complex network of corners and ramps. The dark grey rock is utterly unlike slate, much more rounded and weathered, without any of the sharpness or clean lines. I see white veins of quartz. One is particularly prominent, and I watch as it seems to sway in the breeze. I think it is an optical illusion, but as I look I realise it really *is* swaying in the breeze. It is the severed end of Sam and Rob's rope, still up there.

'I'm not fucking going up there,' I say to Lee. I'd known I wasn't since I got out of the car.

Lee nods. 'Alright, then.'

I relax and look at Rob's rucksack. His walkie-talkie is still clipped onto the shoulder strap. Inside is his expensive jacket, and one of his approach-shoes: a glorified trainer soled with technical rubber. The other one must have bounced clear.

I unzip the top-flap pocket. Inside are Rob's Jaffa Cakes, he always takes a pack with them as a reward for finishing a climb. Some of them have been smushed into crumbs; they must have taken the impact of the fall.

Well, waste not want not. I open them and fish inside the spongy mass, hooking out a couple of intact ones. 'Jaffa cake, Lee? They're Rob's.'

Lee laughs and takes one. 'Good,' I say. 'It's what he would have wanted.'

Lee solos up the first, easy pitch. At the top, on a big grassy patch is Rob's other trainer. Lee chucks it down to me. It trickles down the cliff, bouncing from ledge to ledge, slowing and finally deflects, right at the bottom, just as it runs out of power. It falls into my hand.

We find the impact crater of the smaller of the two rocks that caused the trouble: this one fell and cut Sam's rope 95 per cent of the way through. It is like a kerbstone, and Lee can barely lift it. The larger rock, about the size of a fridge-freezer, which took Rob off the hill and left him to dangle halfway down the cliff, is nowhere to be seen. I don't like to think that it might not yet have got all the way to the bottom, but be up there still, perched and waiting to swoop. Better that it had rolled and bounced much further, down the slope and is just nestled amongst other rocks, now deprived of kinetic power and slowly to be grassed and mossed over.

For the next few days, Sam and Land Rover James drive up to see Rob at the hospital. He is pleased and grateful that his pack and his trainers have come back.

When Sam returns, he tells us details of the accident. There are a lot of jokes, we are all willing to boom out laughter. Some of the details are sad, though: Rob not thinking he would live and wanting a message taking to Becca, Sam's thought of whether to cut the rope on his best mate, and some of it – a boulder fall, the rope torn by the impact of that first rock – is frightening. I get flashes of the reality of his situation, on your own with your best mate badly injured on the ledge below, no phone reception, hoping for rescue, waiting for a helicopter, not being able to do anything meaningful. Not just frightening but boring and lonely.

Sam tells us that Rob is a big hit at the hospital. He remembers everyone's name and is unfailingly polite. 'Oh, hello Sandra, have you come to change my dressing? Thank you so much.' We all laugh at that; it is very like him.

Sam approaches me awkwardly. 'Erm. Rob is going to be released, or signed out or whatever, from the hospital. I think I would like just to take him straight back home, but I know you might want to stay a bit longer. Have you got any thoughts?'

'Yeah, it's alright; I've asked Lee and Becky. I'll go back with them, they'll take me as far as Sheffield, then I can train back from there.'

The day before Rob is discharged, Sam walks with us into the quarries. He feels he wants to climb so that his last climbing experience is not him sitting on a ledge waiting to be rescued. We go up the galleries to do some fairly easy sport routes. I lead up one and lower down, pull the rope and leave the clips in. Sam ties in and confidently leads up. His moves are good and he is under control, up clip rest, up clip rest, then ties in at the chains and lowers down.

Everyone is pleased and smiling, trying to restrain it so as to not overcongratulate him. We don't want to turn it into some weird pity-tinged super-praise event.

'Thanks everyone,' Sam says. 'And now I think that's enough. I'm going to go back.'

Becky, Lee and I stay a few more days, as planned, then leave. Everyone else from the club goes the night before we do. The three of us are planning on going to the Heights in Llanberis and have a burger.

In the eighties, the Heights was closed, then reopened as a club through a loophole in the licensing law. To come in, you had to be a member of the BMC, so loads of the local youths joined the BMC even if they had no interest in climbing or mountaineering. There was a big round table in the window where climbers would meet up and work out where they were going next day, sort out lift shares. Then they'd all get plastered – cash permitting – and the big challenge was to climb the next day with a blistering hangover. You couldn't worry about falling when you were concentrating on not throwing up.

Tonight, the place is rammed with people. Perhaps there has been a freak convergence of organised and televised sporting events. People are crowded up to the front door; it would be a challenge to tunnel your way through to the bar, finding a table would be impossible. We look at each other, and head to the chipshop. The queue there is out the door, and everyone has that fixed expression of being hungry and not happy, but not complaining because it's no one's fault.

We decide not to add to the hassle. In the Spar, we pick up beer, two pizzas and a pack of garlic bread, and then drive back up to Tŷ Powdwr. Under the light of the kitchen we eat our pizzas while we all flick through books and magazines. Becky pulls out her laptop and works for a while, using her phone's Wi-Fi.

The tip of her tongue sticks out of the corner of her mouth, then she shows us a webpage she has built and how she can tell which bits people click on.

It is peaceful and nice. I miss my son a bit, but I'm glad to have all this time to myself; such a luxury. I'm not bored with it. The climbing takes up most of the day, like work would, then you just eat and lounge around and have small chats. Time spent with your friends.

After a while, I head up and pack what I no longer need. I leave out my clothes and sleeping bag, book and headtorch. We sort out what leftover food can be chucked, and what will make an odd breakfast.

The next morning, we eat, drink a few cups of coffee, mop the floors and lock up. We drive out; I'm in the back of Lee's Astra, Becky up front with him. I'm slightly surprised when they turn north and west and head for Bangor and Caernarfon.

'We're going on the coast road, Pete. Me and Becky always stop off for a swim, if you don't mind. It's the ritual.'

'Sound by me. I'll have to swim in my shorts, though; I've not got swimming trunks. Where are we stopping?'

'Colwyn Bay.'

Colwyn Bay, remembered from holidays in Llandudno as a kid. Conwy Castle; how I loved it there, running around the battlements, leaning over the edge to look so far down while my mum, granny and grandpa had heart attacks through fear.

We stayed in cheap old Victorian guest houses. One day I looked out and saw a group of punks walking down the street, it might have been '83 or '84. I asked my granny, 'Should we call the police?' Who knows, maybe it was some of the punky climbers of the era: Stevie Haston, Jerry Moffatt, probably a bit early for Paul Pritchard, on their way up to the limestone at Parisella's Cave. They deserved the fucking police calling on them, for neglecting the slate in favour of limestone.

As Lee drives, I am quiet, thinking about childhood, and wondering how my son will remember the times I am spending away from him. Dad didn't like to come on holiday with us; he might spend the first day or the last with us and drive back. I remember him once buying me a bag of soldiers – he told me he was going to steal them, and I was terrified, a bit excited – but then he paid for them with one of the brand new pound coins. I liked the nobbles on the grenades and the bullets in the belts of the machine guns.

We drive along the coast road. Inland are steep rounded hills, to the left are dull orange beaches and the sea. Lee turns off without needing to think about the turning and pulls down a road towards the beach. There are hundreds of parking places against a low concrete wall, only a few cars of dog-walkers.

There is a changing room in the toilet block. It smells foul, like backed-up drains, lain over by a fresher smell of recent shit. I quickly shrug out of jeans and into a pair of shorts. They are cheap climbing trousers that zip off at the knee.

Lee emerges, followed by Becky; he starts to stride confidently towards the sea: strong legs, strong back. Becky has a blue two-piece costume on, and she doesn't meet my eye as she walks out. She's holding her back awkwardly with her arm across her body, and I suddenly realise she's self-conscious about being in a swimming costume. So I look out to sea and follow Lee towards the surf; I don't want her to feel uncomfortable.

I've never really been one for looking women up and down. I was shy as a teenager but you wouldn't have known it as it was hidden behind a loud voice and being funny. I had acne, and because I smoked, I was skinny, though muscly enough. Sometimes I missed my cue. In the pub recently, a mate said he had no regrets, except he wished he'd fucked all the women who had wanted him. I laughed, I knew what he meant: opportunities missed. I thought of a girl in America coming into my room for a chat with only a towel on, her hands above her as she combed and fixed her hair. I was lying on my bed; I could have reached my toe out and pulled the towel off her.

The sea is pleasant and warm on my feet and then ankles, a dark orange-brown that I remember from being a kid around here on holiday. I thought the water was mucky because of the colour, but Grompa explained it was just the sand being picked up by the water. I didn't like the occasional bit of seaweed either, when it swirled against my legs, but Grompa just said it was like the grass of the sea, and I didn't mind walking in a field, did I? Grompa was a clever man. Childhood polio – no vaccinations – had left him with stick legs and a hunched back, and he'd only been fit for clerical work. He didn't leave for war, he didn't learn a trade and he didn't go down the north Staffordshire pits either. He just worked for the GPO when they were in charge of the phones, married my granny, who was from a farm, and taught himself astronomy as a hobby. He made his own telescopes, and models of the solar system out of pieces of brass meccano, with different coloured map pins for each planet.

The water is warm: shallow, but quickly cold. At thigh height comes the bit I hate most: launching yourself in to get your head wet, the gasp of the cold slap through your body. A few desperate strokes to generate muscle-warmth, then stand up and calm the deep panting, fuck... fuck.... Lee is ahead swimming with powerful strokes, then stands up. I settle for wading out.

I look back, and Becky is a little way behind, crossing her arms across her chest, against the cold, I think. I stand about waist deep, letting the sun warm my back and arms against the chill of the water.

There are gulls overhead. I look up and see their thin spiky wings and forked tails just as one wheels then dives into the sea. Not gulls but terns.

'Lee! Look at the terns!' I'm not sure he hears properly but he catches my meaning and looks up. I wade closer, we are both up to waist height. Only a few metres above us, they flap around, then shoot like arrows into the sea. We must be amongst a shoal of sand eels or something.

'Did you see that one?' Lee shouts about the one that has come closest to us so far. As it dives, it pulls its wings in, then bucks and sweeps back and flies back up again. We watch them; they quickly lose awareness of us and dive closer to us, unthreatened.

Becky shouts that she's going back; she looks cold already.

'Too right,' I say.

'The cold water's good for you. It is a tonic for the kinaesthetic system,' says Lee, putting on a slightly funny voice. The cold of the water will shrink down the bulges, the swellings, pockets of fluid around joints, tendons and muscles. Blood will flow faster around our bodies, carrying the nutrients needed for quicker repair. Professional athletes, such as endurance runners, take ice-bags for the same effect: to reduce swelling and promote repair. We aren't professionals, we don't have sports physios, or even a freezer good enough to make enough ice for a bath. So we swim in the sea.

Not for long. We wade back out. Soon we are back on the road. The three of us play a game of Oss. The rules are that the first person to see a horse says "Oss" and then the other two have to say 'Ahhh' appreciatively. For advanced players, seeing a fox, you say 'Ginger!' and a dead badger must be greeted with 'BBBaaaDDDDDGGGEEERRR!' The drive passes beautifully.

They drop me off at Sheffield station and we hug goodbye. On the train, I wait until I see a horse out of the window then text 'Oss' to both of them. Becky texts back 'Nice' and Lee texts back 'Well played'.

CHAPTER 19

Moving Being

May 2017, Thetford Forest

I would have liked to have left hours ago, but it's Friday morning, which means my girlfriend has to go to work, and my son needs to go to school. So I have to take him. It's the normal struggle to get him ready, fed and into his clothes.

'Put your lid on,' I say, so he gets his helmet and walks round the back gate to get his bike, a black and green one I got him from Halfords a year ago.

Ned, our dog, watches us go from the front window. At the gate in the hedge we turn back and wave at him. Dog language is all about body language, so us waving probably means something to him: 'Stay there; back soon, everything is normal'.

My son rides along on his bike. I walk behind, him; pointlessly, really. He will soon be old enough to go himself, but it seems expected for parents to walk their kids to school, proof against carelessly driven cars and child-snatchers. I thought about riding my bike with him to school, but I'd be expected to be off the pavement, on the road, and I don't fancy the traffic.

He whizzes off away from me, balanced beautifully, upright. He doesn't do any bunny hops over kerbs, no wheelies yet. He has books that tell him how, but he's never bothered to read them, never bothered to practise it. He's still young. If he wants to, he will. Every time I suggest maybe reading the book to learn a trick it puts his back up and his voice goes shrill and shouty, then I shout back and it's on. He's old enough for that.

Past the pelican crossing, he turns right. By this time, there are always a clan of children mobbing towards the school, herded by the village childminder. The kids are younger than my son, and I can tell by how straight his back is – he is pretending not to look at them – that he loves this next bit. He pumps hard on the pedals, leans into the turn, and undertakes the lot of them on the fresh green spring grassy slope, whipping between the Perspex bus stop and the old brick wall of the old school.

He leans hard out and pumps harder. A couple of the little boys always try and race him, but he's off, between the end of the wall and the street sign pole. Ten yards later he's stuck behind a mum with a pram; when she notices, she lets him by. The headteacher is at the front gates. He wants to show he's being good, so stops and gets off and wheels through. If she hadn't been there, he would have whizzed straight through, taking a perfect line so his handlebar tips barely get by the galvanised steel of the security fence.

When the bike is parked, he walks awkwardly, swinging his book bag. He walks head down, clops his feet, stumbles through the school door, oblivious to the parent holding it open.

It's when he speeds up that he is graceful. When he runs and skips, swims, rides his bike, climbs a tree, when I take him to the rock or the climbing wall, that is when he is moving well. He has long limbs, he's skinny like I was.

On the way back, I don't bother with the pelican crossing. I don't want to hold up the traffic, put a few more seconds onto all those people's drives. Instead I time my sprint: a truck is taking its time to accelerate from the roundabout and that gives me the time I need. My girlfriend drives past and waves, taking the car to work.

Back at the house, Ned the Dog is waiting, still up in the window. When I put the key in the door, he runs through, tail thrashing, and hopping around like a slimline seal. He bounces at me, and jumps in my way. He licks his lips, which means 'You are the boss!' in Dog.

I wrestle him into his harness, laughing and annoyed: Labradors, especially when crossed with collie, do not care about pain. If I walk him with a collar he'll pull against it, ignoring the choking while making horrendous death-rattle sounds. I find that embarrassing, people will look at me as a cruel owner, so a harness it is.

When we get through the kissing-gate and up to the woods, I let him off. He bounds forward, but then looks back, and I make him wait before I say, 'Go on, then'. Off he belts. He's fast and muscular, but his back legs look odd; he bunny-hops instead of running evenly. He's got hip dysplasia, his hip sockets didn't form properly. It's not uncommon, especially in pure-breds, which he is most definitely not.

Our last dog, Stella, there was nothing wrong with her hips. She was collie-Lab cross but much more collie than Lab. She could run. I would be on my mountain bike down a forest track and I would really start to sprint, highest gear as fast as I could go. Then she would shift up a gear, without any apparent effort, her head still and level among the whirl of her legs. I couldn't have kept her on a lead; she needed a lot of exercise or she'd get depressed, moody, neurotic. So I ran her off her lead, until one Boxing Day when she scouted out too far and couldn't hear us. She was clever and I knew she could work her way back, which is what she was doing when she tried to cross the road and was hit by a car. I found her, when I saw hazard-lights of cars up the road, and there she was, dead or in the very last moments of dying. I think she wasn't quite gone, that maybe there was enough nutrition and oxygen in her brain left for her to know I had found her. That evening we all cried as we buried her, my son helped dig the grave, and Venus was bright in the sky. She was only a puppy. Eighteen months old. I could have kept her on a lead. If I'd kept her on a lead she'd have taken ten years to die, rather than minutes or seconds; she had to run, she needed it.

We keep Ned exercised. We regulate his food. He must not put on weight or his joints will start to wear, become arthritic, too painful for even the indestructible collie-Lab cross to bear. His back legs are rippling with muscle; I like to squeeze them when he snoozes on my lap in the evenings. If he starts to lose that muscle, that will be a bad sign; the pain and debility will start to creep up.

If he ever gets to the point where he cannot run or swim, he will decline quickly, because a dog needs to run. The wolf in him needs to feel like he is hunting, that he is useful to the pack. Sometimes he runs in his sleep, squeaking out a high-pitched *whif – whif – whif*. He dreams he is running and barking, hunting, though for him this is never anything other than an imaginary hunt. His food comes in a bowl three times a day. Turkey and rice.

There will come a point when we call the vet. When that happens, it will be because he has not run for a while and will not have any purpose. He will look at me, and I will know it will be time. For now he is a puppy; he's got years in him yet.

Back home, a treat of a greasy pig's ear, and leave him in his crate. He feels safe there, sits and then curls up. Nothing else to do? Have a sleep. Tanya's mum will pick him up once she's done her couple of hours cleaning work. She likes him for the company, and he likes her. He recognises the name Nanny, and goes crackers when he hears it because he likes to be in her bungalow, skidding around the tiled and laminate floors, snoozing on her settees, coming up for a cuddle while she watches telly.

I kick the van into life and head out.

CHAPTER 20

The Very Big and the Very Small

May 2017, Rainbow Slab; Trango Tower

Lee is not having a good trip. The conditions, the 'connies', are out.

The day is humid. Anglesey is barely visible for the lurking blue haze over Caernarfon and Bangor. The air is dead still. No breeze to either move the heavy damp air mass or dry sweat from hands.

I'm belaying: paying yellow nylon rope through my belay plate, inching out how much Lee is allowed, ready to catch him if he falls. Which, I think, might just be coming.

On the climb, I see Lee's fingers are leaving sweat finger-prints on the rock. If I was closer, I could see the lines and whorls, then they quickly fade as the sun dries them.

He moves left, still low on the cliff face, flicks his right foot out and toes onto a foothold. Still for a second, then clenches his thigh and shifts his hip to stab out his finger, like a man throwing a dart in a pub. The handhold is small, no bigger than the end of a box of matches, and sloped. Lee catches it, but his fingers surf down the slick layer of sweat, and pop off the edge: he has greased off.

I catch him easily on the rope, and he swings from the stainless-steel bolt. These are sport climbs, safer than the drive here because of the bolts drilled at regular intervals into the rock.

'Fuck! Fuck. Conditions, Pete. Wait for the fucking

conditions.' Very angry.

'Going again?'

'Nah. Fuck off. Down.'

I pay out the rope and he lands gently, feet on the floor. He looks – furious – at his fingers. They are soaked, oozing sweat, hardly any chalk left on them.

'Conditions are out. Connies – are – out.'

He takes off his shoes, unties, gets his rucksack.

'Might be better in the evening,' I offer. He nods and we head out.

Lee is quiet, anyway, but he has different types of quiet, and this is the kind where he is not at all happy, locked-up anger at something he can't change. I chatter away, trying to distract him out of it. There's no distracting someone who cares so much about what he does, but who cannot – this second – do it.

We head down the swerving levels alongside the stream running down the hillside through brick and concrete before breaking out down the hill. We walk across a single giant slab bridge of slate, about twelve feet long, six feet wide and balanced from bank to bank. Walking across it is nervy: it is about four-inches thick, but that seems really thin. On the far side is one of the old quarry huts, a blue tarpaulin slung across the roof. Someone is living there in secret; it might well be a climber, or a local lad fallen out with his missus or chucked out by his folks.

I'm telling Lee about a mate I had, years ago, and how he fucked me over for a girl I fancied. I've turned that old pain and embarrassment into a funny story packed out with lies, something to spike through his unhappiness.

'I was downstairs getting beer and I heard one of my other

housemates burst in on them, shouting, "What are you doing?" And he says, "Reading!" I heard her giggle, you know....'

Lee's silence is now about listening.

'Anyhow, I just swallowed it: last year at uni before I could fuck off to America. Next eight months – they didn't even want each other. You'd go on a night out, and he'd pull some random lass, or he'd be about to get in a taxi with some other lass on the course, and you can't say anything because it's your mate, you know?'

'He sounds like a 24-carat cunt,' Lee says, and I crack up laughing. The old pain is suddenly less; all those people we hang onto, thinking they're better than they are. That energy we spend on people who were never worth it.

We walk through the short and leafy oak trees, no more than forty years old, spreading out along the edges of the worked quarry. It smells green and loamy, then the sudden strange stink of feta cheese. The wild goats have just passed through; they graze calmly. I'd be unafraid if I had horns like that.

We drop down further alongside the stream, past other old quarry buildings; one of them is filled with an enormous Ingersoll steam engine and a foot's depth of wild goat droppings. There are also a load of empty cardboard crates, empty cans of lager, empty alcopop bottles, and hundreds of thumb-sized metal capsules that look as if they hold a gas – nitrous oxide maybe? I can't keep up with the modern ways of getting high.

Lee lowers me down to the ground. We are at the bottom of *The Take Over* and I have just fallen off.

'Come here,' he says and grabs my hands, turning them so

he can see my fingertips. His look is of disgust, tempered with amazement. My fingertips have hardly sweated at all, even in the humidity of the day. The chalk is still white on my fingers; only a few tiny patches right on the whorls of my fingerprint betray any sweating at all. His hands would be soaked.

'It's alright, Lee. I'll leave them to you in my will. I saw on telly, they can do transplants now.'

'You going to try that again?' asks Lee.

'Nah. That's it, nothing left in my fingers. What do you want to do?'

'I was thinking of dropping a rope down the Rainbow and having a look at *The Very Big and the Very Small* – not have a try, just have a look at the moves.'

For thirty years, *The Very Big and the Very Small* was the hardest thing in the quarries. It was originally graded 8c, which was groundbreaking; controversial for a slab climb.

We scramble up a grassy slope, scrubby small trees. At the top of the slab there are a cluster of old quarry buildings. They are still roofed and watertight, with wooden doors. Maybe those buildings are the reason that the Rainbow Slab survived. It's hard to believe that sweep of rock isn't natural, but no, it was unearthed, sloughed free of block after block, a handful of black powder at a time.

I walk out on a narrow spit of grassed-over rock. I stand, wobbly at the edge, looking down; can't stand it, so I lie down to peak my head over the edge, looking down the Rainbow. The lump of rock I am on is still balanced up here, overlying the clean sweep of the slab. It's like an Easter Island head, left like a totem, watching over, first the quarrymen and now the climbers, who crawl around below; and below again, the hydroelectric power station.

'You need a hand, mate?' I ask. No, he doesn't; I am left to watch him and the view.

Lee steps carefully along the edge of the cliff and finds a pair of bolts. He turns the rope through and clips in to abseil, throwing the rope out behind him. As he starts out down, he walks over a small niche, packed with slate rubble. He stops and wraps the rope around his leg and picks one up. It is sharp and jagged and the size of a brick. There are dozens like it, poised and ready to fall.

He looks up at me. 'Any one of those would kill you. Might try something else.'

He unclips the rope and walks along the cliff. If he stands by the side, he can reach out and clip a pair of bolts on the face. He steps back from the edge, gets it all ready, carefully and neatly. I've never seen him make a hasty move, and definitely not here, with forty metres of fall below your feet.

He steps back out to the edge, reaches his hand around and clips the carabiner into the bolt-hangers; carefully does up the screw gate. He has already got his GriGri – an abseil device – on the rope, so he simply steps out into space, leans back and slips smoothly and silently down the rope.

Nothing for me to do but look out and think. Below is the S-shaped bridge, the power station buildings. Above the oblong offices is a spiky tower of rock – with imagination, a legendary Welsh castle – we call Trango tower. In the March rains, tons of the loose slate avalanched and cascaded down, threatening the offices and workshops. Twenty-ton diggers have been clearing the rubble; from here they look tiny, but you can hear the *glakakakakakakaka* as their steel track links turn and tread. Woven-wire gabions, like big lobster pots, have been filled with slate waste, and stacked to make walls and revetments.

Up here it is peaceful. We don't scream when we fall or shout when we succeed, and their security guards won't come up here to chase us off. We know their risk assessments say it's too dangerous for them. So the truce holds.

Lee's rope starts to bounce, I know he is coming back up. His head appears. He is grinning, the angry silence has been blown away. He looks much younger, happy.

'How was it?'

'Amazing. The holds are tiny. Unbelievable. And the moves between them – just –' he sighs and shakes his head. He's struggling for the right words out of reach. On the rope he has felt the holds, played with them, seen how they would work with the shape of the body. How the angles of your limbs within that six-foot space could stretch and balance and make a workable sequence to be able to move up. 'The more I see of that man's climbs. Every one is just unique, such character, such character.'

In the late eighties, Nick Harms had found some blank space on the Rainbow Slab, in between the existing classic lines. This was a horribly controversial place to drill three bolts in: the climbing equivalent of advertising Starbucks at Stonehenge. He got threats of a kicking if he fucked about with the Rainbow, but the bolts were there now, so he started working out the moves. Harms had done the hardest single move on slate (he nabbed the third ascent of *Windows of Perception* by Johnny Dawes, a prestigious early repeat) and he was at home on hard slabs

Dinorwig Power Station from the Rainbow levels.

like *The Medium* (by Johnny Dawes). So, to Harms, the hard slabs just didn't feel that hard any more. This slab was more part of his climbing past than his climbing future, he was attracted to more powerful body-tension climbing – big grips and bold lunges – rather than balancey moves on the tips of his toes.

Having said that, this slab was different to anything else he'd ever climbed. It was tough: 'there isn't a single move below 6c and most are 7a'.[62] Some of the holds were as small as matchsticks and horribly sharp, needing just the right amount of fingernail to grip them. Because of this, 'You don't get many attempts per session before your skin gives out... that's if your frustration with stringing it all together doesn't get the better of you first. I began to feel guilty at dragging people up to the Rainbow to belay, particularly as the power station folks blocked off the lower path... and I just couldn't get the shoes right.'[63]

Frustrating enough, but even success would have had its own problems. 'One of the final nails in the coffin was the grade. I knew it was hard, but not how hard. Johnny had proffered a suggestion [of the grade] after he'd had a go on it. But I thought if I did it, no one would believe me slapping an 8c tag on it. There just weren't that many routes of that grade around at the time. I thought I'd be a laughing stock. Bearing in mind that the 3 bolts I put in this line were the cause of the threats to get beaten up, I thought grading this 8c would be like a red rag.'[64] It was so hard that Harms would have called it *The End*, had he climbed it. The culmination of all the world's climbing to that point, and something beyond which nothing was possible any more.

So when Dawes asked if Harms minded if he did it instead, he gave it away. And almost immediately regretted it. Dawes climbed it. He knew about kickings from public school, and fully embraced being a laughing stock, his ego battle-tested against the scorn of others. Dawes declared it an 8c. Dawes named it *The Very Big and the Very Small*, the 'big' being the number and the 'small' being the holds: fucking tiny.

CHAPTER 21

Dawes of Perception

February 2016, The Roaches, Staffordshire

A few months before Sam and Big Rugby Rob's accident, Sam and I head out with ice-axes and crampons for a few days' attempted climbing in the Scottish winter. The weather is total shit, though, so we end up in Lee's new house in Sheffield, checking out three different weather forecasts. Nowhere looks good. Out of the lot, only one place is remotely viable.

The wind blows hard at the Roaches in Staffordshire. The weather is terrible over Wales, which is why we are here. It isn't slate but it'll do; at least we are trying to climb something.

Sam leads away up an easy route, but we can't hear each other and he's out of sight. He hasn't pulled all the rope through, so I can't start climbing. I'm 90 per cent sure he thinks he has, though, convinced by the rope drag through his gear. But I can't go until he pulls that rope tight.

Suddenly I hear his voice; it sounds quite posh, although, actually, Sam is not. 'Climb when ready!' The standard climber's command. It sounds like Sam, but something makes me a bit unsure. It's shouted from closer than it should be; maybe it's a trick of the gusting wind.

'Pull the fucking rope through, then!' I shout back. Something muffled happens at the top. Is someone up there with him? Then the rope snakes up and I'm free to get going.

When I climb around a corner, I see Sam, and he makes faces at me.

'Climb up here, quick,' he says, hurried. I do and as I get closer, Sam is mouthing something at me.

'What the fuck are you on about, Sam?'

'It's Johnny Dawes!' he hisses. 'That's who shouted down to you!'

A figure is walking away over the golden-red gritstone. He has a red vinyl roll-top rucksack, the kind kayakers use, and wears a cloth pillbox hat, very hippyish. He skips along the edge of the cliff then drops easily out of view down the path.

We walk out down the path, drop into the pine plantation, thick brown needle carpet after thin moor grass and heather. There he is again, on his own, looking up at a slab of rock and thoughtfully drinking from a bullet-shaped flask. You don't get chances like this twice, I think: be bold.

I walk up to say thanks for shouting down. He doesn't notice me approach; he's in a world of his own, and jumps when I say hello.

'Scared the shit out of me! Hold on,' he says, 'I'll walk down to the car with you.'

Sam and I exchange glances. We are walking back to the car with Johnny Dawes!

'Look at us,' Dawes says, 'there's no one else, but we're out here trying it.' He frowns and looks out over the west; the sunlight is leached pale yellow. 'It seems like over the east side of the country you can see further.'

'It's hazy out to the west,' I offer.

'It *is*.' He is delighted.

At the car, he grins at us. He's got a boot full of copies of his book, *Full of Myself*, and a cardboard box with copies of a

DVD called *Stone Monkey* in it. I buy a book and Sam buys a DVD. At one point, Johnny upends the contents of his red vinyl bag. There is a tatty old abseil rope, and an ancient harness, wide purple webbing and no padding. There is a single nut on a quickdraw, and that's it. It is the weirdest collection of climbing gear ever, and there's something about the way he tips the bag up that makes me think it's part of the show.

Stone Monkey is the best bloody rock-climbing film ever made, and everyone knows it. It's a bit odd, there's some funny sequences in it. Johnny being sent to bed by his posh mum and dad and climbing up the side of the stairs then over the bannisters. A bit where he's wearing school uniform – he was never tall – climbing a concrete underpass in Manchester.

There's loads of scenes of him climbing on the grit. He is young. He wears Lycra leggings and patterned jumpers. His legs look strong, his arms are well muscled but not blocky from weightlifting, he is in perfect physical nick. The blurb for *Stone Monkey* calls him the 'Nureyev of the rock', and it should sound silly, like some wanker declaring that Gialvadini's goal against Juventus is balletic. Until you see Dawes climb, and you get it: the shapely limbs, those straight legs and the moves; the moves. They look rehearsed and seamless and it is like a dance, swirls of powerful shapes, control, flowing up the rock.

The big sequence is Dawes going up the middle, groove pitch of *The Quarryman* in Twll Mawr. When I first watched it, I didn't get it. It didn't mean anything to me. The way he climbs, there's no strain to it, often no apparent effort. He just bounces up, sometimes with his tongue stuck out like a kid faced with a tricky maths problem.

I see a video of James McHaffie climbing the *Quarryman* groove and it frightens me. The effort on his face, the way his feet skid on the rock. He moves up, braced between the two faces, then skitters back down. He breathes hard, he looks uncomfortable and afraid, then his feet slip again. There's barely any friction on the smooth glass walls of slate, and only the occasional hold.

In *Stone Monkey*, Dawes' moves are confident and precise. He flicks his feet onto holds, braces his arms with the elbow up, folded like a chicken's wing. He wedges in, and his face concentrates, but he looks totally in control. He is wearing stripy leggings and a vest top, his hair is a mid eighties near-mullet like a synthesiser player's, sideburns shaved high up to where the ears join the scalp. He remembers to put on a look of extra concentration as he becomes aware of the camera at the top, before flopping onto the bed-sized belay ledge called New York. He made it look easy.

1986, ledges, beams, underpasses, squash courts; Vivian Quarry

Johnny Dawes came to Llanberis with a spiky carapace of withering scorn and open rudeness. Unlike a lot of the other climbers around, Johnny was from a wealthy family who lived in a manor house in the lee of the Malverns. He was sent to public school, an exuberant child, with intelligent and sensitive ideas, expressed as stream-of-consciousness speeches. He could talk for hours about sports cars. Therefore he was a target, a lightning rod for teenage aggression.

Under pressure, he learned to detach himself from the

violence and emotional assault, create within himself a space of calm from which he could operate. The one good thing about school? Being introduced to rock climbing by a couple of sympathetic teachers who took a green Transit van of kids climbing rather than teaching them how to fire a Bren gun and march up and down with the Combined Cadet Force.[65]

Johnny Dawes knew that Redhead was the 'best' climber in north Wales, and set his sights on him. This was the old story, the old challenge – which Redhead disdained – fed by the climbing mags. Dawes' trick was to quickly repeat Redhead's climbs and then claim they were not *that* hard, downgrade them.

Redhead was five foot ten, and with long arms, could reach out, slow and steady, for those tiny crimps. Johnny Dawes was five foot four, which is way below optimum height for a climber. He couldn't reach the holds other climbers could, so very early on, he learned he had to jump for things, get some spring out of his legs so he could reach. If he was taller he probably would never have done that; he would have just reached the small hold, wrapped his strengthening fingers around it and pulled hard. You can't train to be taller.

Dawes spent hours and hours and days and days climbing everything that was around. Not just the traditional climbs on Peak gritstone, but the brick ledges and wooden beams of the manor house he lived in. At boarding school, he climbed the brick edges of the squash courts, lay backing on the corner of the bricks. He used metal pipes to grab on to, mantled onto the tops of buildings. When he went to university in Manchester, he climbed the concrete underpasses of the Mancunian Way, putting up graded problems along the irregularities of poured concrete.

He did so much of this that any natural talent was massively amplified by experience by the time he was in his late teens. He could hit moves and jumps accurately and at high speed. He had fantastic balance – not just a static balance, but a heightened awareness of the momentum of his body in movement and how to change its direction with a rapidly placed hand. A human gyroscope.

All these hours of playing on the rock, and rock-like materials, had also resulted in a lot of falls, hitting the ground from pretty far up; usually lucky, leaving dents in flowerbeds, or turning a crash into a run downhill through bracken until momentum spent itself.

Dawes thought a lot about it, obsessing, his mind spiralling thoughts in unusual ways. He described himself as an 'autistic wild boy'. That sounds like just a cool climbing star title, pre-rehearsed, but not when you see him on camera saying it. He is trying to explain something about himself; his mind is racing and plucking words out of anywhere. Autistic. Wild. Boy.

* * *

Redhead, after his successes on the Rainbow Slab, found fresh ground to work on. In Vivian Quarry there were blank walls with nothing you could grip, faint thin cracks too small to slot gear into, neither handhold nor foothold.

Right, thought Redhead. This blank face was a canvas, ready for art. He abseiled down it, watched by his mates. Subtly, he worked a fine chisel into the cracks and levered out an edge. 'Where there was a crack, he just opened it out, and you get a little triangular hold. Or not.'[66] *Manic Strain* was very skilfully done; climbers today who don't know the history wouldn't believe that it was chipped.

Dawes did not like this. He understood rock in a different way to any other climber. The rock had its internal rhythm that you could feel and dance to. If you danced well to it, it might let you climb it, if you shuffled out of time then you would fall. Breaking and chipping the rock destroyed its song, like a second-rate DJ interrupting the song you love to do his own dickhead jokes.

Dawes climbed all the routes on the Rainbow Slab, until he got to *Raped by Affection*. What he didn't know was that there was a sling missing from the high bolt, which had allowed the dangerous clip to be made more easily by Redhead, necessary even with his longer reach.

Dawes reached his toe across space and landed it on an edge the width of a penny. It held. But he couldn't reach to clip the bolt with the carabiner. He couldn't go back down; he was nearly a hundred feet up the slab, with few pieces of widely spaced gear below him, which might slow his fall, but probably wouldn't stop it.

He pulled out his quickdraw, the gate facing the wrong way to clip the bolt. He had to move, but he had to get it right, too. With only one chance to do it, he tossed the carabiner in the air, it flipped around, he caught it and flicked it at the bolt. The carabiner pierced the eye of the bolt-hanger. He grabbed the hold and made the clip. Johnny called his version *Draped in Affection*.

Having done Redhead's hardest climbs, Dawes needed to put up his own incredibly hard routes in Vivian.

Dawes of Perception ran up a slab with tiny little pieces of poor gear. Just at the hardest point, the crux, Johnny drilled in a bolt for protection, which was safest clipped when it was at knee height. The landing was razor sharp teeth of slate. 'Lose contact and your only hope is to immediately crouch, briefly ride the slide, then push off at right angles to the plane just before to avoid losing a leg.'[67]

Redhead accepted the challenge, but being taller, tried to clip the bolt from lower down. He fell. His belayer, Dave Towse, immediately jumped off the ledge and into the pool of Vivian, pulling enough slack out of the rope to keep Redhead – barely – off the ground. Redhead broke his thumb on one of the rock fins, lucky to get away so lightly.

After *Dawes of Perception*, Dawes put up *Windows of Perception* with slate's single hardest move, a rockover from fingernail edges, a move so difficult that climbers would later debate how to do it as two separate halves.

'*Dawes of Perception* had nearly killed [Redhead]; the technical ones like *Windows of Perception*... were beyond him. His crown was stolen.'[68]

So what?

CHAPTER 22

The Quarryman

May 2017, Capel Curig

I walk into the Siabod Cafe in Capel Curig. The day is hot, but a lot of people will still be up on the hill. The cafe will be very busy later on, as walkers come down from Snowdon or the Glyderau and bikers finish the mountain bike trails along the valley. The menu is above the counter, white paint faking chalk on a blackboard.

The man standing behind the counter is average height, wiry, cropped hair, tanned from the weather. But it is the way he stands: he is a climber, perfectly balanced and still, like a martial artist. When he reaches for the pen and the order book his hands go straight to them without looking, like finding a crimp.

'Alright mate?' he asks and it's no surprise to me that his accent is Liverpool.

'What's that there, then? Austrian rarebit?' I ask, and I hear my accent go more Scouse than it normally is. My accent wanders around, Liverpool, north-east, you could hear it as Manchester or Yorkshire when my dad's Staffordshire rises to the surface. When I do electrical work, I drift straight into Estuary – asking for 'side-cu'ers' (side-cutters) so I can cut 'cabuw' (cable). Just because everyone I've ever worked with on electrical had that accent.

'Austrian rarebit? Well, it's like Welsh rarebit, except you get a free doll of Hitler.' He is absolutely deadpan; he summed me up and knew he could risk a cheeky joke. 'But we've run out of those, so instead we put smoked bacon on top.'

'Go on then. One of them.'

I tap my card on the card-reader but it doesn't want to play. Try it again.

'Come on bloody thing,' the man says. 'It's the internet connection.'

'No it's not,' I say. 'It's karma for your Hitler joke.' He grins at that; fair enough, one point to me in the great cafe game of making strangers laugh.

I walk over to a table near the window with my coffee. There is a pile of old copies of *Climber* magazine. I grab one at random; it turns out to be from late 1985. In the news section, there is a short paragraph stating that Johnny Dawes has climbed two new routes in the slate quarries; the name of one of them, *Dawes of Perception*, being described as typically egotistical.

1987–89, Llanberis Pass; Plas y Brenin training centre

Raining again. Johnny Dawes and Bobby Drury would roll a joint, get into the car and drive up the Llanberis Pass, then down again, twisty thrilling mountain roads. Dawes drove the same way he climbed: with his tongue poking out in concentration. Dawes loved racing cars. He loved the cornering, using the power in the engine to balance between throttle, brake and the friction of the tyres.

Left at Pen-y-Gwryd, then down the long straight to the north of the llyn to Plas y Brenin. This was a big old Victorian hotel, now the Plas y Brenin National Outdoor Centre, teaching people to climb, kayak and navigate the hills. It had a climbing wall, with new resin holds bolted onto boards. Its real function was for school kids and adults attending courses to be able to learn the basics of belaying when it rained, but off-duty instructors and local climbers could use it unsupervised.

As they climbed around the plastic holds on the indoor wall, they noticed that if they sprang or jumped, there would be a 'moment of weightlessness'. They kept doing these moves and started to realise that in that moment, you could change motion and direction, jump and add new movement. That weightlessness was the quest, having emerged from a game.[69] No one else was doing this, although across the world, similar advances in movement were happening in skateboarding; tricks based on the 'ollie', which pops the skateboard into the air.

Egging each other on, sometimes with other mates, they would try more and more ridiculous jumps and leaps, runs across a low level of sloping holds. Perfectly timed running smears using blank patches between the holds for a toehold, where if you hit it just precisely with the pad of your shoe, it would generate a tiny amount of friction; thrust, enough to keep the orbit of your run from degrading, then jumping to catch on the edge of faraway ledges.

It was a step beyond. These moves had an extra dimension to them, they took place in time as well as space. As Dawes and Drury ran across the walls, they were cornering like sports cars, riding dynamic skids intuitively based on the subtle repetition of their play.

Back out in the climbing community, Dawes' achievements were given respect. He was the 'best'. But when other people got involved, desire and achievement got warped into something different and troubling. The acclaim, the social role of being the best, being worth knowing, worth talking to because of what you had done, not who you were.

'To a young, socially immature person, that grew as a cancer,' he wrote, about a climb called *Indian Face*.[70] 'The end of this lies in photographs, sponsorship and in ugly tights, and in a dead end with a bolted door.'

Movement was the only thing with any real point for Dawes. The futility of life in an uncaring cosmos was obvious. 'Friendship and activity are some compensation for deep-seated hopelessness, but only climbing appeared to have a little germ of profound depth in all its excited little plays of life and death.'[71]

At the same time that Dawes was receiving the acclaim of others, few understood, really, what it was that he was doing. Onlookers who understood climbing were often conscious that something different and very good was going on, but how could you express it? Crooky (Martin Crook), with classic understatement, noticed he had 'an extra spring in his foot'. Andy Cave, climbing with Dawes in the Peak, 'stared incredulously as he stood on non-existent footholds and jumped dynamically for a pathetically small pebble with his fingers. What he had, more than anyone I had ever met, was balance. He really was dancing on rock.'[72]

Then Dawes would try and explain it. His long intense stream-of-consciousness speeches would have been recognisable to the school bullies as the 'Johnny Classics'. Instead of offering only dismissal, people now tried to understand, but when Dawes asked them, 'Do you understand what I mean?'

their responses revealed they were nowhere close.[73] They hadn't been there with him.

May 2014, The Quarryman *groove*

On my first Wales trip, Lee had disappeared for a day while we all went multi-pitching up Tryfan. That evening at the campsite, everyone was glowing from the light and the air. Lee walked in as we all lounged around. He was contained; we were all pleased to see him and tell him what we'd done.

'How was it?' Garry quietly asked him.

'Alright. Got two moves further than last year.'

'So that year's worth of training was for two moves? Basically, nothing?'

'Nah,' said Lee. 'I was out there, trying it. It was cool abbing down.'

'What were you doing?' I asked.

'*Quarryman* groove; it's a pitch on the Dawes route from the eighties. Megaclassic. A flaring groove, just less than ninety degrees, like the opposite of a knife's blade.' I imagined a bowie knife pushed into molten rock and leaving a weird slash.

'It's not really like any other type of climbing,' he went on, 'you've got to use your whole body to generate friction.'

'Like chimneying?' I asked. I know chimneying from old mountaineering books, squeezing your back knees and palms on opposite sides of a rock chimney to lodge yourself in place.

One evening, when I was fifteen or sixteen, I went out with mates one Friday night, walking around Newton Hall estate. We were looking for action, any kind of action: girls who wanted to get off with us, or trouble, or getting out of our minds.

We smoked tack: cannabis resin. I never heard it called tack outside the north-east. It was easier to get than to chance the embarrassment of trying to bluff a shopkeeper to let us buy cans of lager. Behind Martin's newsagent and Greggs bakery, a substation formed an alley with another wall. We all managed to lodge ourselves in the alleyway, backs against the wall and knees against the other, sitting there like weird floating monks, discussing fights and tits. When we got down, eventually, deciding that neither fights nor tits were going to happen to us in that alley, we anxiously checked our jeans to see if the rough brick had worn through the fabric.

'It is. Not really. More like an off-width crack, but it's glass smooth, there aren't any real holds until much higher up. You've got to chicken-wing and then roll into the groove to get into it,' he explained, miming the moves, 'then put your feet out, but if you push too hard you just skid out quicker.'

'Cool,' I said lamely. I'm not sure I understand half the phrases. 'Disappointed?'

'No. Not at all. When I was resting on the rope, I saw an ant crawling up the rock face, just doing his thing. I wouldn't have seen that if I hadn't been there.'

Late eighties, west wall of Twll Mawr; Llanberis scene

In the morning, the climbers and slateheads would start to emerge from their pits, piecing together the previous night's events, and dealing with hangovers. For most, it meant a fried-egg sandwich at Pete's, and see where your mates were going. Hangovers are endurance events, like alpine routes. Food and company help until adrenalin can flush the fatigue away.

'Last night at a party, Nick Thomas had tried to smash my head into a basin, Steve Andy tried to ram my head down the bog. Today, Skinny Dave and I abseil down off an un-cemented slate hut to inspect the untouched West Wall.'[74]

Dawes hadn't been able to understand why no one was talking about this wall. Sheer, unbroken, like a cliff of granite from El Capitan or Lofoten had been sliced off and air-dropped into an obscure quarry in north Wales. Why *wouldn't* you want to climb this wall?

Because no one else had Dawes' vision to look for routes up it. Back when they had explored Twll Mawr, Joe Brown and Claude Davies had thought it looked too blank and steep, which it probably was for the gear and standards of the early seventies. From the bottom of the pit in bright midday sunshine, the features flatten and detail is lost. Everything fades yellow in the bright sunlamp light.

In the morning or evening, the wall looks very different. The sunlight at an angle reveals cracks and shelves and ledges, features to be climbed. If you ever look at the moon through a telescope, the greatest detail of the topography can be seen along the terminator, the line between the light and the dark, where the shadows pick out craters and ridges.

'It was gold and red and all wavy, like a celestial butterknife had put the aurora borealis down it. And it was glittering! It was amazing!'[75]

Hanging from a dirty oil-stained rope of dubious history, Dawes found large features. There were big shelf-like belays, which he would name *London*, *New York*, *Paris* and *Rome*. He saw the groove that would become the iconic part of *The Quarryman*, which intrigued him.

Modern graffitied art in one of the tunnels – a tribute to the quarrymen.

The wall had everything going for it. It looked incredibly tall, like El Capitan, but wasn't, only being about 200 feet. The routes that Dawes had the vision to see weren't too hard, and weren't too easy, a perfect Goldilocks zone of difficulty. The angle of the wall was just off vertical but *looked* vertical, so was 'flattering. So you feel like you're doing impossible moves. And then you're doing another impossible move.'[76]

Over the next two years, Dawes looked for sequences and routes between the belays. He found them. It was outrageous. It was audacious. Friends came with him, like Bobby Drury, Skinny Dave, Moose and Carlos, all outstanding climbers in their own right.

There were big features like grooves, cracks and ledges, and on the blank patches in-between, Dawes started to look for, and find, matchstick-sized edges that could link together into intricate sequences. 'Where else has space-time been woven so wackily, the impossible and the easy overlapping so unpredictably? Features at a generous kinaesthetic angle: big broken toffee features coding for waist's *hippy hippy shake,* the wall's installation of links angled for creative flick of limb. Look at where the hold should be and use that instead, put your foot in a position you never thought possible, on a hold that doesn't look like it would work, setting up for a hold that looks tiny, that turns out excellent, putting you in a "hands off" with unrivalled views of Snowdonia. That's why you can wear Lycra on slate!'[77]

The Quarryman was the first. It took many visits to drill in bolts, work out the sequences and be ready to climb it from the bottom.

Bobby Drury was living in the caravan in Johnny Redhead's garden. He woke up one morning to Dawes knocking on his caravan door, wanting to go climbing, telling Bobby he had a great new wall, 'and I just didn't want to go out that day. He kind of dragged me out, "Come on, I've got a car we'll have a drive up there."'[78]

On the wall, to Bobby's surprise, it was actually climbable: amazing for such a blank-looking wall. 'We started abseiling down... thinking, "Fuck me, there *are* tiny little edges on this; you can actually hang on this stuff."'[79] It was hard – yes – but it wasn't *that* hard; it was actually climbable, and the two of them did each pitch relatively quickly, with only a few falls.

The groove itself was a bizarre gymnastic sequence. It wasn't like the rest of the climb, which was basically thin edge-holds on a big beautiful wall. It was mainly holdless, rolling into the corner to press with your back, hands and feet. 'I remember thinking at the time that the reason we could do this was because we were small. I'm five foot seven, Johnny's five foot five.... We can get a larger percentage of our shoulder and back into a groove, which helps us get in. If you're a big lad, you can only get your shoulder in.'[80]

There was just enough to move up. Drury later likened it to 'a bizarre dance. Left hand and foot are on the left wall, and your right hand and foot are both on the right wall. In some kind of horizontal bridge, and through a series of flic-flacs your hands are now on the right wall and your feet are now on the left wall, so it's like some bizarre gymnastic sequence.'[81]

They didn't finish the climb that day. After they had done the groove, Drury dragged Dawes, not too unwillingly, off to a party. They came back the next day to finish the last pitch. 'The top pitch was the hardest; that had a rockover that was really savage, the holds were so small that I cut my finger on it.'[82] This was typical of the time: a climb escaped from because the day was running out and different priorities were taking over.

* * *

Coming back into the village, the slateheads and dole climbers would load up on cheap food – between Pete's and the chipshop – then hit the pub. Which generally meant the Pad (Padarn Lake Hotel), or the disco at the Dolbadarn on Thursdays. Having altered your consciousness with some extreme climbing, it was time to get fucked up.

The Pad had been the social hub of the village for a long time, popular with climbers since the sixties. 'The forecourt of the pub was jammed solid with vehicles – mostly old vans and station wagons full of climbing equipment. Shuffling through the car park, the sound increased, and opening the inner door, a shattering roar hit me like an explosion. A smoke-filled room, milling with casually dressed climbers, tables piled high with empty glasses, beer slopping everywhere: Saturday night at the Padarn!'[83]

Everyone banged elbows together. 'Farmers, the girls from the chemist and the Co-op, the hairdressers and the builders, the walkers and the climbers.'[84] This was not some tarted-up tourist trap, and it wasn't a climbers-only pub, with wooden-handled ice-axes or antiquated gear to display its identity. No. This place was real.

After the pub, the party. Already semi-loaded, everyone would walk down to someone's house; the one on Goodman Street was notorious. Hot knives would vaporise blocks of hash – imported from Pakistan and Morocco – into steam. Magic mushrooms, scavenged from playing fields and grassy areas every autumn, would be brewed into tea. LSD was harder to get, since the hippy chemists cooking it up on remote Welsh farms had been busted. But amphetamine was still common, easy to make in a bathtub or crude kitchen lab, although the smell created was unbelievable: a chemical vapour: part fish, part smelling salts. Some climbers might be selling bottles of ripped-off booze, and the temperature would rise.

'For those who had taken the full dose and moved to Llanberis, parties formed part of the local structure,' said Nick Dixon. Nick would ride his scooter, a Honda C90, from Staffordshire where he was studying at Keele University, then crash on the floor at a friend's houses or in the toilets at the Vaynol. 'I find parties frightening. On many occasions, I unwittingly ended up at one with strange strangers, and narcotics which were also frightening. I remember the shouting and the fighting and the mess.'[85]

CHAPTER 23

Supermassive Black Hole

May 2017, Twll Mawr 'Not Allowed' section

The young couple are walking along the Dinorwig quarry road along the hillside above Llanberis. They see us already climbing, so stop for directions.

'Hello,' he says, 'do you know where Twll Mawr is?' He pronounces it right.

He is pleasant and she is Californian – and hot – so of course I offer to show them where it is. Becky turns, holding Lee's rope, and raises an eyebrow at me. The couple wants to do *Supermassive Black Hole,* which is becoming a classic. I think they are on a climbing date. They are carrying climbing-brand rucksacks – if we looked down the valley we could see the DMM factory where his was stitched. We walk towards the twin slate pillars called Watford Gap, chatting as we go.

There is a barbed wire fence sectioning off Twll Mawr, but the end post doesn't quite meet the sheer wall of slate next to the road. We squeeze past it, and now we are in a part of the quarries where we are 'Not Allowed'.

We walk around the edge of the pit. Above us are huge high walls, the clean, barely possible wall of *The Quarryman,* the quarries' most famous climb. Below us is the sheer drop into the pit, seventy metres straight down. The drop gives you a specific kind of fear, where you think you should throw yourself off the edge just to get it over with.

I point out the route. Far below us, a tiny, orange-rusty ladder leads up to a tunnel entrance. The route is next to it, up an arête and finishing on the quarry rim: seventy-five metres, longer than most ropes. We are standing well back from the edge, heather and grass have bonded tiny fragments of slate together, but it still feels as fragile as sand.

The girl looks over and sniggers nervously.

'Ohmigod! It looks really *outthere.*'

I don't think they're going in.

May 2016, Twll Mawr

'You got a plan for this week? What are you getting on?' I ask.

'I've a few things I want to do. Start high on the levels, Gorbals maybe. There's a few things I want to look at. Then I thought we could go and have a look at *Supermassive Black Hole*, if you want, Pete?'

I look at him, pleased and surprised. I grin, I think.

'Really?' I ask, like a boy being told he's being allowed to go on a treat.

Lee and I hop over the five-bar gate. A path leads down the hill, and two terraces down, we head left. We go around the hillside, across level ground. In places, the train tracks from the quarry still survive. We scramble over a dicey mess of scree, then through the mouth of the skull you can see from the valley road. The tunnel is cool, despite the heat of the day, early for May. At the end of the tunnel, we take the right fork – the left one ends in a thirty-metre drop. It's where that tiny, orange-rusty ladder is. It no longer reaches the floor of the pit, wrecked by rockfall, the steel dangling like two stray strands of spaghetti.

The tunnel mouth is at the top of the first pitch of *Supermassive Black Hole*.

'What we'll do, Pete, is have a go at this first pitch, see if you get it. Then I'll have a go, and then we'll head on up through the rest of the pitches.'

Good idea. Lee is on a mission: he wants to climb as many of the 7a pitches in the quarries as he can. He ran into Johnny Dawes in Sheffield, who told him to do this so he would know how slate had to be climbed. My project is another 7a pitch that Lee can climb and farm his skills with, recruit himself for his true goals.

We walk past the quarryman's hut. The roof has fallen in as the timbers rotted. All around it are mattresses of soggy moss and shell-bursts of bright green ferns growing out of any crack their spores landed in.

We step onto the glacier of slate scree, walk down it like uneven steps. This is less scary, now. There is the same wariness of the sudden tilting block, the same CLOCK CLOCKY CLOCK, as the slate shifts with our footsteps. The buzzing of the power station is loud today.

Lee and I drop our backpacks onto the ground. We look around for 'crag swag'. No luck; there are barrels and bits of cars, bones from a wild goat. A daisy chain of old climbing rope has been stashed here, now it is rat-chewed; the white of its core fluffs out from the nibbles. No one sane will ever use that again. I wonder where that old carabiner I threw away is, amongst all the rock.

Harnesses on, shoes squeaked clean for maximum grip. Lee always spits on them and rubs them clean on his trouser legs, with long strong strokes like a carpenter planing wood. When I do it, I tend to rub them quite quickly. I'm sanding it, little swip-swip-swip-swips of movement against the polycotton of my trousers. It always leaves black smears, a hot skid of tyre rubber on tarmac when a lorry brakes hard. We are using my new Spanish rope. It is turquoise blue, the colour of the Med. It twists and tangles. A few routes and it will soften, the twist curled out, but just now it has its own life.

Lee flakes the rope out, I sit on a handy block, getting ready. I watch my hands tie the knot to my harness. They know what they're doing. I take a breath; Lee sees it and clips me into his plate.

'Nice one, Pete. Enjoy it.'

'It's only climbing,' I say, making him laugh. As if we care so little about it.

Off I go, up the cracked fin of rock, big ledges to stand on and pike heads for handles. I haul myself up easily at first, clipping the bolts resined into the face. It isn't hard to keep the fear small.

Then I get to the bit I've been waiting for. The holds run out. I have to leave the fin and step across space onto the smooth cliff wall. There is a little seam, a ridge to use. It's the width of the edge of a light-switch fitting. That's big for slate. I can reach across with my foot to find a little ledge. But I'm spread out too far, so I rock my weight onto that foot, drop the other foot, and my hand flicks and reaches for a perfectly round hole at waist level.

I stack my fingers in. It is a shot-hole, where a quarryman drilled into the rock and then poured a handful of black powder down. The explosion was small, a puff of smoke rather than a cloud of splinters, just enough to open up the natural seams of the rock so it could be levered off. Big fucking metal bars, mate. Wherever we climb, we are on what the quarrymen chose to leave us: the rock faces that would be no use because they were rippled or had a dolerite seam, or just couldn't be got at easily enough.

I come into balance, and my fear releases itself into a string of words that pop like bubbles across the still air: 'Ineverexpectedtogethere....' and echoes off.

Not over, though. Stepping onto the wall and the shot-hole are only half the crux; now I have to move up and lean and get back onto that fin, only higher up, past the lack of handholds. *Shitshitshit*. Okay. Go. Foot on, breathe and go. My fingers stack in upside down now and I try and stand up; my thigh clenches, up I go. Wobble. Wobble, my hand out – grab the fin – to brace against it; fuck, I can't do this.

I whip my hands back in to hold the knot of the rope back to my harness. It is a touching ritual, checking you are still attached to the rope, that the knot has not unthreaded, that in half a second's time you will be safe and not still falling, down, down, unsurviveable.

The rope comes tight, I bounce and dangle on the end of my rope, which runs back to the last bolt I clipped. I've hardly fallen a metre, quite safe.

Two hours later, we're on the second to last pitch of *Supermassive Black Hole*, and the hard work is behind us. The stance is small, no more than a few shelves for our feet, but the bolts are good. Lee rigs up and I get ready to go, taking a second to look for the quickdraws.

We are high enough on the wall to see someone wandering

about around the rim of the quarry. He's got a young collie dog, and he's shouting at it in Welsh, *'Na! Na, Medi! Na,'* because the collie hasn't any sense of the danger and is nervously trying to find the edge of the scree.

This could be anyone, and we tense up. Sometimes kids throw stuff in, just for the thrill, and it wouldn't take much to take us off this wall: a brick-sized lump of slate or a stolen car radio.

Concentrate. I look at the rock of the last pitch. It is very un-slate-like; at some point in the deep past, some geological process has happened. Perhaps superheated steam blew through a crack and into a chemically different area of baked mud: the slate here is converted into a coarse-grained grippable rock, almost like swirly brick. There are pockets, like leeches' mouths filled with quartz crystal teeth. They will make good handholds, and I plot the moves from one to the other.

Just as I am about to start climbing again, the man with his dog walks back down the scree and looks over the edge below, studying the pit. He's got some business here; he's no straying tourist. He's not a security guard either; they never come away from the road. Then he looks left and sees us on the stance. He walks straight over to the edge above us, untroubled by the exposure. He looks determined and he's coming straight for us.

'That's one of mine, you know!'

And I know who it is.

'Alright, Ian!' I laugh.

Ian Lloyd-Jones is the climber who first put up *Supermassive Black Hole,* bolted it and named it. I had recognised him and spoken to him the previous year.

'You two all right with all the exposure? When I did it, my

mate was shitting himself up there.'

Lee and I look down at the drop below us, as if noticing it for the first time. 'Nah,' I shout back. 'I'm rope-access and he's a tree surgeon.'

Mid to late eighties, early nineties, the Karakorum; Clogwyn y Grochan

Ian Lloyd-Jones was one of hundreds of climbers around at the same time as Johnny Dawes and Paul Pritchard, but who weren't doing anything like what they were doing. People like Dawes and Pritchard were there, drinking in the same pubs, but they were on a pedestal. It wouldn't have occurred to someone like Lloyd-Jones to try what they were doing.

In the mid 1980s, he had recently returned from a year's college in London, unhappily drinking far too much. He picked up climbing where he had left off, finding a circle of mates to go climbing with. The slate quarries weren't his favourite place: he liked Clogwyn Du'r Arddu or the Pass, or a trip down to the Pembrokeshire sea cliffs if they could get transport. The quarries were okay, and Ian and his mates put up a few new routes: *Igam Ogam* (Zig-Zag), *Rhyfelwr* (Warrior), *Squashing the Acropods*. Good enough lines, but nothing to set the world on fire after Dawes and co had begun redefining the limits of kinaesthetic possibility.

One evening, Ian saw an S4C documentary about John Silvester, who had newly taken up paragliding. The documentary was exhilarating, beautifully shot by Alun Hughes. The images filled Ian's head.

John Silvester had become entranced by the sight of paragliders wheeling over Chamonix, bright blue and pink wings circling like condors. They would take off from the Brevant and land in one of the valley fields. Silvester had a go, looking for an easy adrenaline fix. He loved it, and managed to borrow four off a manufacturer to take to the Himalayas, where he'd visited several times, looking to climb an enormous 6000-metre wall. 'I unintentionally gave up climbing after that first summer and became a pilot.'[86]

It turned out that the paragliders – 'wings' – could be made to go up, as well as just descend. John became very good at all this, his enthusiasm and attention to detail fitting well to another dangerous but exciting sport.

There is footage on the internet from 'The Birdman of Karakorum'[87] where he and filmmaker Alun Hughes swoop around over snowy Himalayan peaks. John is enthusiastic, it seems like he is clapping his hands in glee, although actually he is slapping them to get blood back into his fingertips and warm them up. In the footage, John burbles excitedly, 'No one's ever been through this col, it's like a first. And we're climbing! It's getting better! I think we might make it, Al,' while Al groans, 'Don't get too clooooosse....'

The next day, Ian was hiking up the pass to go and repeat *Brant Direct*. At HVS, it was well within his grade. Looking out, Ian saw a paraglider floating and wheeling, its bright colours the same bright pinks and blues of climbing Lycra. The pilot dangled underneath, pulled the controls and whirled over the pass like a condor.

Ian couldn't lead *Brant Direct*. His heart wasn't in it. He went home, made a phone call, and started to research how he could fly paragliders. From then on, he would put all his energy into being a paraglider pilot.

* * *

May 2016, Twll Mawr

It is a short pitch, ten metres or less, and I go up it quickly and confidently. Almost before I know it, I am peeking over the shelf of rock at the pit-rim. I reach up, grip, then simply walk up the last shelves of rock and mantel up onto the flat edge. Here I am, on the edge of the pit where I have walked so many times before. To my left are the double bolt-hangers. I clip in and shout down '*Safe!*' and Lee takes me off the belay.

'Well climbed!' says Ian. He chats as I set up my belay. 'Anyway, I'm giving up on the new-routing for the moment.'

'Really?' I ask. I am a bit surprised; since the early 2000s, Ian has been one of the most prolific new-routers in the quarries.

'Nah, I'm over it really. There's still a bit of an anti-bolt brigade who don't like what I'm doing. Someone nicked the bolt-hangers from one of my belays over there.' He points to the back wall of Twll Mawr. 'So, anyway, never mind. I've just started leading dog-sledding expeditions in Finland. Something to do in winter. And I've bought myself a yacht. I'm spending most of my spare time on that.'

I sit with my legs over the drop, unafraid, as I pull the rope through my belay plate, and Lee comes up to meet me. I look down, taking it all in. It is a bit anticlimactic. If I've done it, I haven't done it well. I dogged those first two pitches, but did all the moves. A good day; a day to be proud of, but still no great feeling of satisfaction.

I think back to the night in the pub back home with Darryl

and Land Rover James. They wouldn't have any feelings one way or another about this achievement; Darryl rarely climbs now – he got into photography – and I haven't seen him for ages. What I've done here doesn't affect them.

Lee reaches the top, and vaults up over the edge with style and control. 'Thanks, Pete,' he says. 'Safe, by the way,' as he steps away from the edge.

Ian Lloyd-Jones heads off with Medi, the collie looking round at everything, tongue lolling. Lee and I take a few minutes at the top of the pit in the sun; we eat some smushed Jaffa Cakes from my pocket. Lee rigs up the rope, ties it differently, a Y-hang to the two bolts. In a second or two, we will step back over the edge and abseil down, back to the tunnel mouth at the top of pitch 1, and get our bags then walk out. As I stand there, some satisfaction does grow inside me. I might not have done it well, but I was out here, trying it.

CHAPTER 24

Mister Blister

May 2016, golden hour to blue hour, Australia

Early evening and up high on the levels, where I did my first ever 7a. The evening wind is blowing cold. The sky is quite clear and the detail of the rocks up the pass – Cloggy, Parson's Nose, Crib Goch – are sharp and clear, pink-lit rocks as the sun sets. Slightly along is a slab which is constantly wet enough for a grainy, black algae, like tyre-rubber, to have grown. In places, the slate is glass smooth; wet as it shines, and the algae hasn't been able to get a grip.

But it hasn't rained for a week; I've been checking the weather from far across the country. The climb underneath – *Mister Blister* – is, unusually, dry enough to attempt.

'I don't like it, I'm coming down,' says Becky.

'Just keep moving,' says Lee, but she is decided, sits back. Lee shrugs and lowers her down.

'It's too cold,' she says crossly. 'I should have led this last time I was here. I did all the moves clean on the top-rope and now it's too cold.'

A few minutes later, Becky has wedged herself behind a fragmented spire of rock. She is wearing my down jacket; I'll be alright in just a jumper and with my blue wooly hat under my lid. Becky doesn't like the cold and feels it badly. The sun hasn't set, we are in Golden Hour, a good time for climbing as the temperature drops and humidity lowers. Lee reckons most of the world's hard climbing gets done in Golden Hour. I think I'll have a go; it's not one of the routes I've obsessed over, but it is the right grade, and these ones can surprise you. No weight of expectation.

'Try hard, Pete,' calls Becky.

'Thin slab, Pete,' says Lee. 'Trick to it is just keep moving.'

Sounds fair enough; off I go. The holds for my toes are thin, matchsticks and hyphens. Among the algae, tiny clumps of moss grip on and try hard to make a living. Each spore only has one chance, and they're taking it. Deprived of water for a week, the moss is going crispy.

The fingerholds are small and sharp. I latch them confidently, knowing my tendons are like catenary wire, cable, braided fishing line, strong and unsnappable. Neither hands nor feet will slip, the challenge is to keep my body tense so I stay on the wall and don't rotate off, but just keep floppy enough to move a limb at a time.

It is working. Stretch my leg out left for a hole like doing the splits. Flick up for a pocket, a seam of staccato dashes good enough for three fingers at a quarter of a tip. Hard move coming, here is the crux, high toe and I grunt as I try.... And fall. Another one for the collection.

I work my way through the rest of it. It is strange to move up on such small holds, but satisfying. The trick is not to stop-shift your foot, move a hand up, don't camp out on any of it. As soon as you find your toe-end taking your weight, then you move up whichever limb is now too low, too scrunched up. A big sharp flake feels incredible, and you can stand on that for a rest. Up and up, the chains of it.

'Well done, Pete, good effort,' Becky shouts up from below. Her voice is small but thick with emotion. She means what she is saying because we are friends, but, as I thread my rope through the lower-off, I know she is choking on her own frustration. She did all these moves before, she should be able to do them now and that would be a good tick. The cold has got to her and she is small and miserable in my jacket.

I haven't done it of course, but now I know it could be possible.

'I'll rest and go again.'

She takes off my jacket and gives it to me straight away so I don't lose heat. She doesn't ask if I want it, she just takes it straight off. If she asked, I wouldn't want to say give it back.

For a few minutes, we all crouch at the bottom of the route, low and out of the wind.

'Okay,' I say to Lee, and quickly we get ready; Becky gets my jacket again, thanks muffled by the thick down pile. I start up again, feeling good, and more confident again on thin moves. I know it all works. Get up to the crux, a bigger move than I remember. I fall as I'm moving, not far from the bolt. Ah, I missed something. I was in the wrong position, trying to do the move from too far out to one side rather than using similar holds to the left. Lee told me last year that the heart of technical ability is remembering what you did before and then repeating it.

Okay. Down again. I leave Becky with my jacket this time, keeping hold of the core warmth from my muscles, plenty. We are into Blue Hour, if anything colder and drier than Golden Hour. I couldn't ask for better connies.

I feel my tendons, check in on how tired I am. I've got another go in me; my fingers are tender but nothing like sore. I strip my shoes off quickly before the big-toe bone aches. Slab work is hard on your toes, so much of your weight goes through them.

I could have a few more goes. If I rest properly.

'What do you think?' I ask. 'Can I have one more go?'

'You should. Perfect conditions, Pete.'

'One more. I don't want to keep you up here in the cold.'

'It's fine,' says Lee.

'Have another go,' says Becky. 'I'm okay.'

One last go, I think, and it takes the pressure off. Doesn't matter whether I get it or not, we'll be going down after this. I glide up to the crux this time and, as I press up, my heel rotates out so my toe can't stick where it should be. I'm off. I'm down.

We pack up quick, rope coiled, gear stuffed recklessly into rucksack by me and Becky, the same neat order as ever from Lee. We walk through the short tunnel and the hillside opens out. Becky trails behind.

Becky follows a way behind; she doesn't want to catch up. I feel guilty – but only a bit – for keeping her up in the cold without having done the route. But if I had done the route maybe that would have made her feel angry or cheated, unacknowledged competition turned inwards and gone sour.

'She alright?'

'Yeah. Gets angry with herself if she can't do shit. Just needs a bit of time.'

Lee would happily walk down in silence, but I never like it too quiet, me. I ask him a question about what his favourite comedy is. With Lee, this always works. Behind his quiet, he loves to laugh. As we trudge down we are reminding each other of different episodes of something that was on five years ago, the characters, swapping quotes – precise from him and half-remembered paraphrases from me – laughing at the memory of it. Moving, and in our jackets it is soon warm, calories burning from our thighs and trapped by layers of goose down. Now the breeze has dropped, and in the precise sharp light, everything starts to look blue, except the hillside catching the last rays of light, which are soft pink.

CHAPTER 25

Time Bandit

Spring 2017, Norfolk; Upper Australia, Vivian Quarry revisited

Lee buys an old van, a long-wheelbase Transporter, off another climber in Sheffield. On the phone, he tells me it needs a bit of work, but he and Becky are going to head off around Europe. It is the right time to do it: they are together – firmly together – no kids, still renting houses, renting rooms off their mates. Becky is sick of where she works, sick of the drive, sick of the fact that she can do the same amount of work as everyone else in about twenty minutes on a Monday because she understands spreadsheets.

'Should be alright with my job,' Lee tells me. 'Spoke to my manager and he says he'll keep it open. They know I can climb and cut trees, they know I don't turn up still pissed off last night. They'll have me back.'

The metal of the van is white, but the wood of the cabinets and fabric insulation are bright yellow, a lurid shade like a dandelion with the resolution turned up high. 'Fucking hell, Lee, it'll be like living in a hardboiled egg.'

'Hmm,' he says. 'Yeah. I was thinking of repainting it. He pauses and looks at it. 'It's a bit much,' without a flicker of humour. His wry understatement catches me just under the ribs: I start to laugh, and in seconds I am doubled up, not just my cheeks hurting but the muscles on the back of my neck. Lee laughs at me laughing.

I've always been a generous laugher. Like the first time in the pub with my mates a few days after my dad died and long before I climbed. They all expressed sympathy, and then we got on with our night. It was what I wanted, and what they knew I needed, something normal: laughter at bad taste jokes and ripping the piss out of each other within our carefully defined ritual boundaries. Something struck me as funny – fuck knows what, it has been lost to my memory – but I laughed in the same way as now, uncontrollably. My mates chuckled at first, but then looked at me in horror across the picnic table at the back of the Irish pub. I had lost control and they were scared. But I needed it.

Each time we speak on the phone, there's a new addition to the van. Becky finds things on eBay, such as a front seat that spins around when you clunk a lever, a twelve-volt fridge, a solar panel kit for trickle-charging the leisure battery. Lee's brother, a boatbuilder and outfitter of yachts on the Norfolk coast, runs up a unit for the gas hob which barely takes him an afternoon. It has a drawer with a special recessed handle, spare from a very posh boat sold to a Russian.

When I speak to them, they tell me of somewhere new they want to try climbing. Sweden. Norway, maybe as far as the Lofoten Islands: huge sweeping granite slabs out of the freezing grey sea. Fontainebleau. Magic Wood in Switzerland. Italy, generally, then down into Spain for more granite slabs in La Padriza, just north of Madrid.

Becky starts to disengage herself from her job, setting up her website and getting bits of contract design work, troubleshooting websites. All she needs is her laptop and Wi-Fi, which she can get out the back of any McDonalds.

My fourth annual Wales trip. I will spend a few days repeating the climbs I did that first year: *Orangutang Overhang* and *Gadaffi Duck* – this time without a fall. *Looning the Tube*, led, rather than top-roped.

Lee has told me that this will be the start of their big tour. 'We'll come along to Wales and then drive off from there. We've got the ferry booked from Hull.'

In the quarries, we sit about. Garry and Alice are there with their year-old son, Henry, close eyes on him as he toddles around the levels in the sun. They are staying at a guesthouse in Llanberis; the hut doesn't allow under eighteens and Henry doesn't yet sleep through the night: they don't want to wake everyone up changing nappies and jogging him until he dozes off again.

The day before, Garry and Alice took Henry up Snowdon. They have a baby carrier to pop him in, with mesh side-pockets for packets of Wet Wipes and spare dummies. Other walkers stopped to tell them 'Well done', as Henry dozed under his sun hat, in his greasepaint of suncream.

Henry is small and blond, with fine features like an elven child. He has socks with a rubber sole, cheaper than shoes. He stumbles around the slate chips, picks them up before Alice stops him licking them. It is nice to have him there. This group of us, sitting around in heather on the wide landings between levels, feels like a tribe. It reminds me of the big groups of aboriginals I saw in the real Australia, peacefully sat under the shade of spreading trees next to a modern dual carriageway.

Lee and Becky explain their plans again, in detail to

everyone, several times.

'I want to go and do something on a mountain, don't I, Lee?' says Becky sweetly. 'He's not keen, though.'

'Bit boring.'

'We'll be in Switzerland, though. May as well.'

'Okay.'

Lee and Becky have bought little Henry a Sweep glove puppet. He already has a Sooty one that he likes people to play with him. Lee picks it up and bobbles it next to his ear as if it's speaking.

'What's that, Sweep? Yes. I know. Yes. The hardest bit *will* be living in a van together.'

Becky giggles. 'I've had this all week since we bought the bloody thing.'

'What's that, Sweep? Yes. Yes. Murder? You'd be out in five years, eight, tops. Yes. You could do a PhD in prison.'

'Oh, good grief,' says Becky. 'Bit too convincing, pet.'

Sweep's head swivels to 'look' at her. Then back slowly, whispers something in Lee's ear.

'Shush, Sweep. Don't let anyone hear you say that. We'll talk about it later.'

Lee still has Sweep on his hand looking balefully at Becky. The effect is quite disturbing but also very funny; my cheeks are tight from laughing and cold tears plop out of my eyelids.

'So, anyway,' says Becky, 'Lee wants to go to the Gränsfors Bruk axe factory. But, after this, I'm not so sure.' Lee looks panicked and whips Sweep off his hand, putting him in Henry's backpack.

'Sorry, Becky.' We all start to calm down.

'It's alright. Alice, make sure that fucking puppet goes home with you and not him.' And that's it: we are all hysterical again.

Garry and I walk down the levels from the gate. It's early enough, about eight o'clock, and we need to get going by nine, really. Four pitches up the wall, you don't want to be taking too long and getting flustered about it, start to make mistakes as the light fades. We should be in good time, but *Supermassive Black Hole* is pretty popular. Safe, nicely bolted, good grade. We can't rule out the possibility that other climbers will be on it, then you'd be stuck in the fucking queue.

We're travelling light, anyway: just rock-shoes, rope, harnesses and quickdraws. Helmets, and a fistful of muesli bars – how very alpine of us.

'We should have brought Sweep down here,' says Garry. 'He could have belayed.'

'Not sure I'd trust him.'

The walk in is familiar to me now. I've been down here a few times with Lee and with Becky. Here is the half-buried rail for the slate wagons, where once a ring ouzel, like a blackbird with a white collar round its neck, flew out from under mine and Becky's feet. We stopped, said, 'Cool!' Then walked on quickly in case it had just left its nest in a crevice a few feet beneath our feet. Later that day, in the shade, Lee did *Set the Controls for the Heart of the Sun,* then the first repeat of *Dark Side of the Moon.* I just watched.

Here are the blocks with their spiders' webs across. I always try and avoid breaking them; I like the big bubble-shaped spiders with their tiger patterns of black, orange and white. But even with care, you sometimes crash though one of their guy-lines with your shorts on, and feel the silk tug against your leg before it breaks, understanding how strong spider's silk actually is.

Through the tunnel, a first for Garry. He is plainly enjoying the adventure of it. A day out with a mate; time away from the family will sweeten the return to domesticity. Past the little building. Garry points upwards.

'See up there? That's where I came in with Lee a few years ago.' He points halfway up the *Quarryman* wall, far above our heads. 'That's the Alcove.' It's a huge square-sided bay that could fit a townhouse into it, packed with a slope of slate waste. 'You walk across these ledges. It's fucking terrifying, man, I mean, they're big ledges but there's nothing but the drop on the other side. As I was going past the slope of scree, I just heard a rattle and ducked for no reason. A piece of slate just went flying past my head: if it had hit me, that would have been it.'

I have never fancied that scramble across the ledges. In the guide book it's down as a roped approach to the Alcove. Nothing hard, but with no second chance if you slipped: a clear drop, right to the bottom.

We walk down the scree slope. Here is where I traversed it last year when Lee and Becky were busy with *Set the Controls for the Heart of the Sun*. I could hear the buzzing of the power station. On the far side of Twll Mawr, just below the start of *Hamadryad*, I put my hands on the rock. They tingled with the vibration, like the rock contained an electric charge. I pressed my fingernail against it to see if I could get it to rattle. The buzzing felt stronger through my fingertip, but at too high a frequency to make it rattle against the rock. I pressed my ear against it: behind the buzzing I could hear faint pops and crashes – *pok! ASSH… pok, pok Cashh!* – as the millions of gallons of water

sloshed down the huge pipes, forcing giant bubbles of com-
pressed air up and out of the vent near Nuremberg.

It is quiet today. Down the bottom of the pit, Garry and I
rope up and get going. Familiar moves, then the crux.

A familiar fall. 'Fuck!'

Again and again. Not wanting to practise the move, in case
the practises will tire me out. I can't see that just to repeat the
one move, the one fall, would be a better use of time and energy
than repeating all the work to get up there each time.

I sit on the ground, pissed off. I'm not sure if I'm tired or
not. Maybe I'm just warmed up.

Garry looks at me. 'Do you mind if I have a go?'

Not really, is probably the answer but it does get me a bit. I
stand up. 'I'll have one more go.'

And then I get it.

A couple of hours later, with the hard work behind us, I fell
on the second pitch, that wiggly insecure move across a loose
block, then swore, then did it. I offered the lead to Garry but
he grinned and said, 'Oh, no mate. This is *your* day and *your*
route,' and I couldn't tell whether he was being nice or being
lazy, which is what having mates is all about.

Just as I move up the pockets of leeches' teeth, I hear voices above. I wonder very briefly about someone trundling in a
rock or throwing a car stereo, but I'm more comfortable in the
quarries now. Then I realise that some of the voices are female.
What could be better than to top out of a scary-looking pit with
women to admire you?

When I emerge over the lip, the two women there are
amazed, the instructor with them, less so. All are wearing

industrial access harnesses in wasp colours of black and yellow. Much chunkier than climbing harnesses, with big steel D-rings to clip gadgets onto. I recognise the instructor from Plas y Brenin who led a course I did a few years before.

As I belay Garry up, I hear the instructor tell the women, 'What they've just done isn't necessarily *that* out there,' but I don't think they care. When Garry comes up, one of them says, 'I can't imagine doing that!'

'That's because you're sensible,' says Garry, instantly becoming modest, likeable and slightly funny.

It turns out that they are geologists about to go on an expedition to Bulgaria to map rock formations. They've done a rope-access qualification. Now the instructor is showing them real-life rope skills, to give them an idea what it will be really like, away from the training centre.

I wonder what it will be like in Bulgaria. Amazing, probably. I can't imagine doing that. All those years of study, learning about crystals and sediment and karst landscapes. Then abseiling down to do real science.

Garry pulls our trainers out of his tiny rucksack and I coil the rope. Today we will just walk away, no need to collect anything. We exchange a little grin. Nice to have an audience.

On the last morning of the trip, Lee, Becky and I walk down from Tŷ Powdwr, down the steps that run right the way down the height of Vivian Quarry. We stop at each level and look across, identifying the climbs. 'That's the Dervish Slab. There's a bad step across that; I didn't like that, did I, Lee?' says Becky.

It is a Saturday morning, and as we get to the bottom level, the carpark at the bottom is filling with tourists. We walk through them, past the little tea-rooms and under the arch into Vivian Quarry's bottom level. Back around the path over the deep green water, under those same shady birch trees.

I feel self-conscious. Down here, you aren't really hiding the fact that you are in a place that someone in authority has decreed you shouldn't be, and made the point with signs. I know that it is accepted that climbers will just walk across a stile, and start climbing, responsible only to themselves. But I hate it, I hate it. I want to go up to a ranger from Gwynedd Council – though I've never seen one and don't know what they look like – and say, 'I'm breaking your rules being here, is that okay?'

In Liverpool, when I was a kid, we lived near Allerton Park and the golf links. It's a nice part of the city, leafy and suburban. When I tell them I was born in Allerton, the automatic response from other Liverpudlians is 'Ooh, ver-y posh', the inverted snob-bery of people who consider themselves more authentic because of their postcode, like a gang of teachers and social workers in the pub arguing about who is the most working class.

I remember once, before I even went to school, my mum pushing my sister in her pushchair while I toddled around, walk-ing on the footpath through the golf links. There was a gale-fallen tree trunk, truncated by chainsaws and left like a park bench, yellow wood turning to grey-silver, and Mum let me climb on it. Through the trees, a golfer started shouting at us, moustache and Pringle jumper and mulletty seventies hair. 'Get him down now. It's not safe. He'll get hit by a golf ball.' I was frightened and felt ashamed: early rules about power, and how easy it is for an ag-gressive man enforcing the rules to shout at a woman and a child.

Hundreds more incidents like that. Farmers shouting that

there isn't a footpath there, actually. Gangs of lads surrounding you and asking what the FUCK you think you're doing on their street. A red-faced man, drunk, running out of his back gate and shouting at you all for playing football behind his house. Snarling and growling at young teenage boys as if they were other men. All these washes of paint, mental patina, that where you walk doesn't belong to you and you are only tolerated as long as you aren't noticed.

Lee doesn't give a fuck. Becky doesn't either. I wish I was more like them. I also wish I was off to Europe climbing for a year in a van.

I lead off up *Mental Lentils*. First thing I ever saw climbed, first thing on the slate I ever climbed, and it's not how I remember it. Good, though. I start in the cold shade, place gear, clip a bolt from a ledge. The easy moves, then the holds up the finishing slab, emerging from the shade into the weak sun. Pad up to the top as my fear rises. The first lead of the day is always scary. Up to the top, and, in the moment after I feel I have balanced on the top footholds, I reach and grab the chains with relief. That could be considered bad form, if you did it and held them, taking your weight onto them, then you might have to wrestle with your conscience – had you really done the route or not? But fuck it. I'm ticking it.

On the ground again, Lee is looking at the blank slab that cuts out to the left from *Mental Lentils*.

'What you looking at, Lee?'

'*Time Bandit*. I tried it a few years ago, fell off it loads. I did *Poetry Pink* after. Probably because of the falls,' he says. Typical Lee analysis, and I file that away for my own use later. 'Anyway, it'd be nice to get this today, start the trip off nicely.'

I watch him and Becky set up. They've got a bright fluorescent yellow rope, but Lee ties both ends to the belay loop on his harness.

'Right,' he tells Becky, 'Left-hand side on the bottom of your plate, and right-hand side on the top.' Their set-up is a normal one for climbing with half-ropes, but usually it is two separate ropes in different colours, so you can just shout, 'Slack on green'. But Lee and Becky climb so much that they can manage this, can retain the focus of identifying the ropes, just hold that detail gently in their mind, and use it when it is relevant. Either of them would be a good climber, but together they multiply each other.

'Look,' I say. 'Before you get started, I'm going to head off. Get home and see the boy.'

'Okay,' says Lee. 'Been a good trip, look after yourself.' We hug, briefly and awkwardly, like wooden carvings, arms around each other's shoulders, the ropes and harness in between.

'Have a great trip.' I turn to Becky and hug her too, closer and warmer, less awkward because I can lean down to her height.

'Bye-bye, Pete. We'll see you in a year.'

'Don't kill each other in the van,' I say, and I walk away, laughing.

Through the arch, I turn, and start to head up the quarrymen's steps up the side of Vivian. It occurs to me that if I get to a certain point on the steps, I can watch Lee climb. I reach it two flights up, lean on the post of the three-strand wire fence. There is a gap through the trees and I can see the slab Lee will make his way up. He is there: just hidden by the trees, I can see him resting at the last good ledge before he starts to edge across the tiny holds of the blank slab.

There. He starts to move, flicks his hand onto a crimp and edges his left foot out, weights it and stands. His limbs move like a spider's legs, deliberately and sequenced. A step and a flick, and his hips rise as he loads his weight onto his toe-tip, then a flick to a new handhold then a wobble and he falls.

Not too bad a fall, that. I can see the fluorescent rope he dangles from; he sits in his harness, looks down towards Becky and puts his hands under his armpits, his feet flat against the wall. Looking, thinking, resting.

If he had made the move I would have shouted to him when he got to the top and waved. As it is, I just turn and start the long walk up the steps.

CHAPTER 26

The End

In an interview with a climbing magazine in the early nineties, Paul Pritchard was asked, 'What is the greatest threat to UK climbing?'

His reply was, 'Dance drugs.'[88]

Nineties, Llanberis scene's ending

The climbing scene had replaced work for the lost generation of dole climbers. Kids who followed them – new generations of school-leavers – were emerging into a radically changed society.

Thatcher had got lucky. North Sea oil had come along, pouring revenue into the economy and the government tax coffers. The economy had picked up, boosted by a booming deregulated 'financial services' sector – banking and stock-broking. Flash bright kids could make fortunes buying and selling imaginary computer numbers, and were rewarded with equally fantastical sums of money from the banks and brokers who employed them and provided their gamblers' stakes. This was presented as: Success! The ultimate goal of society was now to make sure that everyone (especially those with existing reserves of assets and private education) were free to make piles of money, and fuck everyone else.

If you had loads of money, the goal was obviously to spend it: not wisely, either, but through buying designer clothes and brand names. The idea of a branded piece of clothing is to advertise how much money you spent on it. That is its entire point, there's little difference in quality, they often look fucking ugly, or stupid, but you can recognise them, and thereby know it cost lots. Which means the dickhead wearing it must have had that money to spare: so by implication has more money than that, because they wouldn't buy a Lacoste T-shirt if they didn't have that money spare, would they?

At the same time, a new drug was on the scene: Ecstasy. Originally devised as an aid to marriage counselling, the cousin of amphetamine produced feelings of love and wellbeing, therapeutically useful to couples who hated each other sober.

Taking Ecstasy as a street drug was an awesome experience. The pills were large, and chunky, almost the size of cookies. To take one was to hang around for about half an hour, wondering if you had been ripped off, but then to notice a speed-like tingle rushing up through your body. It was hard to keep still, you twitched and jolted as your body needed the outlet for the energy being released by the huge dump of brain chemicals activated by the pill. Dancing was the natural outlet for the movement, the music became a physical force, but meant even more than music usually does. True chemical rapture.

The nervous system was also flooded with hormones like serotonin and oxytocin, the same kind of chemicals released during sex, but also when you hold your newborn child for the first time, or cuddle your lover, skin touching skin. These chemical feelings of love, friendship and affection transferred onto the friends you had come out with, the other young people you were dancing next to, the crowd in the field or in the club. Plus, your hair would stand on end, as though your whole body was holding a charge, a biological capacitor. You would look at your mates dancing beside you and realise they were the greatest and best human beings you could ever have known, and so were you.

The whole experience was unbelievably pleasant. In poor, northern ex-pit villages where the main buzz used to be fighting the casual gangs from other villages, the pre-arranged fights stopped overnight. In order to get these new drugs, you had to know and speak to other people, you couldn't be head butting them on a school-playing field or throwing milk bottles at the side of a bus. The emergence of these drugs knocked all that on the head, for the time being.

Llanberis was generationally due for some anti-English/anti-incomer/anti-climber sentiment – drunken beatings and hassle outside the pub – but no one could be fucked, and instead organised coaches to take them to raves, everyone all in together. A lot of the climbers who had been the backbone of the eighties scene were moving onto other things. The scene itself wasn't doing anything new.

The recovering British economy, now stripped of coal mines and steelworks, had huge opportunities for communication and computing. Home computers were rapidly becoming the norm, not for household accounting, but because of the games you could play on them. IT was now important for businesses wanting to send letters, run their payroll and cut down on their expenditure of paper-clips and pencils.

Nick Harms enrolled for a degree in computing, and spent the next ten years in London doing IT engineering contracts. He left behind climbers of incredible talent who were routinely doing very hard things.

'I didn't appreciate – because everyone was doing that – how out of the norm that was. I think if I had appreciated my own abilities, I would have stayed, kept climbing. When everyone is climbing 8a, 8b, 8c around you, I didn't think it was particularly special.'[89]

The climbing did leave a gap. Nick filled it with motorbikes. 'Riding motorbikes very fast, then crashing them very fast, too. I managed to walk away from every crash I was in, but the last one left me with a bit of a buggered-up neck and I haven't had a bike since.'

Up in the quarries, things continued much as they had always done. Rain storms brought down collapses of fickle walls of slate, the scree slid down the glaciers. The cheap 8 mm Troll bolts rusted and weakened, some popped out or were hit by rockfall, sulphur-salts leached out of the slate and efflouresced out of the drilled hole, like a fungal bloom of white crystals.

A few went up there, the occasional lonely soul out for a personal adventure, or groups repeating a lower-grade classic, but once more the quarries were quiet.

CHAPTER 27

Staying and Leaving

Early nineties, Liverpool Anglican cathedral (E3 5c); ethical shoplifting; ascents on UEA campus, Nelson's Column; hopping up the peak

Some of the dole climbers stayed on in Llanberis and made lives there. Their children would go to the local schools and be taught in Welsh and English. There would be enough 'climbing brats' around to renew the scene in later years, when they came of age.

Others moved away from the eighties climbing scene, drifted on to other opportunities.

Johnny Redhead had spotted his own complacency, now that he wasn't at the cutting edge of climbing or controversy. He could have stayed comfortable in north Wales, but instead went out looking for conflict, edge. He took his art to Liverpool, setting up a studio on the edge of the city, near the notorious L8 postcode, still riot damaged from 1981.

Nightly, the city's clubbers and drinkers went out on the primal hunt; this was his new field of savagery: bare flesh and vomit. Meanwhile, bullshitters talked out what art they were making in the cafe. 'To talk "is" to do. Everyone seems to be a people's poet.'[90] Amongst the bullshit, grants were to be had, and Redhead railed against the form-filling, the box-ticking needed to get a subsistence level of grant funding, while not compromising his painting. 'When I paint, I mean it!'[91]

Perhaps his greatest triumph was to be paid to hold an

entirely obscene art exhibition within Liverpool's Anglican cathedral, while climbing the south face of the cathedral, filmed for Granada TV. He rated the climbs E3 5c, technically easy but necky, though not compared to what he could do. The intricate carvings of the apostles provided handholds, and he looped slings around their heads for protection. 'I took great delight in chalking their noses as pinch-grips as I climbed by.'[92]

Johnny Dawes left for college, to do the legendary Sustainability Studies course at the University of East Anglia.

One night at my local climbing wall, I talk to my friends Serge and Tim. I know them both from going on climbing trips to Scotland in the winter. It's the British Isles' statistically most dangerous climbing activity. When you are on snow, you aren't held to the mountain by very much, and every winter brings news reports of deaths of climbers, avalanched, slipping and falling and dragging their mates with them. It's not through people not knowing what they are doing, either. The biggest predictor of being caught in an avalanche is to have previously been on an avalanche awareness course.

Fuck that. We must be mad, although the views are incredible and the snow, beautiful. Tim suffers very badly from fear when he is up there. I hide it better, but barely sleep for the week of a trip. When I camp at Llanberis campsite on a slate trip, I often wake up chuckling at my own dreams, a happy laugh that makes me feel child-like again.

The subject of Johnny Dawes comes up.

'I knew him, actually,' says Tim.

'Oh yeah, of course, you were at UEA with him, weren't you?' says Serge.

'I did the Sustainability Studies course at UEA. Johnny Dawes started it at the same time as me.'

At the age of twenty-seven, Dawes went back to university. 'The intellectual side of me was neglected with climbing and I'm now just balancing things up really.' Dawes looked at the state of the world and wanted to do more. 'I don't think that you can divorce the fact that we have cheap coffee with the fact that these countries are poor.... Awareness of people in the west isn't very high, really.'[93]

On campus, Dawes had developed routes and boulder problems up the concrete pillars of the campus. Today, many of the necessary pits and pockets have been filled in by the maintenance programme, and university security rapidly intervenes if people are spotted climbing the structures on CCTV.

Tim explains how amazing the course was; inspirational lecturers who knew every student's name – of an intake of sixty – within two weeks. 'But by the end of the three years of being told there was no hope and everything was fucked, I just decided the only alternative was political action.'

I look at Tim when he says this. I love having mates who are climbers; they have always done *something* worth hearing about. Tim has sandy hair, still in quite a youthful centre parting, he doesn't look his age. He is nice and bright and comes across as a bit shy.

He tells me of some of the stunts they did, like ethical shoplifting. Tim and his mates would go around and shoplift items made of tropical hardwoods which had been illegally logged from south East Asia. They would just boldly walk into a furniture shop and confidently pick up and take a mahogany lamp, leaving a printed letter stating that they were removing the item but that it could be collected later. They would then meet up with other ethical shoplifting teams outside a police station, and would all walk into the booking desk with their nicked gear.

'This is stolen,' they would declare and the duty sergeant would groan.

'I know,' the copper would say, 'you've stolen it.'

'No. In fact, the wood this is made from has been stolen from the Penang people of Malaysia.'

The luckless policeman would bury his head in his hands and plead, 'Just *please* fuck off.' Then reach for the paperwork. At the time, perhaps, it might have felt a bit fruitless, but today the provenance of something made of wood, its environmental origin and credentials are taken for granted.

Johnny Dawes came on some of the actions with Tim and his friends. Some protests could utilise the highly specific skills of climbers: for example, scaling Nelson's Column in Trafalgar Square to fly a banner in support of indigenous peoples around the world.

'He was nice,' Tim tells me, 'a nice bloke. You'd talk to him and he'd have these incredible streams of consciousness. Wow.'

Tim ultimately gave up political protest when, having been convicted of a few 'crimes', his next court appearance would entail jail. I look at him, radiating pleasantness like the carving of an affable sun. 'I didn't want to go to jail,' he says, and I don't fucking blame him. Tim became a wood-turner instead.

Johnny Dawes lived in India for a while, a fully paid-up hippy, then had a house in Sheffield. He put up further incredible gritstone climbs, like *Jumping on a Beetle* and *Angel's Share* at Black Rocks, while playing computer racing games like Tocca 4.

The levels of Upper Australia, Garret to the quarrymen.

With age, he put on weight, but never lost his underlying climbing ability. He decided that no-handed climbing was the way forward, as he hopped up slabby routes in the Peak. For years, he travelled a core-circuit between Llanberis, the Malvern Hills (where his parents lived) and Sheffield. He recently made side trips to places like Lundy or La Pedriza north of Madrid, where he would still be able to climb slabs of incredible difficulty, with beautiful footwork that made empirically great climbers feel like they were beginners again.

CHAPTER 28

Tambourine Man

2014–15, California

Through the double tunnels above Dali's Hole, past the Guillotine Block into California. This is the same way that Lee, Environment Agency Tom and I took to go and climb *We No Speak Americano*. Halfway up the scree-slope, overlooking *Americano*, is a little natural garden. Cushions of mosses – water-holding mattresses – give enough growth for birch and rhododendron seedlings to lodge and have a go at living. In the middle of the cliff glade is a rowan tree, planted deliberately and growing out of the plastic rabbit-spiral that protected its trunk when it was small.

This garden was Will Perrin's favourite place in the whole of the quarries. The tree was planted in memory of him by his friends. Every year on his birthday, Pete and Rachael Robins, two of those closest to Will, come up here with wine and fireworks. They get a bit drunk and fire rockets into the big cave across the quarry.

The fireworks explode, using the same black powder that carved out the quarries. Metal salts add hot colours as they burn. Chrysanthemums, willows and peonies, fish, spiders and palms, different effects made by the charges within the paper tubes. The brightest are the mag stars – aluminium burning hot white, like magnesium in a science lesson – or the blinding spark from an electric arc welder. The best shots of the rockets fly into the cave and detonate inside it, the sparks bouncing off the wall, ricochetting and lighting up the dark until the quick-fire dies.

Late nineties, Rainbow, Seamstress Slab, California

Will Perrin and Pete Robins became friends after Pete moved to Bangor to study oceanography in the late nineties. Tony Blair had come to power, a landslide election win wiping away the uninterrupted period of Tory rule. The economy started to prosper; Britpop and Oasis fought Blur in the charts. Huge numbers of students were now enrolling at university, loans incrementally replacing grants. Students in that period had a level of material comfort far beyond what had been available the previous decade. Each September, a new intake would unload at university halls of residence, some with cars of their own, many with electric kettles, portable TVs and new Playstations. In 1998, if you opened a student bank account with Barclays, you got a free mobile phone, so suddenly everyone had one.

In his first year at university, Pete often sacked off studies in order to go climbing. It was easy to meet up with Will in Dinorwig and walk along the road into the quarries – they didn't have a car. As a local boy, by his late teens Will Perrin already knew them inside out, going for a climb with friends on summer evenings, or soloing increasingly hard stuff when no one else was around.

Will and Pete played a tactical game with each other, taking turns to lead and belay pitches. You could sacrifice a lead – oh, no, you do it – in order to get onto a better one later, but try and avoid getting scuppered. If you took the middle lead of a three-pitch route, you would get one lead and your mate would get two.[94]

By about 2000, Will and Pete were climbing well. They had a pattern of trying a route, failing on it, then getting back on and doing it easily. They did *Cwms the Dogfish, The Untouchables, Dark Destroyer, The Dark Half, Heatseeker*. All hard 8as.

The climbs Will and Pete went on were now established classics; little was new. The bolts and occasional pitons left over from the eighties were gradually corroding, reacting with the salts gradually efflorescing from the rock around them.

Will committed suicide at the age of 24 in 2004, an action that floored the local climbing community, particularly his closest friends. Had he lived, he would today have been one of the best trad climbers around, a truly exceptional talent. Pete Robins still looks back on Will's climbing as some of the best he ever witnessed: the time he did *Raped by Affection* on New Year's Day with the hangover and wired sleeplessness you could only get away with when you were twenty; watching him easily ascend every hard climb on the Seamstress Slab – *Windows of Perception, Heading the Shot, The Medium, My Halo* – then soloing a few E4s.

Round about 2006, there were rumours of a new guide book being written. About the same time, there was recognition that the bolts in the quarries were – generally – fucked.

You could put the routes in the quarries into four categories. There was classic trad where you had to place your own gear, like *Comes the Dervish*. There were sport routes, like the later routes from the late eighties that Nick Harms or Johnny Dawes had put up, like *Cwms the Dogfish, The Quarryman* or

The Dark Half. These were relatively safe if you could trust the bolts.

Then there were the routes of 'designer danger', the likes of those that Johnny Redhead and Dave Towse had put up, including *Raped by Affection* and *Cystitis by Proxy*. These had been deliberately bolted so that they didn't necessarily guarantee safety. Some were slightly out of reach or awkward to clip. Others were placed just *after* the hard bit of climbing so provided a reward rather than a safety net. This reflects an accepted ethic: climbers who were there for the mental benefits of a game of skill vs death would not feel cheated.

But there was also a fourth category – 'designer danger by default'.[95] These were climbs that – for whatever reason – were badly bolted. Maybe the dole rat who had put them up hadn't got enough money to afford more than a couple of Troll bolts. Maybe they hadn't been able to borrow a power drill, so had to hand drill and couldn't be fucked to put loads in. These climbs were not mega-classics that were worth risking your neck for, and so most people didn't bother climbing them.

Pete Robins was one of the climbers who found himself doing a lot of the re-bolting. They 'just had a load of money for new bolts'.[96] It was a lot of work. Each new route had to be abseiled down and the old bolts removed: sometimes, climbing, you find the old hole with the expansion collar still wedged in. Then the mighty Bosch power drill would hammer a neat hole about 10 centimetres into the rock. Blow out the silica dust, or run in a bottle-brush with water, otherwise the dust would just stick to the epoxy resin, like flour over bread dough. The epoxy anchored in a brand-new, high-grade stainless steel bolt. Most of the retro-bolted routes had between three and ten bolts sunk in.

View from *Solitude Standing* as the cloud begins to lower

The climbers who did it struck a deal with the bolt fund, that for every so many bolts they put into old routes, they could get some bolts and resin for their own new routes. Pete Robins found two great lines, an immaculate clean groove – *Rowan* – and an immaculate clean arête, *The New Slatesman*.

Underneath the moss garden with Will Perrin's tree in it, Pete found an unlikely sequence of moves up a blank face. He climbed it, and called it *Tambourine Man*, after his friend's favourite song and artist.

CHAPTER 29

The Meltdown

May 2018, Bus-stop turning circle; Australia

Lee and Becky are back from Europe, in a new house in Sheffield which is very cheap because it is being renovated piecemeal around them. It has no curtains and there is no point cleaning the floor because it will be stripped out next month.

Not that Becky is there much; they cut their year travelling short for her to start a new job, back in the outdoor clothing world, near Newcastle. She is away most of the week and they miss each other badly after their time in the van. That closeness has tied them together rather than driving either of them to a murder to be implausibly blamed on a glove puppet. The risk is that day-to-day life is just tediously routine. Lee has returned to his old job, and is on his own through weekday evenings. Not great.

Lee picks me up from Bangor station: his old van is not as unreliable as my old one, now parked in its perpetual space at the local garage. This time has been booked and I am not missing these few days climbing because of any fucking fuel leak. We travel through the dusk, from Bangor to Llanberis, with clearing rainclouds and a suddenly emerging moon that lights up the edges of the clouds. We land at the campsite, trusting the weather forecast that it won't be a washout.

The next morning is bright and dry, and we drive up – short interruption to get pork pies from the Spar – and around the lake, higher still through Deiniolen and Dinorwig, past club huts and climbing instructors' houses, before the long straight down to the bus stop turning circle, where we park.

We are early, but there are a few cars parked up on the wide cinder verges. Notably one absolutely tiny car, less than a year old, a modern little hatchback, white with red trim, which for some reason screams out HIRECAR! Lee drives a little past it before we park: our climber-radar is on. We are fascinated.

All the doors of the hatchback are open. Alpine grade sleeping bags hanging off the back doors, ropes and bits of gear strewn behind the car like the tail of a comet, and, amidst it all, two men, sitting and gabbling away to each other, very rapidly, about something very important.

Not that we can tell what. Lee switches off the engine; he and I quietly start organising our kit and rucksacks. Very methodical, us: Lee has everything he wants to hand, and because I have taken the train, I really have very little to carry. We are slyly listening to what the hirecar guys are on about. What language is it? My brain cycles through some options: I hope I would recognise English, Welsh has its own sound, but then I catch 'pericolo' (danger), and the rhythm resolves itself into Spanish. I don't speak Castiliano – but I recognise it when I hear it talked, and this is as multilingual as I will ever get.

These Spanish climbers are intriguing. Lee and I keep catching each other's eyes and muttering, 'Wonder what they're up to?' to each other.

They look fit and skinny. Their skin is not just olive but a really deep brown, darkened from being outdoors and constantly in the sun. Spain is just like Britain, there are enough indoor and office jobs where you can become pasty-faced, but these two clearly don't have one. With glee, I notice that they are rolling cigarettes and drinking coffee: there is a percolator cooling over a camping stove. But better than that! They do not have cups, and have instead cut the tops off clear plastic bottles, raggedly, probably with a pen-knife, to make improvised handleless mugs.

I hoist up my rucksack, neat coils of rope looping out the sides from under the flap-lid of my rucksack. I walk close enough past them to be able to catch their eye and say hello.

'Hi,' they reply, with a barely perceptible 'y' sound. 'Hi-y'.

Lee and I get onto the footpath and fall in next to each other, normal conversation-formation.

'What do you reckon?'

'Dunno,' he says, 'with foreigners you can't tell if they're wads or not. I reckon they are, though. I think they're here for something specific. Caro Cialvidini just did the first female ascent of *The Quarryman*. Maybe they're here for that.'

They look good enough to be wads, proper wads. It sounds like an insult, but it's not, it's climberese for the best, the cutting edge of the hardest climbers.

It's exciting, but whatever they are up to is their business, really. Climbing is a strictly participation sport, at least from where Lee and I are dangling, and we have got our own climbs to do.

Early next morning and we are high on the levels, walking up the faint scree path up the side of Australia, heading for one of the big slabs. There are some long climbs up there, a single pitch of forty metres, but a nice easy grade. They get a lot of stars, they're meant to be good.

Between the blocks, orange and black spiders with white scales have spun webs. I don't want to break their webs, it would be thoughtless and unlucky, so I carefully pick my way through.

The slab above us looks good, not some sheer ramp, but a fractured blunt spike, with shelves and cracks that promise ways to the top. There are Joe Brown routes up here – *Antiquity, Dolmen* and *Menhir*. That last one amuses me, makes me think of Asterix and Obelix: the cliff does look like one of Obelix's menhirs.

We get our harnesses on just at the bottom of *Plastic Soldiers*. As we do, another couple of climbers cross the blocky rubble and walk over to where we are. One has a beard and turns out to be Scottish; his mate has hair died a lipstick shade of bright red.

'You on *Plastic Soldiers?* You mind if we do *Clash of the Titans?*'

'Batter in, mate,' I say. The two lines are next to each other but quite independent, a good six or eight feet apart at any point.

As I start to climb, I hear Scottish Beard start to swear.

'Fuck. Fucking hell. I have forgotten my GriGri. Fucking hell. Fuck's sake.' A GriGri is a belay device, a gadget that helps catch the rope when you climb. It's a safe little thing: useful if you think you're going to be falling and resting on the rope. No big deal, really, just use your belay plate instead, except there is an underlying embarrassment in Scottish Beard's rant.

'After all that –' his red-haired mate says.

'I know, I know. I was telling you again and again to make sure you remembered yours.'

Red Hair looks up at the climb. 'What grade is this?'

'Oh, 6a. Yes, 6a.'

Red Hair looks up at it, the length of the route. '*Is* it 6a? Is this going to be another sandbag? Is it going to feel like 6-fucking-c?'

I catch Lee's eye – both our expressions are carefully fixed, not a twinkle of amusement – and I start to climb. We'll have a laugh about it later.

Through the climbing, top out onto a grassy flat platform right at the top of the obelisk. The sun is glorious. 'LEE, SAFE!' I shout and hear 'Pete, off belay' drift from below. I walk back and find a bolt in a huge lump of slate to belay from. It's funny. From the climbs along the side – *Slab Rog, The Olympic Torch, Mynd am Aur, Mister Blister* – I've watched loads of people climb *Plastic Soldiers* and *Clash of the Titans*, silhouetted against the view of the valley beyond. One pair, a few years ago, was Rob and Sam the day before their accident. Now, though, I am the one silhouetted, as I sit right on the edge and bring Lee up.

As I start to pull the rope through, Scottish Beard emerges from the right-hand side. 'SAFE,' he yells, and starts muttering, 'Find a belay, find a belay.'

'One back there on the rock I'm on. Bolts and a thread, feel free to share. Plenty of room on the edge too.'

'Thanks, mate. ON BELAY!' he shouts below.

As we both belay, paying the rope through our plates, we can chat, it's sociable. I can feel what is happening by the tension and slack on the rope as you pull it through – you could do this blindfolded – and anyway I won't be able to even see Lee until the top ten metres.

'Hey,' Scottish Beard says. 'Guess who we saw in Llanberis. Johnny Dawes.' We could have known each other for years and been talking about someone we went to school with. 'There's two Spanish guys here to try *The Quarryman*; he was down in V12 giving them the beta. They were about to set off, and Dawes was just like, "I assume you're coming for coffee at Pete's?" to them.'

I laugh. 'Sounds right. We saw them Spanish lads at Bus Stop. They looked like right wads.'

Lee emerges about six metres below me. I call down to him, 'Dawes is in town.'

'Hah, yeah, is he?'

Shortly behind Lee is Red Hair, climbing nicely up the moves of his route.

Lee tops out and, as we coil the rope, we hear Scottish Beard say, 'See? What did you think?'

'It was okay.'

Lee and I wave goodbye – we have somewhere else we want to be – and, as we walk off, Lee tells me he was talking to Red Hair while they belayed. 'Them two were in Pembrokeshire on the sea cliffs before this, but the weather's turned shit so they're up here. They've been climbing together for a week and they're starting to get on each other's tits.'

I start giggling.

'Yeah,' I say. 'I think I got that. The GriGri.'

'The GriGri.'

We head down a level or two. I'm still on my mission to get the grade of 7a well and truly ticked, and there's one down here called *Slatebite*. Lee has done it before, reckons it's soft, but definitely not any lower than 7a. That will be good for me, a good confidence builder. It's meant to be fun too, not terrifying. It looks odd for slate, one of those blocky climbs, unlike the classic slabs where you are on your toes the whole time. But if it was set in a climbing gym, on fluorescent resin holds, it would look pretty normal.

The ritual. The shoes, the knot, breathe and feel yourself change, then I am off up the blocky start. A quarry spider has put its web across a useful little niche, and a small green jelly-sac of a plant – thoroughly Martian-looking – has spread itself across the step. It isn't too hard for me to use something different, though, so I leave them alone to pursue their own lives.

Maybe I'm getting used to it. I feel less frightened, like this is less important. It might just be the route. I want to climb it well enough, but my thoughts haven't lingered over it. I haven't climbed it as I drift off to sleep, tested the holds with my thoughts.

It is no giveaway, either, though. I pad out along an awkward ramp, big holds for slate but which all slope the wrong way. I need to use a lot of finger strength, taking a proportion of my weight just to give me the confidence to use them. If I was on gritstone, I think, I would just trust my feet, I would drop my heels so that the butyl rubber of my soles would grip the coarse grains and tiny silicate crystals, mould and squash onto them, all friction. But I can't, and I reach into an unstable position, something too strenuous. I match, but I can't imagine making the move I need to to reach balance. Half seconds tick, strength fades and I choose.

'Take!' I say, clear.

'Yep,' says Lee, and I feel the rope snake tight on my

knot. Then the familiar fall, like dozens of others. Maybe hundreds by now?

'Bollocks!' I say.

'Have a rest, try again. Do you want to try the move?' Lee asks.

'Nah. Down and from the beginning I think.'

A few minutes later, not many, because my fingers aren't tired, and I'm up again. Past the ramp quicker, with a bit more confidence, the unstable move. This time, I just do it – classic slate – then there is a rest to look at what to do next.

'Right,' I shout down. 'I think I've got to get my toe up to here, undercling and then reach for that up there. What do you reckon? Is that a good hold?'

'I'm not telling you.'

What? What the fuck does he mean? I'm asking for help here. He has done it before, why can't he just tell me? I look down and he shrugs.

'I want it to be a surprise. You're a good enough climber now, Pete.'

I look up at the hold above me, a triangle of rock. Might be good, might not. But it is the clear thing to go for. He's right. I was looking for reassurance, looking for permission to do what I knew I had to, but permission is bullshit. I don't need it.

I open my hip and pad my toe up. Total concentration: a tiny part of my mind notices that I cannot think of anything else, no room, no spare brainpower. Then the release as my toe finds the hold, space left by my clever old finger for it to join them and pop up my hand for an undercling.

My other leg dangles free and pads on the rock, my arm stretches far up for the hold. My fingers land and curl into a great hold, something I could dangle from all day. Other hand up and the rest is not hard. I'm at the next clip, then the chains before I know it.

Another 7a, then. Fist bump with Lee at the bottom.

Lee heads back on the Saturday night; he has work on Monday. Becky will be back home waiting for him. I don't mind losing Lee to that, priorities and all. Plus, the club are up, so as Lee leaves I meet up with them, and I catch a ride down to Tŷ Powdwr with my gear on everyone else's laps and me hanging onto the outside of a Land Rover Discovery, riding it like a hobo on a freight car.

After a quick cup of tea and settle into the club hut, I take a few of the newer club members for a walk. We go into some of the tunnels, some of the semi-secret parts of the quarries like California; we go and see Will Perrin's tree.

We walk down the quarry road to look into Twll Mawr. Walking along the edge, above the sheer drop, looking up at the *Quarryman* wall is one of the showstoppers of the quarries. Fear and inspiration mixed, I remember the intensity of the feelings as I stood there for the first time. It feels the same every time I go back, too.

As we slide through the gap between the slate wall and the fence, I hear voices echoing around Twll Mawr. I tell the other two we must be quiet, someone is on something, and it might be something very hard indeed.

As we walk along the edge of the pit, I see a bouncing rope on the centre of the cliff, and a man resting on it. He is on the *Quarryman* wall, but maybe five metres lower than us. He has probably ascended at least sixty or seventy-five metres from the base of the pit.

I look, tap Andrew and Nick on the arms, and point at him. I can see him and his belayer. They are on *The Meltdown*, the hardest climb of them all in the quarries, and the hardest slab climb in Britain. He is top-roping, trying all the moves out, so he can learn them. The difficulty of *The Meltdown* is so great that no one could just start climbing and guess their way through the intricate sequence.

The climber notices us, feels the weight of our eyes on him.

'Hi-y,' he says, and his belayer, the other Spanish lad, looks up and then waves.

I can't fucking wait to tell Lee. Someone on *The Meltdown*.

1989, Twll Mawr

Below *The Quarryman* groove, Dawes found a slab that fascinated him. It had holds, and features, but they were all – weird. Underclings and side pulls, big holds but all of them in the wrong places, and over-small, awkwardly placed footholds. This was what Dawes wanted; not blank, but a 'maelstrom of possibilities, that movement could add grip to'.[97] The rock had a weird melted texture, as though a blowtorch had liquified it and let it gloop and run, like roofing tar. He called this *The Meltdown*.

Dawes top-roped it, and linked the moves, but broke off a hold which he resined back onto the wall. But that was the end of it, so he went looking for something else hard. What Dawes had envisaged as *The Meltdown* just sat there, that being the nature of rock.

When the Ground Up guide came out, it included a picture of Dawes' topo that he had drawn for the *Quarryman* wall, done in blue biro on lined paper, snaking dotted lines with numbers all over the place showing how hard the moves and the pitches were, little 5s, 6s and 7s dotted around. He put a key in for features like a spike, a bolt, a peg, a nut and – Johnny be Johnny[98] – a symbol for a peanut butter sandwich and a drawing of a surreal telephone box. There is a lot of information there, and if you could be fucked, you could work out how to do the climbs, or at least protect them.

The guide also included a brief description of Dawes' project line:

18. The Meltdown *(project)*
An old project of Johnny's rumoured to be F8c.

Innocuous enough, if you read it casually. To the right climber, it would be the slap of a gauntlet, a challenge thrown down.

2005, Twll Mawr

In 2005, James McHaffie, known as Caff, climbed *The Very Big and the Very Small*. By this point, he had climbed all the existing hard sport climbs in the quarries: everything with a grade 8 attached. Later that year he rappelled down into Twll Mawr to have a look at this one near-impossible project.

'We'd heard he'd pulled a hold off; we were curious and thought it would be fun just to try out the moves on it. There were four of us. It was evening, it was midgy, we all had a very small go, a twenty-minute effort. It was all very fraught with the midges.'[99]

Ignacio Mulero, belayed by Talo Martin on *The Meltdown*. *The Quarryman* groove is the vicious slash above them to the left.

Nineties, Lake District; noughties, Twll Mawr

Caff had grown up climbing in the Lake District with his dad,
Ray. Early on, he had been taken to Dalt Quarry, to lead up an
easy enough sport climb: *Blue Oyster Cult*. It was a minor quarry, but there were other good ones in the Lakes, notably Hodge
Close. The Lakes are better known for big mountain routes, but
there is slate, too (Cumbria is as wet as Wales – the same damp
Atlantic air – so slate in both areas is great because it dries so
quickly). Even, Caff found, some routes that could be climbed in
the wet, because the holds were so positive you could get away
with it.

Near Coniston, a winding road turns off from Yewdale. The
road climbs and hits a plateau, and at the end of it is a network of
quarry workings. On the right-hand side of the road are Hodge
Close and Parrock; the easiest way is to walk down the rough
path through Parrock, slate slabs overgrown and smeared green
with moss. Parrock is linked to Hodge by a slate tunnel, but not
the small ones of Dinorwig which would allow a narrow-gauge
railway. This was on a church or cathedral's scale, a cavern well
lit by its generous openings, dripping rooves and shallow pud-
dles. As the cavern opens into Hodge Close, a lake fills the bottom of it, clear dark water, horribly deep.

If you go to the far side of Hodge, you can find small trails
running down from the top edge of the quarries; little worn
paths amongst well-set larch and pine trees, clusters of birch.
Along the top edge of the quarry some of the tree roots are undercut, by mini streams and waterfalls that wear away the primitive earth, leaving roots overhanging the air in big plates, the
strain taken by sinuous cables on the far side, the tree growing

straight up like the tower on a suspension bridge.

Among these trees are the wrecks of two or three cars, trundled over the edge of the quarry. The tyres are still on, with thick treads and all the radiator hoses, the paint is still there, so you can tell that one is red, another white. If a car is burnt, the rubber of the tyres goes, leaving fans of thin wires; the paint bubbles, scorches and burns clean off. This hadn't happened with this car: someone took the handbrake off and pushed it, watching it gather speed down the slope before the car went over. That someone felt safe in the isolation, safe enough to enjoy the moment of destruction; Hodge Close is remote enough for that.

Climbs run up the sheer sides. Caff did *First Night Nerves* when he was about seventeen, and *Ten Years After*, which was a big lead for him at the time. On *Limited Edition*, he found quite good smears, using the friction of his rock-shoe to hold his weight: much less likely in Wales, but possible on the rougher slate of Hodge Close. Caff soloed routes like *Malice in Wonderland* and *Main Event*, so he could reasonably conclude that he 'always got on well on slate'.

So on trips down to north Wales with his climbing mates, one of the main parts of the trip would be 'hammering it onto the slate'.[100] In the late nineties, Caff would climb with Will Perrin and Pete Robins, 'knocking off the classics, E5 and E6'. Then, when Caff moved down in 2002, he 'got properly stuck in', living in Llanberis for a while. For a period he had no car, so the quarries were the only place to go, and, by 2005, he was looking at *The Meltdown,* getting midgied with his mates.

It was too hard for him, really. When he came back to it in 2007, he started to put a bit more effort in, and found he could do the first half. 'But the first half is the easy half, really, until you hit this traverse left which is hard. And weird. Hard and weird. Double duo.'[101] Just at the wrong time, just as he could have been starting to make a dent in it, the quarries were closed for six weeks to be used as a film set for *Clash of the Titans*. That was it for years, then; he couldn't be arsed to drag someone in there to help him belay. He hadn't got close enough to it for that to feel worthwhile, put himself into his mate's debt for belaying favours.

2011, Twll Mawr

By 2011, things were a bit different. The new Ground Up guide had come out,[102] and Caff, Pete Robins and a few others had put up new routes that had got into it. Robins and Caff had nearly fallen out over climbing *The New Slatesman*. It was clearly Pete's route – he had found it – and after Pete had fallen on it, he offered Caff a go, though Caff was temperamentally unable to do anything other than try really hard. He nearly did climb it too, but just dropped the last move. Pete exploded and told him to fuck off and find his own 8a, which Caff did, putting up *Sauron* deep in Mordor, and another strange hard route, *The Serpent Vein*, which ran up a seam of dolerite that looked like a snake, parallel sided and banded at regular sections with quartz stripes.

By 2011, Caff was much stronger and fitter than he had been, climbing hard limestone, including a limestone route on the coast called *Big Bang*, the hardest sport route in Britain. You can't climb hard limestone without being really fit, training your strength, stamina and power. Success on steep hard routes directly equates to how long you can hang on a fingerboard for.

Slate doesn't give a fuck how strong you are. It's about technicality of movement, being flexible, being bold. But *The Meltdown's* holds were weird enough to need real strength to use them. Caff's enhanced fitness meant that this time he could do it quite quickly and do them all hanging from a rope with only a couple of rests. If you can do a route with only a couple of rests on the rope, then it should be clear that you can do it clean: very little is stopping you.

That very little took another year to overcome. Caff used some of the strength-training regimes, and crucially lost some weight, sweating out a few pounds under his waterproofs while teaching a scrambling course at Plas y Brenin. He began to understand about rest days: if you train regularly, your body comes to crave the release of energy, and then when you don't train for two days it is fizzing to actually *do* something.

What was it like? Before Caff climbed *The Meltdown*, *The Very Big and the Very Small* was the hardest slab climb in Britain. But the moves were almost standard for hard slate slabs – Nick Harms had felt that they were nothing new; rather, nose-grinding rockover after nose-grinding rockover on tiny holds sharp enough to split a fingertip within a few goes.

But *The Meltdown* was not like that. It was weird. The footholds were small, or odd shapes and angles. You had to use all the handholds either as undercuts – so pulling on them from above, like lifting a piano from the bottom – or sidepulls, so trying to pull them like an archer drawing a bow. The moves between them had to be quick and precise, then a hard pull, locking core muscles before moving a foot. Then immediately after a hard move, the handholds would change, and the same shit foothold would become really good, almost but not quite a rest. Weird. Just weird.

May 2018, Twll Mawr

The Spanish lads are Ignacio Mulero and Talo Martin. Ignacio climbs *The Meltdown* the week after I head back home, and in a quiet way, it hits social media. A post on Instagram, picked up by UKC (UK Climbing) website, all very low key. People's comments are very low key. Thumbs up and okay hand-flash emojis:

> *felicidades*
> *venga*

May 2019, Twll Mawr

A year after that, Talo Martin releases a ten-minute film showing Mulero climbing it. These short films are the currency of climbing, either on YouTube or Vimeo, picked up by a few keen climbers, those who might understand what they are seeing. They are still a vehicle for advertising and sponsorship, but don't achieve anything like the advertising income of a fashion-conscious blogger talking about being anxious before going out for pizza with her friends, or an ex-bartender from Hampshire playing Minecraft with his friends.

I wonder if the camera will pan up and show us as figures in the background, watching him climb. Of course not. When we watched them, he was on a top-rope, not lead. He had on a black T-shirt, which he took off to flog the holds dry and clear of chalk. His back was roped with muscle fibres, an anatomical drawing. In the video, Mulero is wearing a bright red T-shirt. A dull grey or black would have been a poor choice, but red stands out against the slate.

CHAPTER 30

Instructor Job

June 2018, East Anglia

The building work has run its course, and my insurance is due. Nearly two thousand fucking pounds, with all the Working at Height and Rope Access clauses. Plus, the agent at my main client has left. I liked him, he was sensible, specifying Sadolin Superdec rather than wasting everyone's time with linseed oil paint that doesn't fucking dry now there's no lead in it. But I could also tell he wasn't swimming well at the job. He left a few months ago and they haven't replaced him, so no one has made a decision on any of the work I've priced for. No. Time to jump.

Anyway, I've had enough of working on my own in old buildings. Even with the radio on, my sly negative internal voice would start up: why are you doing it like that? That could be better, couldn't it? What will they think, what will they think? I've had enough of it, especially when the autumn comes around. I tell close mates that it's my dad's voice, which is half true. It does sound like the things he'd say at his most peevish. But he's been dead ten years now, all these conversations are imaginary, the criticism cannot come from him. I have to accept that the voice is mine, and it echoes in my ears loudest when I am on my own.

What I need is some company, something I can just turn up for and do.

One of my son's friend's mums talks to me in the playground while we wait for them at hometime. 'You should apply to Center Parcs,' she says. 'You know loads about climbing. I'm on Sports Booking Desk and half the kids running the climbing wall haven't got a clue.'

I don't know. The money won't be great. A bit of me worries that I am just too old for it.

When I was at university I went to America in my holidays to work at a hotel; the visa was easy to get. The chip dropped off my shoulder as I enjoyed the sexual benefits of a British accent amongst a gang of attractive resort workers, all of us in our early twenties. It was great, the Americans were great, they thought you could do anything. The United States Republic of Hell, Yes! rather than the Constitutional Monarchy of No, I Don't Think That's Allowed. I never thought I'd settle back in the UK, but I tried to bring the best bits of the US back with me. But you shouldn't go back, and I am wary of just trying to rerun a previous success now, nearly twenty years later.

When I check on the website, they're hiring.

I don't know what to expect from the interview. I'm wearing a blue checked shirt, black trousers and uncomfortable black shoes that look like a NYPD patrolman's, the hard leather step of one heel digging into the sole of my foot. My socks are thin, and cushion nothing, or barely anything. My foot moves in the shoe and I feel it rub as I walk. I tighten the laces one more time, and one of them – as thin as coarse fishing line but not as strong – breaks, and so I have the fuck-on of rethreading it and tying it up with the world's smallest bow.

The job is as an outdoor activity instructor at Center Parcs, about five miles – or two villages – from my house. I've driven past the entrance hundreds of times, the plastic logo sign mounted on wood. Every winter, they spray white snow made of recycled paper pulp over the pine trees around the gate. It looks magical – but also slightly stupid. Around the gate, the other trees are normal, snow-free in the now-normal Yuletide mild weather. On either side, green mesh fencing, very high, blocks off the site. You can't see in, and I have no real idea of what it will be like. This park is a big employer in the local area; I've seen the housekeeping minibus collect the women who clean the lodges. Some of the mums who pick my son's classmates up wear the coloured polo tops of the various departments.

Walking through the park, it is actually nice. People ride by on bikes. The day is cool and dry, but sunny, and it feels to me like how woods should be on the Pacific coast of California. I remember a friend at school going away to Center Parcs in Sherwood Forest. He couldn't explain why it was so good – there was apparently a swimming pool, it was warm? – but he couldn't convince me. Now I'm here, it feels sufficiently like its own world to be interesting.

At the interview venue, two men greet me, Paul and James. Part of me wonders whether the 'Action Challenge' Department might be absolutely full of climbers, people who have routinely climbed E4 to E6 every weekend since university. On first impressions, no probably not. The two men are friendly and wouldn't be out of place on a building site. This will be okay, I think. I'm going to play the Climber Card.

'These questions aren't really specific to the role, but just answer them how you like. Can you tell us about a time you surprised someone?'

And we're off. I like talking, anyway, and who wouldn't want a chance to talk about themselves for an hour?

'...slate quarries. Which in themselves are incredible places. So you're going through old tunnels and abandoned pits, abseiling in, amongst all the machinery and the quarrymen's huts....'

I can see them responding to it, too. They like me; I'm funny, but they're half shitting themselves that they've got a right nutter on their hands. I reign it in a bit.

'...teaching my son, and I've always liked helping people, new starters at the climbing club, or apprentices when I was in the building trade....'

All going well, I think. Balance just right, between someone who has done stuff but isn't such an extreme personality that he will be unmanageable, unable to fit into the sensible but onerous safety requirements designed to keep children alive on zipwires.

'Can you tell us about a time you've taken a risk?' asks Paul, the older of the two.

I raise an eyebrow and we all laugh. I tell them about some trips up to Scotland in the winter, in the snow, with Serge and Tim.

'The thing is, with triggering avalanches, you never do know how close you've come. A footstep either way could have made the difference.'

I can tell they would have loved to have said that themselves.

A week later they offer me the job. I take it.

Eighties and nineties, Liverpool; Tremadog; Llanberis; Himalayas; Gogarth; Chamonix

You couldn't make money at climbing. Not real money, not enough money to tell anyone you wanted to fuck off. You might get a living, a handful of people did, or you might have a job for a couple of years at Plas y Brenin, but that was as high as you could reach.

Climbing instructors had been around since the sixties, more or less. Some were ex-army commando types. Some were outdoor education teachers, people like Colin Goodey. Some were elite climbers; Joe Brown instructed at a centre in the Peak District before he moved to Wales.

Some of the slateheads, like Andy Newton or Mike Raine, were in the right place at the right time, doing a PGCE and emerging into the world of education with a load of real-life climbing experience. Slateheads like Bobby Drury and Paul Pritchard were surprised to find themselves actually being paid to climb, enough perhaps to call themselves 'professional' climbers. By today's standards, what they got was next to fuck all. A bit of money, a few flights, or some gear direct from the manufacturer. Still, after the years of dole dwelling, it would have seemed like a lot.

For Bobby Drury, this ultimately provided a level of acceptance from his family. Bobby had been adopted as a child into a religious middle-class family in Liverpool, 'where my dad was a consultant anaesthetist and my mum was a teacher. And they had grown up in public schools since the age of three. And I'm adopted, so I come from a very different stock of people. I just didn't fit in, and for all the loving... and support they gave me – I just didn't understand the kind of life they expected, of O-levels, A-levels, going to university.'[103]

Bobby literally left Liverpool immediately after sitting his O-levels, knowing he had fucked them up and not really caring – he was free now – and hitched to Snowdonia. With teenage thoughtlessness, he just vanished, no concern given to how his parents must have felt. 'It took Mum two months, I hadn't made any contact at all, she'd been ringing round and I was living in a caravan opposite Eric Jones' cafe [in Tremadog] and all I was doing was climbing, climbing. She rang Eric's number, and he knocked on the caravan one night and said, "Bob, I think your mum's on the phone." She was crying, "Bob, you've failed all your O-levels."

Bob already knew that. His realm of achievement would be measurable and tied up with climbing grades instead. 'No, Mum, I'm leading 5C! O-levels? I've led *Vector.*' His mum and dad didn't get it, but shortly afterwards, Bobby moved to Llanberis, where his climbing started to take off even further: dole; Pete's Eats; the quarries, climbing, climbing, climbing.

Four years later, by the time he was twenty, he could speak to his dad and tell him he was going off to the Himalayas.

'The Himalayas?' asked his dad, public-school tones down the phone.

'Yes, I'm going with Joe Brown,' and his dad recognised the name, perhaps from the Old Man of Hoy climbing broadcast in the mid sixties. The penny dropped for Bobby's dad, who liked classical music and fell-walking in the Lakes with his socks pulled up to his knees. But his parents could not understand that Bobby wasn't just hanging around in a caravan doing nothing – although that was a part of it – but actually doing something and getting respect for it, even if they would not choose it themselves.

'I never even got him to put a harness on, all those years; not even [for] abseiling. He's dead now; just wasn't his bag, you know? I suspect now, a modern parent has been exposed to far more rock climbing and they know about [it], and it's all a lot more understandable.'

Bobby was able to show them articles from climbing magazines in which he was mentioned – 'Mum, I'm in this.'[104]

When paragliders started to appear, he became entranced, just like John Silvester had been. While climbing, he had felt it would be amazing to just step off and float away from the cliffs. As a paraglider pilot, Bob found he could do just that. The small six-foot box you climbed within was nothing compared to the cliff you were climbing on. But, in turn, that cliff was just a small feature on the entire landscape: the huge landscape opening up from the view above.

Soon he was writing his own articles about paragliding and editing *Cross Country* magazine. Despite his failed English Language O-level, he wrote descriptions so vivid, of going into a spin and deploying a reserve chute, that they would leave you sweating for weeks.

'I think we should all get massive amounts of money from Gwynedd council, because essentially we created a great climbing area,' said Crooky.[105]

Andy Newton was already training to be an instructor when he started climbing with Johnny Redhead and Crooky, in the early eighties. Going out to the crag with Redhead and Crooky had been a 'total laugh. You'd get back... after a day and your muscles would be aching. In your sides. From having a laugh.'[106]

Andy had got to know Johnny Redhead when he had gone to borrow a chainsaw from him – an obvious stitch-up. At the time, Redhead was getting a lot of flak for apparently cutting down an oak tree that obscured the start of a new route in Ogwen, so of course Redhead had looked at him oddly – a fucking chainsaw! Andy didn't know how to use it, so Redhead cut the wood, while Andy held it, the whirling teeth inches from his fingers. It was almost a test of nerve.

'Climbing with John was always an eye-opener.' Redhead's climbing was exceptional, beyond most other talents. Andy wanted to look after him as much as he could . 'Even just belaying as best I could. That was my part on the team.'[107] For himself, Andy liked doing trad climbing on sea cliffs like Gogarth. 'I liked being able to look after myself.'[108]

Doing this for years, alongside formal instructor training, meant that Andy became really good – not just at looking after himself but also other people. In turn, he could further teach others how to do the same, and he built a career on this, as an instructor and a guide. This would later encompass training and auditing large, tame leisure parks which might have high-ropes courses and a zipwire.

Better climbers didn't have the personality for instructing and guiding. Stevie Haston had moved to Chamonix, where he was extremely unpopular with the local French guides, who called him *Le Vache Folle* (The Mad Cow).

Haston's climbing was still extraordinary, including extremely committed alpine ascents with little margin for error, like the first free solo ascent of the Walker Spur. He considered that he was leading the world at ice-climbing – and that's a fair assessment, putting up as he did the first grade VII ice route in the world. Haston's list of achievements continued to grow, and he continued to climb at the highest level even into his sixties.

But when Haston came to do his guiding exams, he famously failed, marked down for his attitude rather than his skill and judgement. Guides didn't have to be great climbers – they had to look after their clients. They had to be safety-conscious, attentive to the needs of city-types and doctors who could afford to pay to be dragged up to height.

CHAPTER 31

Between the Here and Now

July 2018, Norwich, local climbing wall

I drive up to Norwich, round the outer ring road. Near the airport, where occasionally you see a small passenger jet or a Sikorsky helicopter taking oil-workers – or, increasingly, workers on the enormous offshore wind farms – out to the North Sea, I turn right and down a small road. On the industrial estate is Highball. It's a climbing centre in a cheap industrial unit no one else wanted.

The car park is busy, so I slew into one of the reserved spaces for the parcel delivery depot next door. They are the last spaces to fill up; the yellow road markings and the RESERVED FOR DPD signs keep people away. Once you've been going to Highball for a while, you know that DPD is closed in the evenings so they don't care. Rarely there'll be an HGV and a load of blue-pogoed Sprinter vans, and cones all over the place – their turn to use Highball's parking places.

Inside, chalk floats in the air in harsh white fluorescent light. The climbing walls stick out at weird angles like the prow of ships, like the strange angles of dazzle camouflage or a twentieth-century Communist art sculpture. The resin holds dot around them like jelly beans. When the routes are newly set with clean holds, it takes only a few days for the bright colours to get muted by white and black: white from the chalk and black from the shoe rubber.

It is night-club busy tonight. A man with a Tough Mudder 'finisher' T-shirt clumps clumsily up an overhang, an accessible entry level climb. His mates look up at him, false casual stances. They all wear sports gear, gym goers with sculpted blocky arm muscles. Tattoos. There are a lot of hats, beanies and baseball caps, carefully chosen to reflect *something* about the wearer. Flesh tunnels and piercings, no requirement to take them out before you climb.

Two young women step past the group of men. One wears painted-on leggings and a sports-bra. Her stomach is flat and muscular, her tummy button small and interesting. She pulls on to another climb next to the one they just did; the muscles in her back flex, then her buttocks, thighs and calves, as she points her toes into the holds. Her friend watches her; she has similar leggings but a peach-coloured T-shirt over her sports bra.

The men all notice her, but there is no overt leering or sexual comments. Climbing walls aren't like that. There are more and more women coming climbing – not yet equal numbers – but far better than the few of the eighties. During those years that Llanberis' dole-funded slate scene was in its heyday, climbers, like Lynn Hill in the US and Catherine Destivelle, started to show the male-dominated scene just how good they were. Lynn Hill was the first person to climb *The Nose* on El Capitan.

In 1995, British women Airlie Anderson and Lucy Creamer put up a route called *Venus Envy* in Greenland. Indoor climbing competitions are regularly won by Shauna Coxey OBE, and Hazel Findlay is one of the boldest trad climbers in the UK. Any leftover notions that climbing is something that women cannot do is fast disappearing, as more women are trying, and succeeding, at every level.

Garry is getting his shoes on. When I join him, he pretends to punch me in the face and shouts, '*Duzsh, Duzsh!*' – playground punch noises. I normally hate people play-fighting. In grown men, in boys, it is aggressive. An assertion of dominance, a threat display. But with Garry, I couldn't give a fuck. It's just Garry; he gets on my tits but I love him. He is short and very skinny, little on him that isn't muscle. He jumped on my back once and I couldn't believe how little he weighed. He is very strong, very powerful, and has little excess to drag up with him.

We walk across to the competition wall, an oldish set – the holds have been up for two weeks – so less busy. Garry and I start up the easier problems, a long warmup, trying to climb the problems perfectly, with no noise.

After a while, Ben wanders over; he has been patrolling the poor behaviour of the inexperienced.

'Look at this,' he says to us. We watch a bloke with a beard make a desperate snatch for a faraway jug, a wild swing, all strength. His feet are badly placed; he is standing on the middle part of his foot, his arch, rather than the toes. He has socks under his hire shoes. He makes the move, swinging wildly, then bangs the finishing holds triumphantly. He drops down to his mates, spinning in the air, then fist-bumps everyone, somehow looking both delighted and aggressive at the same time – 'I-bet-you-can't-do-that'.

A moment later, Tilly – one of the talented teenage female climbers at the wall – steps onto the same problem. She climbs it easily, silently, with a cat's grace. Slick moves. It makes me laugh, because I know what she's doing. She calls it BMB – Big Man Burning – hopping onto a climb to do it better than one of the macho blokes; she uses it to motivate her to climb hard.

'Well, Benny. Have you decided yet? Are you coming to Wales?' Garry asks.

'Hmm,' he says. 'Yes, I think I will. I've booked the time off.' Garry and I cheer and high-five.

'You'll love the slate, you will. It'll be just right for you.'

'I had my doubts,' he confesses. 'The thing that sealed it was: out of everyone I asked, nine out of ten said, "Slate? What the fuck do you want to go and do that for?" but then the tenth person would be like, "It's fucking amazing."'

'Who said it was shit?' I ask.

'Everyone. But then I thought "I like shit".' He says this leering.

At ten, Ben and the other staff of the centre will call out 'Last Climbs Please' and then try and force us all out of the door so that they won't be late home.

August 2018, Thetford to Australia then down into Tasmania

The next Thursday night, I go to the wall, Highball, and pick up Ben. He comes and stays the night at my house, crashes on the floor in the front room. The next morning, Garry arrives in his truck; we take a few seconds to load up, then a bit longer to eat bacon sandwiches I have made, with grilled tomato in between thick bread, and cups of instant coffee.

My son gets up, sleepy headed, keen to see Ben. Ben is always rude to him, which is his way of being friendly. All of my climbing mates are good with my son. They treat him like one of us, a grown-up who just happens to be shorter. None of them swear any less, but they don't spoil him, either.

We drive out, in Garry's big work truck. It's one of those

Japanese four-wheel-drive pickups, and it's got leather seats and a checker plate bed at the back that we load all our gear into.

'How the fuck do you afford this?' I ask.

'It's from work,' says Garry. 'It's not too bad on fuel. Are you looking forward to PopMaster?' That is it, I think; we have become old.

Garry manages a chain of local hardware shops across Norfolk. He has his phone linked through the console. When a work phone call comes through, it blots out the radio.

'Then Jenny is going to need cover for the Attleborough store. Can we send Dave? What about Helen? Not Scott, I want him in Swaffham....'

On the way towards the Midlands, everything has changed. While Lee was away, I came up less, so I missed the start of the big roadworks around Cambridge. I love it. Miles and miles of rollers compacting Type 2 sub-base; that yellow rock the same colour as the big machines. Diggers grading it out; it takes real skill and delicacy of touch to bring the bucket back dead flat, tiny little twitches and eases of your hands on the twin joysticks of a fourteen-tonner. I remember those jobs from when I worked on sites; never on this scale, though. I see the men in the cabs, sunburnt red, cropped hair and orange jackets with hi-vis stripes. A gang of steel-fixers tie cages of rebar, rusty skeletons soon to be drowned in concrete, poured at fifty slump.

'Look at it all,' I purr at Garry and Ben. 'The concrete! Brutalist, you know.'

We pass a long straight stretch, bulldozed through the flat agricultural fields. Big yellow machine after big yellow machine, steel and circuitry and paint. They have company names decalled onto the engine casings and jibs: O'Donnell, Maclean, Quigley. Nothing clever by PR companies, no brand image, just a bloke's name. Then, cranes, readying to assemble a ship-sized section of box steel: the span of a bridge.

I suddenly realise that my favourite graffiti is gone. The brick building with THE FUTURE has been demolished, probably run straight through by a D9 and ploughed into the foundations of the A14 extension. Fuck, no. But I saw at least three versions of that graffiti since I first ever noticed it; every season the owner must have painted it out, then it sprang up again like mushrooms. The artist is still out there. When the road is finished, he will have the cathedral-scale trioliths of the bridges for a brand new canvas.

Another phonecall for Garry. 'Yeah. On the road to Wales. Away for the weekend. Nah, nah, that's alright, I'm only driving, what do you need? Yeah. No, we can. Or could send Dave. Not Dave then, Carl or Sophie....'

On past Birmingham, by Telford, Shrewsbury. We see the first hills, but above them the blue sky is giving way to stacked white cloud. Further on, past Oswestry, and the summer light is gone. Past Corwen, the signs are in Welsh and English. ARAF SLOW. Toilets Toiledau. The sky is dark and soon splots of rain hit the windscreen. We look at our phones for the weather forecast, but there's no longer any point hurrying.

* * *

Later that evening, the rain has stopped but the air is humid. Low cloud hangs just above the big cwm of Australia, very white, full of droplets. The three of us are up on the Sidings

Level, railway tracks still running under the slate waste. Piss-easy climbs, really, most of them; not very high, just six or seven metres. Three or four bolts, safe as houses. They have a theme of names: *Thomas the Tank, Ivor the Engine, Gordon, Hogwarts Express.*

'What's this one called?' asks Garry. *'Sonar?'*

'Sodor. It's the island in *Thomas the Tank.* You'll know that in a year's time.' Garry's son is nearly two, a bright little blond-haired boy. A tiny bit young for Thomas. I read the stories to my son, trying to remember them from when my mum had read me them. Then the TV series with the little model trains. The toys, the lunch boxes, new books, never-ending.

The climb itself runs up a thin crack-line up the slab that starts next to a graffitied face in black and white. The artist who came here wanted to do a huge mural across it; he left the Aztec face as a statement of intent. Maybe that is a thing in the graffiti world, like a climber would expect other climbers to leave his project alone. But the local climbing community, not the quarry owners, didn't want the graffiti and fucked him off.

The climb is polished by many hands and feet. Relearning how to clip, how to climb, how to thread our rope through the chains. Ben moves beautifully up the rock, slow and balanced and controlled; we had thought he would. Garry is light and powerful and the most experienced. He started climbing with Lee years ago. By now I've caught up with the mileage that Land Rover James and Darryl thought I needed a few years back.

At the end of the level, there are two fractionally harder climbs. I get onto one of them. It is way below the grade I need to concentrate at. I am standing at good ledges, there is one last bolt to go before the chains. I reach to my gear-loops and there is nothing there. No more clips.

'Fucking hell. Twat. I'm out of quickdraws.'

Ben looks up from where he is belaying me. 'You *are* a twat.'

'Wait a minute,' shouts Garry. 'I'll throw you one up.'

Garry aims carefully, right for my body. I'm on a great ledge and Ben has taken me tight, so one hand is completely free to catch the quickdraw with. They are good for throwing with weight at both ends like a gaucho's bolas. I see it whirl through the air, right for me, but it's too close to my face. I flinch, and pluck at it as it arcs gracefully past. Fuck. Shame. I am twelve and back in those fucking horrible PE lessons, last to be picked.

The quickdraw goes spinning past, arcing down, past the level and into the void below.

'You're getting that,' shouts Garry.

'Fuck off,' I say. 'You threw it.'

Garry leans flat on the edge of the level, his head over the void, his arms cocked as if he is about to do a press-up. 'I can see it,' he says. I crane my head over, and the 'draw is obvious amongst the scree.

The cloud sinks lower into the amphitheatre of rock. It is still light, early evening. I check my watch and we still have an hour or two until dark. The air is humid, but it is cooler now, heading for cold as the light dulls and starts to fade.

There are a couple of access bolts and we clip my turquoise rope into them. Garry goes first, stepping backwards over the edge and off down the cliff. I go next. I slip a loop of rope through my silver belay plate and clip through it with a big cara-biner. I'm better than I used to be at abseiling, but the first few backwards steps over the edge still make me nervous. I pay rope

273

through the plate, sink further down, then pad my feet flat on the wall of rock. I step down as I start to run the rope smoothly through the plate.

'Look at the holds!' shouts Garry from below. 'We have to do this. It looks great. This is getting done.'

I abseil past the top chains and past bolt-hangers. I don't really look at the holds, ledges and crimps, make no real attempt to look at them or assess them. Not bothered. My mind hasn't linked the thought that this is a climb with any concept that I might want to climb it. I haven't seen it in the book. I don't know its name.

We won't be climbing it tonight. The dark is drawing in, white cloud swirls above, lower. Ben abs down the rope too, feet on the slab until the bottom five metres where the slab is undercut. Ben dangles above a razor-sharp fin of rock at the bottom, touches it delicately with the tips of his trainers and then steps down it. Garry bounds off and fetches the quickdraw, waving it at us. 'Got it!'

Ben looks at him dead-faced. 'Good. Now, where do we go?'

We are in an awkward place in the quarry. The bit we are on is a trodden strip of path, not really a proper level, but pounded slate dust over scree. We walk along the rough path; we know other people have been here, belaying for the climbs above us, but it is not as accessible as the levels above.

'Let's check out this way,' I say. 'Back towards *Looning the Tube*.' At the end of the path is a steep slab. It looks awkward to cross, blocked in a lump by an unstable-looking stack of blocks.

'What do you reckon, lads? I don't like the look of it.'

The three of us look down into the pit. A tumbling slope of

blocks leads down into Tasmania, right at the bottom.

'Well, lads, I think it's down here, really,' I say. 'The long way is the short way. These blocks do lock together, and they should be stable enough. But you've got to be fucking careful, though. Best just to tread where I tread.'

'Can we get out at the bottom?' asks Ben.

'Yeah,' I say, 'there's a tunnel out.'

'Have you been here before?'

'Not down this slope. But I came here into Tasmania a few years ago with Lee. You want to be careful, though, he nearly got killed. One of the blocks he stepped on started moving and he only just skipped out of the way. Right. Anyway.'

We set off down the slope. I'm looking ahead, trying to pick out a plausible way down. The blocks I step on are big, anything from brick or kerbstone, through to telly or fridge-freezer. Then, some are big cubes, like the white plastic water containers farmers leave in the fields for their cattle. A few are bigger still: car or van. Above it, the cloud sits heavy and dark, and the light is weakening bit by bit.

'Try and spread out a bit.' Garry and Ben are quite close behind me. 'We don't want to bring stuff down on each other.' I feel very responsible for their safety. I want to keep telling them to be careful, like a nagging parent.

'Down here, I think – watch that one; nasty drop down there – watch that one too; don't stand on that.'

Dozens of metres below me, I can see the top of a block, like the roof of a double-decker bus. I know it. It is the Dekophobia block; I was with Lee when we came in to scout it out. If I can get to that level then I know can find my way across the scree. But we have flight after flight of uneven stairs to cross first. The slate is dark charcoal grey, black in places, gloomy and threatening. There is no longer enough light to bring out subtlety of shade, hidden pinks or purples. It is near-dusk, and everything is a blue-tinted monochrome.

Down, around the sides of cubes of slate. Lower myself over a shelf facing over the drop. I should go backwards, like going down a ladder on scaffolding, but I am nervous. I've got a Jaffa Cake bar in my pocket, and as I slide over the rock I feel it being squashed, not by the rock, but by the folds of my trousers as they tighten and pull with the movement of my legs. I wouldn't be able to eat it. I would bite into it and chew, with no spit, turning it into a wadge of plasticine, something to have to break down and gulp dry like paper chunks. The sweet orange would go sour and coat my teeth.

Every movement we are losing height, getting closer to the Dekophobia block, but it is slow. I head right, thinking there might be a nice way down. But it ends in a drop; not much, four or five metres, but not one you would choose to chance. There are voids and gaps between the slate rubble; ankle snapping, and no guarantee of the stability of the landing pad. You might land with enough force to set off an avalanche, tumbling you down amongst the hard and heavy debris, rattling you like a dog's toy and burying you in grinding plates weighing tons.

'Fuck it lads – back along here, I think – be careful, be careful. How are you doing?'

Ben snaps at me, tense. 'I'd be a lot fucking better if *someone* didn't keep telling me I was going to die.'

Garry and I laugh. 'Look,' I say, 'we're nearly there, I think.'

A few paces back, and I see a route that will work. It's not too steep: flat gentle planes snaking between car-sized rock. It isn't the way we want to go; it leads back towards the Oildrum Glacier or the Salt Pan Levels. And nothing feels very friendly. The pit has a mood, like it is annoyed by our clatter down its slopes, deciding whether to lash out at these annoying flies.

But the snaking step path works, bringing us down well to the right of the Dekophobia block.

'We're alright now,' I say. We have come down the slope, and there is very little up and down left to do. We follow across and down, and finally we are onto simpler stepping stones, easy across the bottom of Tasmania, now free to pick our own ways across. I know where I am from this point. I even recognise a rusted drill, octagonal sided and jammed between two rocks, a few feet of shaft prominent. It looks as if you should be able to easily wiggle it out, but I remember last time pulling on it, and it being as solid and immobile as Excaliber. Maybe it is waiting for the last true quarryman.

Garry looks back the way we've come. 'Faaaarrking hell,' he says. 'Look how far we've actually come down. And that's not even really from halfway up the side of Australia.'

Along the floor or rock, then we pick up a little path, which runs below *Looning the Tube*. I don't know how long we've taken to get here, probably not more than twenty minutes or half an hour since we came off the abseil, but it feels like it could have been hours.

'Can relax now,' I say. 'Good adventure, that.' Garry laughs and Ben rolls his eyes. 'Anyway, you'll like this bit. We've got a tunnel here, with a squeeze to get out of the end. It looks blocked but it's not.'

The tunnel mouth is wide and there is a screen of drips through a mossy face. The tunnel is dark, but there is a tiny bit of light back from the entrance that lights up the remaining rail as we walk along. Just in time, I notice a block the size and shape of a synthesiser, and step over it – 'Watch out for the block' – At the end of the tunnel I can see the light of the exit, a few glowing threads. The toppled blocks and the squeeze is familiar, I've done this a few times now. I stand on the ledge, twist and put my head up into the gap, each arm follows then I pull myself out. Into the light. I'm on the hill, the col above Dali's Hole. Out of the crater, the evening is not as dark as I thought. It must be an hour or more until dark, plenty of time to walk back up, get our packs, make our camp and eat.

Garry slithers out. Then Ben. 'I liked that tunnel bit. I like underground things. No, it was good, it was.'

He looks up at the levels above then groans. 'Do we have to go all the way back up there again?'

Garry and I grin evilly at each other. 'Yep.'

CHAPTER 32

Le Grandpère

Mid noughties, Dali's Hole, Australia, Bus Stop Quarry

On holiday in Burgundy, in the South of France, you might pull up at a roadside picnic area, with tables and wasps, below big sheets of limestone. French families would happily sit and eat crusty bread beneath the trees, drinking wine or Orangina, with its funny glass bottle styled like an orange. If they wanted, the whole family could climb. Mother and Father would not have had their climbing lives abruptly halted by childbirth and would now be experts with rope. Grandmother and Grandfather might join in, perhaps inspired by the postwar generation of French climbers like Lionel Terray and Gaston Rebuffat. And the children could be top-roped up easy fully bolted routes, perhaps barefoot to save money on quickly outgrown climbing shoes. If it was good enough for Catherine Destivelle, it was good enough for them.

This was not the British model. In the fifties, sixties and seventies, British climbers were 'hard men', climbing with their rugged-faced mates, despite their missus, disdaining easier climbs and the people unfortunate enough not to have surpassed them by punching their way up harder cliffs.

Colin Goodey was not really of this stamp. He had loved climbing since he was a boy. He was lucky enough to also marry a woman – Sue – who loved both him and climbing equally, a perfectly balanced *menage à trois* with no jealousies.

Goodey also knew the quarries well. As an outdoor activities teacher – one of the first to instruct windsurfing in Wales – he took groups of schoolchildren into the quarries for a walk and a scramble about. His favourite trick was to take a group, lead them down a tunnel and switch off their torches, then tell them ghost stories. The kids would listen intently for the whispers of the dead quarrymen. In his pocket, Goodey would switch on a tape recorder with ghostly voices, then pretend he couldn't hear them.[109]

The short cliffs around Dali's Hole would be perfect. They had a few routes on them up the various crack climbs and corners, a classic of Nick Harms called *Telescopic Stem Master*, the pleasant corner of *Zambesi*, and Cliff Philips' *Holy, Holy, Holy,* which looked as easy, but wasn't. A lot of the walls were too blank for gear, but too featured to make an interesting hard climb.

The great rebolting campaign had started in 2006, so Colin invested in a powerful Bosch hammer drill and started whacking the bolts in, accompanied by various members of his family, particularly his wife Sue, or their daughters, or their daughters' boyfriends. Across the course of a summer, the walls around Dali's Hole were transformed into a low-grade sports climbing venue. Goodey named the climbs in French: *La Grandmère, Le Grandpère, La Gendre, Mon Amie, Le Petit Pois.* Then further along the quarry road he rebolted *Fresh Air,* then new climbs *Tomb Raider* and the more respectfully named *362*, the number a reference to the number of quarrymen killed by accidents.

'I got such flak. "Colin, what are you doing on that bag of shit? It's a total bag of shit. Everything you've done there. Do you think they're going to be popular? No! Do you think anybody's going to go there? No. It's a total bag of shit." And that was coming from a lot of people, but I knew they were wrong.'[110]

But, actually, people loved it. They flocked there, bringing ropes and a handful of quickdraws, eating their lunch in the sun trap, above the cool blue pool and the drowned trees. It became very busy, and the local outdoor activity centres started to bring groups. Dozens of people could be climbing within several hundred metres of rock on any given day, or thirty-five school kids brought by reputable centres with well-qualified instructors.

One day, Colin and Sue walked past the gate. A group of white-haired climbers were hooting with laughter and enjoying themselves. They saw him and shouted. 'There he is! Oi! Come here, you bastard!'

On the easy climbs at Dali's Hole were none other than Joe Brown, Claude Davies, Davy Jones and Morty Smith, some of the original ascensionists in Twll Mawr.

Colin walked over. 'What's all this bullshit with the French names? They should be called *Llechwedd*, something like that!' said Davy Jones.

'Ah,' said Colin. 'It is the French style, a little bit of France in Wales. La Petite France, if you like.' He and Sue stayed to watch some other elite climbers of the fifties and sixties climb their routes. At the end, they all walked out together as a group. Colin hung back, breathless – heart and lung problems – and Joe Brown walked with him, now using walking sticks, slowly up the steep incline.

'Can you even name another crag you can just walk to like this?' asked Joe. 'Bloody Brilliant. But can you put into words why you've done all this, Colin?'

'It's so I've got somewhere to go when I get really old, Joe.

An activity pension.'[111]

The security guard's Land Rover drove by, noting the popularity, the children playing at the top of a cliff above the blue water. Dozens of people.

Colin Goodey did not just climb easy stuff. When he found good lines that might be beyond him, he recruited his 'pedigree friends' to help him with the really hard stuff, like *G'day Arete* or *The Road to Botany Bay*.

Colin's daughter, Cath, found an interesting-looking line. 'Dad, let me show you this line, it is going to be two long pitches of very steep rock, but it will definitely go.' Totally virgin. I said I like that, I like that very much.'[112]

There was a piece of heavy rusty chain bolted into the rock at half height that would do for a good stance; by sneaking along the ledge, he could put in an anchor then drop a rope and show that the bottom pitch could be climbed, that it 'does go'. But, getting to the top of the second pitch – a soaring, slightly leaning arête – was a different matter. His friend, Mark Halliwell, came along and the two worked their way up the shockingly dangerous terrain above, blocks barely held in by piles and slopes of scree. They advanced across, belaying each other on double 9 mm ropes, before working their way to the top of the climb. From there, Colin could fix two bolts and a lower off and they escaped by abseiling. Then they could climb it, on a top-rope, to prove it could be done.

'Mark helped me, but he said, "It's your route, Colin, you've got to climb it."'[113]

Colin was now seventy-two (his route, *Septuagenarian,* was bolted, climbed and named for his seventieth birthday), and the climb was only just within his power, especially at this age and with heart disease, which stiffens the grade of any climb.

Colin tried again and again, but fell off the finger crack at the top. He started to get a bit fitter, stopped having a mid-week pint; in fact, stopping drinking altogether. Lost weight. One day, him and Sue went up and he started to climb.

He went through those lower moves he knew so well. This time the crack, where he'd had the problem before, went like clockwork. As he reached up for a hold at the top, he wanted to get a deep breath, but found he couldn't; his chest was tight.

The next thing he knew he was flying through the air.

Sue shouted up to him, no reply, he sat there on the rope. He couldn't hear her. Gradually he came to, hanging on the rope 15 or 20 feet below the corner. He had a terrible pain in his chest, and he could barely speak. He thought he was going to die.

Sue quickly lowered him to the ground. He was ashen-grey and had obviously just had a heart attack, but he didn't want to go to hospital; the climber in him still wanted to get his quick-draws, get his gear, but Sue said no. 'People know you round here, they can go and fetch them.'

At the hospital, blood tests confirmed Colin had had a heart attack and would need a heart bypass. That was it. If he was having a bypass, he was going to climb that climb. He already knew he would call it *Obsession*.

***

The security guards told their supervisors, the supervisors told the management, who sought advice from their lawyers. The lawyer's advice came back: if someone got hurt they might get sued.

First Hydro started negotiating with the British Mountaineering Council (BMC), who had successfully kept Johnny Redhead and his pals away from the levels just above the power station buildings. They didn't really want to just ban climbing. They couldn't officially allow it either, though, and, as someone pointed out during negotiations, 'Climbers knew the quarries better than First Hydro, and they'd always find a way in.'

Around the same time, First Hydro managed to rent out the quarries as a giant film set, for MGM to shoot the remake of *Clash of the Titans*. Perseus and his oiled Greek warriors wandered up and down the quarry steps, skirmished amongst piles of slate waste while rags soaked in kerosene burned on heaps of scree. The quarries looked properly spooky, though the actors probably preferred shooting the scenes in the Canary Islands.

With the money from the studio, First Hydro could erect a fence, which they were legally compelled to do by the Mines and Quarries Act. The fence would be a whopper, not the simple three-strand wire which stops no one: this was eight feet of white mesh and concreted posts, topped with razor wire. First Hydro also wanted the climbs at Dali's Hole debolted. If the centres didn't bring the minibus-loads of kids, if the locals walking by on the quarry road weren't drawn in for a wild swim among the drowned hut and the skeleton trees in the pond, then they wouldn't try and enforce a climbing ban across the quarries.

It was Ian Lloyd-Jones, Colin Goodey's friend, who told him, 'Col, we've got to sacrifice Dali's Hole, mate, to save the rest.'[114] All the work, bolting, all the 'amazing pleasure' it gave to hundreds of children.[115] The two men abseiled down the routes and debolted them one by one, unscrewing the nuts and removing the little bolt-hangers.

'It was sad. It broke our hearts.'[116]

To get up *Obsession*, Colin got the help of Neil Gresham, who was mates with his son. Gresham was a top climber who was just starting to write training plans for people. The one he did for Colin was beautifully typed and in minute detail.

'Step 1, go to the crag. Step 2, set up a top-rope and do all the moves with a very tight rope. Step 3. Breathing exercises…. Do it five or six times. Have a drink of water. Go home. Do your exercises at home. Then go two days later and do it on a top-rope six times.'[117] Gresham also made Colin do falling exercises. Colin had learned to climb after World War II, an era in which 'the leader must NOT fall'. Even if the rope slings held then the shock of the fall, on an inelastic hemp rope with low shock-absorbing properties, might well have been enough to kill or break a back. Learning that it was safe to fall was incredibly unpleasant, but did wonders for his confidence.

'So I went up there with Mark Halliwell and he said, "Big Day, Colin, Big Day."' And I did it.'

CHAPTER 33

Y Rhaffwr

August 2018, Twll Mawr

The next day is sunny, and warm, completely unlike the evening before. By early afternoon, I've climbed something good that took a lot of psyching up, although in the end it turned out to be one hard move, a long reach jump, dangle, then feet on. My first of that grade: you always want to pick an easy one, just to break the psychological barrier of the number. Ben is still along for the ride, following whatever we want to do. So now it is Garry's turn.

Garry, unbelievably, wants to do that same abseil so he can check the route he saw which he reckons will be amazing. I'd hoped he'd forgotten. I feel a lurch. Garry is impulsive like this; he doesn't read a guide book (he lost his last one and still hasn't replaced it), can never remember the names of what he's done. He climbs very well, but his advice about climbing often doesn't work for me – he is so light and strong, whereas I could never get down to the same weight as him, not while keeping the same strength, anyway.

Back up, past the climbs on the *Sodor* level. We walk past a couple and their friend who are climbing the easy routes, nice and leisurely. They have two dogs with them – golden retriever – just like Goldie off *Blue Peter* when I was a boy. The dogs are well behaved, look up at us as we walk across, but stay lounging next to the couple's bags because they have been told to.

We walk along, find the two access bolts drilled into the rock and rig the abseil. Garry threads our rope through the carabiners and starts to equalise them, puts stopper knots in the end so that even if the rope was too short, we couldn't abseil off the end. He flicks the rope to the edge of the drop, and we realise that one of the retrievers has come to see what we are doing. It follows the end of the purple rope with its nose and starts to look interested. For a horrible second, all of us have the same vision, of the rope flying over the side as the retriever follows its instinct and jumps to chase it and catch it so its owners can kill it and they all can feast on their prey. Which in this case would be nylon.

Before it can, we all shout, 'Whoah! Whoah!' and grab its collar. It looks up at us, its face kind and wise, then turns around and wanders back to its owners. They've also seen the threat and tie it and its pal to some climbing rope, looped around convenient rock. We all laugh nervously. The dog lies down and places its nose between its paws and looks out across the quarry.

We abseil down. Garry starts to climb. There is a knife-blade fin of rock under the start. Until he clips the first bolt, I'm scared for him. He moves steadily – precise, nice and light – up the holds. Garry has never fallen outside, never taken a leader fall. Everything he has ever been on has been easy enough for him to do, or he has shouted 'Take!' and rested on the rope. He has never gone for a move which has turned out to be beyond him. I've fallen a lot, and partly that's because I am less skilled as a climber, so more moves are beyond me. Occasionally, amongst the falls, I find a move that I can do despite myself.

I keep paying out and taking in the rope as he goes on,

slowly picking his way up. I keep my attention on him, watching carefully. My neck hurts. When I can, when I am sure he's not moving, I shake my head and flex it to relieve the pain. Relief for a minute as he clips a bolt.

A moment of stillness up there. I roll my neck and look level. Ben is sat on a rock looking up, meets my gaze. He pulls a face which says 'Fucking hell!', a silent whistle of stress.

I look up again. Garry moves up. He doesn't look certain. He edges out left. It is not what he likes. He steps back again. Chalks up. Steps left. Back. Left, then starts to move tenuously up. Up a bit further. Another move, another. Then he stops. I can see him looking. He tests a handhold just within reach. Doesn't like it. Tests another one. Doesn't like that.

Might be a fall coming. My hand is locking the rope down on the belay-pate. I'm ready for it, ready to lock and jump to absorb the impact.

His voice floats down. 'Gone the wrong way. I'm coming back down.'

'Okay!' I shout up, and as he moves down to the good ledge a metre below, I take the rope back in. He is two-thirds of the way up. Best to keep going if he can.

'Maybe I'm doing this wrong,' he says. He rests. I roll my shoulders, shake my neck.

'Okay. Climbing.' Off he goes again, but this time straight up. Almost immediately, he starts to find holds, a long reach, better feet, straight up. He starts to move more confidently. Within a few breaths he is relaxing into his rhythm, and now there is no doubt, he is climbing steadily and nicely. Soon he is at the chains, shining with delight.

'You two need to do this,' he shouts.

'Nah, mate,' I say. I'm still wired from the anticipation of Garry's not-fall, which he still has not taken. 'I'm alright.'

Ben does though, straight up on a top-rope. 'You should have done that, Pete. You could do that easily, as long as you don't go the wrong way.'

I look at the ground. 'Nah. Not psyched.'

Walking back down the same route right the way down into the bottom of the crater. Yesterday evening, the cloud and fading light made the place feel sinister and hostile to human life. Today the light fills the crater, and the way is obvious. There is no less danger; if you step on the wrong slab it would tilt or roll, or run you over just the same, but it just doesn't feel as bad.

Suddenly, from the far side of the quarry we hear a crash.

'Fuck's that?' asks Garry.

'Dunno. Someone trundling something.'

Another crash: huge like a bin full of beer bottles being emptied from a pub carpark. Trundling means rolling the big blocks of slate over edges to satisfyingly explode below. What if the local youth decided to roll a quarter tonne of waste slate right over your bit of cliff, whirling and bouncing through you and your ropes, scraping and tearing you, smearing you down to the bottom? The climbers used to do it too, bored, bong oil drums down the scree-falls. The tube of *Looning the Tube*, which we can see hanging over the edge of the level above, was smashed off the cliff that way. You can see the punctures and dings of the impacts of lumps of rock.

But it is also a thing of the past. All the days, all the evenings when I've been in here, I've never seen anyone doing it. I've seen groups of lads smoking weed, or teenagers heading for parties, seen the aftermath, the cardboard beer crates. Once, a couple, fucked up on cans, him trying to persuade her to climb over a fence so they could hang out in a nice private part of the quarries. We told him a way just to walk around the fence – he wasn't unfriendly – and as we said goodbye, he suddenly said, 'I fucking love cocaine, me.' A lot of the youths in the villages around are climbers themselves, or the children of climbers, or friends with the children of climbers who they all went to school with. They look below them, and don't chuck stuff off the edge.

Klok-BOsh!

Someone is doing it, though. In the light, it doesn't feel threatening. If this had happened last night, we'd have freaked out. We – I – might have scared ourselves into a mistake, taken the scramble too fast, chanced it over a nasty drop.

I look at Garry and Ben. 'I dunno, man. It's regular. They aren't fucking about; maybe they're working on something. Might even be someone cleaning a new route up.'

BOSHboshKlocklock...

Now we can understand where the crashes are coming from, down near where we are headed to the Tunnel of Love. I walk past a block that looks familiar from the night before, but I can't decide if that's because all the blocks look the same or because I actually recognise them. Can't even tell if we're treading the same route, though soon enough we are past the Dekophobia block. As we get off the blocks and onto the faint scree paths, I see an orange line bouncing down the cliff-wall near the tunnel mouth. A rope. That settles it. You don't carry no fucking rope just to go trundling rocks with your mates.

The climber on the rope is about six metres up, with an orange helmet. As we watch, he levers off a loose plate of slate, with tangles of moss stuck to it. It whirls off and falls below – *BOSHH*.

I start laughing. We walk down close.

'Hello Ian,' I shout. Ian Lloyd-Jones, again. 'I see the retirement's going well.'

'Ah, hello,' he says. 'Yeah. Things have changed. The yacht is up for sale. Anyway, you've got to keep yourself sane, haven't you? So here I am.'

I laugh. He's put up another bolted route: *Oyenstikker*, which is Norwegian for dragonfly. Literally it means 'eye-poker'.

'Just on the day I was climbing it, there were dragonflies around, and one of them came right up to me and looked me in the eye.'

'What will you call this one?'

'Dunno. Something will suggest itself on the day. Hey, by the way, I don't know if you went to see Colin Goodey. Did you know he died?'

'No, I knew he was ill. I thought I would have seen that on UKC.'

'It was on there. Calum Muskett wrote his obituary.'

***

2007–2018, Gogarth; Bus Stop Quarry; East Braich (Australia); Twll Mawr, California; Seamstress Slab

Back in 2007, Ian had just about had enough of being a paraglider pilot. He had just seen someone stall their wing – where the parachute folds up and collapses – and do their back in. He had had hard landings himself. He had young kids.

Round about the same time, one of Ian's mates – Phil

Targett – needed cheering up. He had climbed and new-routed with Ian in the late eighties and early nineties. They went to see Paul McCartney one weekend. Then they formed a loose plan to climb the Old Man of Hoy. They went out to the sea cliffs at Gogarth and did *Lighthouse Arete*, an easy enough climb just below South Stack Lighthouse. It is an easy enough climb, much easier than what they were doing in the preceding fifteen years. A lot of climbers do that one as their first ever sea-cliff climb and, quite often, curious seals pop their dog-like faces out of the water to watch the climbers, and puffins look astonished at the clinking intruders above their burrows.

As soon as they did the route, the old buzz came back for Ian. In a fit of new excitement, Ian found a short line in Bus Stop Quarry, which was tough. He bolted it and named it *Mini Bus Stop*.

'I was proud of it at the time; I'm a bit embarrassed now,' he said. 'People came and climbed it because it was something new. We went out and we bolted a load of short, crap routes. What we really lacked was discernment.'[118]

Ian was born on Anglesey and was a Welsh speaker. When Thatcher came to power, Ian was at comprehensive school, with a classroom window overlooking the Nantlle Ridge. On a school trip to Plas Menai (the National Outdoor Centre for Wales as it would become), Ian was taken to Lion Rock. It is a lump of rock sticking out of the trees at the western end of Llyn Padarn, nice in autumn with the trees turning red and gold, and a bog of leaves underfoot, a few old iron stakes banged in for belays and the odd piton here and there. The ideal venue for school kids to be bounced around like conkers, scaling the rough rock in trainers and PE shoes.

One of the instructors turned to Ian and told him, 'You're good at climbing, you.' The right compliment at the right time. Ian spent a summer saving money, working at a cafe on Anglesey, doling out scoops of ice-cream. He had a choice: spend his savings on climbing gear or a kayak. The climbing gear won. He went to a climbing shop in Caernarfon, bought a Troll harness, a Stubai piton hammer, three carabiners, a sling and a hex.

Now, in 2007, Ian Lloyd Jones was back. After *Mini Bus Stop,* more short shit followed, by Ian's own admission. He found lines, went up and rigged abseils to clean and bolt them. Up and down, removing loose rock and checking the moves. It was hard work, so he stuck to shorter lines.

But a chance encounter in the quarries changed his game. 'Oh, I know you,' another climber said. 'You're the bloke bolting all these micro-routes.'[119]

Micro-routes? *Micro-routes?* The other climber didn't mean anything by it, but to Ian it was a red rag. Micro-routes? He'd show him.

Up on Australia's East Braich there were very few climbs. There were loads on the far side of Australia, lines where people had gone to repeat classics like *Looning the Tube.* But the East Braich was in shadow through the day, and harder to access: you had to climb the long single flight of steps (Llwybr Llwynog in Welsh) that ran up to the arête. To the climbers, always prone to making a meal of things, they do recall the Stairs of Cirith Ungol – treacherous, exposed, endless – and leading to the back door of Mordor. Hence their nerdy name for the steps. In reality, they are even, polished and not bad to walk on.

But compared to the simple stroll onto the col that leads to the *Looning the Tube* Level; yes, it would seem a bit of a faff. That had been enough to put everyone off.

But the rock up here was good. Ian's friend, Colin Goodey, had put up an excellent quality route called *G'day Arete,* a semi-bolted mixture of trad and sport, twenty-six metres long. That was no micro-route! Given the amount of untouched cliff face, there had to be other lines.

There were, and Ian cleaned and bolted good lines, all over twenty metres long. *Hogiau Pen Garret, To Infinity and Beyond!, The Garret Slide.* These routes started to creep up in difficulty, from 6a and 6b to 7a and 7a+. *The Road to Botany Bay, Cirith Ungol, Impact Zone.*

Ian's routes tended to be technical; he was good on a slab where he could stay in balance and use his delicate footwork. Most of the routes would have had no place for gear, but a shiny line of bolts showing the way? Dead safe. These bolts were not the poor quality 8 mm bolts of the 1980s. They were tested lengths of stainless steel, with expansion lugs or polymer resins holding them into the rock, which had been used on the continent for years. There was no chance of them popping out of the crack, or being kicked out by a careless foot – an experience every trad climber has had, which by custom costs them a beer to their mates.

Plus, you didn't have to spend any time hanging one-handed, while finding your nuts on the gear loop, unclipping them, selecting the right size, realising it's the wrong size, fiddling it into the crack, putting the carabiner back (being careful not to ping all your other nuts over the floor below) then reaching out a quickdraw, clipping it in, then cliping in the rope. Take too long on that, and your arm starts to fill with lactic acid, pump out and stiffen like cooking steak. The fall might be coming and you better hope that nut holds, as your nerve starts to go....

On a sport route, you climb up to the bolt, unclip a quick-draw. Click. It's into the bolt-hanger. Then swap hands and click! The rope is into the other end and you're safe. Climb on.

Because of the inherent ease and safety, you can do much harder moves. Rather than trying to climb routes you would never fall on (trad), you could now start to try routes with moves on them that only have a given percentage chance of succeeding. Standards of movement could advance, as Ian buried the insult of 'micro-routes'.

'Most people wouldn't realise how much work goes into these routes,' said Ian.

Rigging the abseil, often scrambling over dodgy scree slopes to find a boulder to drape a sling over. Carrying rope and drill. Abbing down, levering off loose rock, to crash on the floor below, careful not to hit and maybe cut your ropes. Then testing out all the moves, checking the line will 'go', which is Climbese for 'be possible'. Selecting places for the bolts, not too dangerous or awkward to clip, but in solid rock not too close to cracks. Drilling the bolt holes with an SDS hammer drill, as heavy as a chainsaw. Blowing out the rock dust, then resining in the bolts, checking them once the resin has gone off. What a fuck-on. Work, pure work.

Ian's climbs were getting more ambitious. As he abseiled into Twll Mawr, to what would become the classic lines of *Supermassive Black Hole, Black Holes and Revelations,* and *Black Hole Sun*, he felt close to his ancestors.

'In a way, we were doing the same work. They went down with just an iron bar; so did I. They were levering off blocks for roofing slates, I was levering off loose blocks to find good rock underneath, something worth climbing.'[120]

He knew his grandfathers and great-grandfathers had worked in the slate quarries, back and back through generations, fathers bringing their sons into work. Fathers and sons tended to follow the same type of work within the quarries: Ian's ancestors had been expert ropemen.

Ian's grandad, Rheinallt Roberts, had been a *rhaffwr* (ropeman). Roberts' job would have been to abseil, using thick hemp ropes or the rubber hydraulic hoses of drills, onto the rock face. Then lay charges, detonate them, and lever off the blocks of rock for the teams below. More complex work would have involved using systems of ropes to haul heavy steel-wire hawsers into the air to construct aerial skylines. The steel wire systems were called 'Blondins' after the famous tightrope-larking daredevil, Charles Blondin. Small trolleys, or 'cars', would be winched up the skylines, lifting and lowering slate blocks to levels where the railway tracks ran.

Other families had operated the narrow-gauge steam trains, others were splitters, splitting slates, which was one of the most skilled jobs of all. By the twentieth century, apprentices would be expected to take a turn on all the different jobs in the quarry. A face-worker levering off a block would better understand what was needed if he had also split slate, a splitter would better predict the grains of the rock if he had seen the huge hillside-scale swirls of the planes through the rock.

Ian had never been able to ask his grandfather anything about it; Rheinallt Roberts had died with dust-filled lungs when Ian was just nine. He could remember some stories of Roberts being in the Royal Engineers in World War II, using his rope and rigging skills for bridging over canals and rivers in the Allied advance on Germany. But nothing about the quarry work.

'I don't know if they ever worked in Twll Mawr. They would have called it 'Matilda', anyway: that was the quarryman's name for it. But when I went down that rope, I didn't feel like I was alone. It sounds a bit fanciful perhaps, but it felt like they were with me.'[121]

Ian's ancestors had worked the slate for their pay, but he was doing it for his own reasons – to make his mark on the rock – and he was fiercely proud of his routes. 'You beat yourself up about it if people criticise them.'

'You are up and down on the rope, trying all the holds, trying different ways the moves can work. It's just like redpointing,' he said. 'I had my first big breakthrough in climbing when I was redpointing *True Clip*, 7b. Then all those sport routes were more of the same.'[122]

Doing all that redpointing made him a much better climber, prepared to try climbs he never would have looked at before. Ian dropped a rope down an 8a called *Tambourine Man*. He did it, and his reward then was to try *The Medium*, put up by Johnny Dawes. He did it. 'The guide book description says that it is in the realms of fantasy for 99.9% of climbers. I must have walked past that route so many times. Never thought to try it. Now I'd done it, in my forties, with slipped discs, back injuries. If I had done that when I was in my twenties it would have meant sponsorship.'

One evening I am climbing with Garry; the conditions are cool and dry. As we work a thin slabby problem, two other climbers are hard at work within the little bay. They are watched by their dog, a brown and white collie, who I recognise as Medi, Ian Lloyd-Jones' dog.

A top dangles down from the chains. Celt, Ian's son, hauls himself up it, pushing with his feet and sitting into his harness in turn. It takes a bit of knack; I used to do something similar for rope access. Some tree surgeons have a technique called foot-locking where they pinch their ropes between their feet and stand up, then push up a Prusik knot to catch their progress. It looks very cool, but there are gadgets that do the same.

On the rope, Celt looks down to his father for advice. Ian shouts up what to do, rapid Welsh. Although I can't understand the words, their delivery reminds me of my own father telling me how to fell a tree — now do this, but be careful of that.

Ian ties on the big Bosch SDS drill to the tail end of Celt's rope; Celt hauls it up and slings it around his shoulder with a climbing sling. He pokes it onto the face of the rock, and Ian shouts more advice. Celt moves the drill a few inches from the left, angles up the drill so the hole faces slightly down, a marble would roll slowly to the bottom of the hole. The drill makes a grinding sound – *grrrrrrrrrrrrrr* – a hundred hammer blows as the drill twists and the masonry bit hauls itself into the soft rock. It takes barely seconds. Celt re-slings his drill, then clears the dust out of the hole with a damp bottle-brush.

More advice in Welsh, while Celt looks quietly down at his dad, taking it in. Celt hammers in the mirror-shiny steel bolt. The hammer sound rises in tone as the bolt sinks further in: *poak poak-pook pook – peek peek – pik*. He tightens on the bolt-hanger with a spanner and abseils down to the ground.

Then Celt climbs the route, easily and in good style, well within his grade. Medi the collie watches from the ground with total attention, well used to the rest of the pack being up on a rope, and not questioning why dogs can't get up there too.

When they're done, Ian chats for a while.

Celt doesn't say anything, perhaps he is shyer and quieter, but he nods along. Not an unfriendly quiet at all.

He tells me that what they have just bolted is an alternative start to *Operation Zig-Zag*; straightens the route out a bit. I'm not sure that was the point, though. Looks to me like another generation is being shown the skills of a quarryman. Physical skills, a right way and a wrong way. Reading the rock.

When it's time, the father and son walk out together, Medi following.

CHAPTER 34

Slippery People

March 2019, in transit; Serengeti; Australia, Rainbow, Vivian Quarry; Thetford Forest

Another drive over to Wales. Suddenly, just past Leicester and round about ten o'clock, Garry reaches into the back and pulls out a carrier bag of cans.

'Holiday. Want one?'

It is a can of blackcurrant-flavoured cider. Funny how that has become trendy. Years ago, snakebite, or diesel, was just an easy way to fastline alcohol into your bloodstream. The big village boys around Durham drank snakebite in the city – pints and pints of alcohol and sugar – fuel for mayhem. Now, apparently, it is made by artisans.

Ben looks up from his book; he's one of the few people who can read when they're being driven somewhere. 'Yeah. Fuck it, holiday.' He pops a can open with a *tshah*.

Ben and Garry laugh at each other, while I keep my mind on the driving, faster cars weaving round us as lanes and slip roads merge and feed into the greater artery of the M6.

'Here,' says Garry, 'do you want a sip?'

'It's fucking cider. I'm driving.'

'Just literally have a sip,' he says.

The road around us is congested enough, but we are moving at a steady forty-ish miles an hour. I wonder if any of the other drivers would see, and be shocked, perhaps call the police. But then my van is higher than most cars. How often do we really look into other people's cars? Only to confirm that we fancy the head and shoulders with its blonde dyed hair, or get a look at that fucking cock driving like a cunt. Not enough to read the alcohol content on a can being passed to the driver.

'Go on then,' I say, and I take the can and take a small sip. It is delicious. Bubbly. The quantity of alcohol is insignificant, but this still feels like a deeply taboo action. It doesn't taste of cider, it is all blackcurrant, or whatever 'summer berries' it claims on the can. I love it; never liked chocolate that much, but a fruity sweet! Opal fruits or wine gums, juicy and lovely.

I give it back and Garry keeps drinking. I shift lanes to avoid a queue of fast cars slowing to a stopstill before they head off to into Wolverhampton.

'Do you want another sip?' he asks.

'No. I'm alright.' Ben and Garry finish their cans and crumple them up. They don't open another.

'We'll be up on The Balcony,' says Lee.

'Aye, righto. See you there once we've had a play.'

Despite the time of year, it is sunny and breezy. Garry, Ben and I head up through the Serengeti to have a look at Yellow Wall. There are two climbers up there already, starting to climb *The Great Curve*. Slow and steady, they know what they're doing. They try and fit gear in; the leader gets a marginal cam in a weird pocket. Then shrugs and keeps going to the next bolt, steady and unfussed. They do it and make it look easy.

None of these lines are winking at me. Garry likes the look of a line in the middle. Only two bolts, *Slippery People*, one I've heard of but never fancied. Off he sets on this bold route, and we hold our breath as he reaches out for an awkward clip.

Someone else walks up behind us, starts talking to the climbers who have now finished *The Great Curve*; they are mates who haven't seen each other for a while. The new guy has cropped hair, while the other two have let theirs grow out, unstyled, wavy and floppy: typical climber. The skinhead talks and talks and talks. Describes his journey, and work and everything he has been doing, apparently, for months.

As Garry ties into the chains, Ben leans into me and says quietly, 'I know more about this dude's life than my own.'

Just that minute the talky skinhead pulls out a plastic pouch of tobacco and starts to make a roll-up. Ben has been giving up smoking – he has a vape that he has been occasionally tugging on, blowing out bubble-gum flavoured steam – but earlier this morning he ran out of the clear sticky liquid, and now he cannot take his eyes off Talky Skinhead's fingers as they compress hairy threads of brown tobacco into a slim paper-wrapped tube. It doesn't take long to decide that he wants one and is going to ask for one. I remember it myself, from when I was a smoker; the nicotine-hunger overcoming social anxiety and fear of rejection.

'Excuse me, mate, do you think I could bum a roll-up off you?' Talky Skinhead says, 'Of course,' and chats away to Ben, who chats right back and before long is inviting him to our Highball wall if he's ever in the area.

I try *Slippery People*. It's scary, it's thrilling. I like it. The moves are easy enough now that I've seen Garry do it; he had to spend more time figuring out what was possible. Ben doesn't really want to follow up it, but then suddenly says, 'Oh, fuck it then, I will.'

P GOULDING

Ben and Garry in Pete's Eats

The sun shines on us at Yellow Walls and, as I watch Ben climb, is warm on my back. The other lads top-rope *Remain in Light*, an E4 with more bolts in than you would expect. It looks good. Maybe I'll do that and *The Great Curve* another time.

We find Lee and Becky on The Balcony, crunching their way through some low-ish grade sport routes. Becky grins out at us from deep within her hood. The Balcony is a narrow defile that cowboys could easily be ambushed within. It is in shadow; cold and sponges of grass quick underfoot.

'This 6a is worthwhile,' says Lee.

'Are you going to *G'day Arete* area?' Becky asks. 'We'll come.' We walk down together, Becky explaining the finer points of social media accounts and how they get used for marketing. It doesn't sound interesting until she starts explaining the psychology of algorithms, and then it feels like we are living in the future, with robots and AI. Maybe AI already exists, lurking amongst the primordial soup of pornbots and Insta-accounts.

'Anyway, one of the guys from work watched *Free Solo* and he came up to talk to me. He was like, "I've started going bouldering. Do you do that: free climbing?" And I'm like, "*Soloing* – you mean *soloing* – in Britain it's called *soloing*." Trying to explain that.'

I laugh. It's been the same in work. Within a year, soloing will be called free-climbing, and we should be into the Olympics then, anyway.

'Don't get me started on the Olympics,' she says. 'I'll be like, "Don't talk to me, climbing is *my* thing."'

On the *G'Day Arete* Level, the wind is howling, stripping heat out of our bodies. We ferret through our bags for extra coats, cocooning ourselves.

Now Becky and Lee hide with Garry in one of the small huts, while Ben – wrapped in a down jacket – tries to belay me up *G'day Arete*. It's too cold to concentrate well and predictably I fall on the technical bit. I have another go, and fall again. I'm laughing as I dangle on the rope, and as I do the wind blows saliva out of my mouth and over my collar.

'Right, Ben. I think that's enough, don't you?' I roar down to be heard through the wind.

'Only if you're sure,' he shouts back, laughing, already running the rope through the belay plate. I hit the ground with some relief, and we run to the cabin to try and warm up.

'You looked good on that,' says Garry brightly.

I laugh. 'Bit fucking windy, mate.'

Down out of the bitter wind, down Llwybr Llwynog, and onto the col of Australia.

Lee and I stand near to the edge, past the ruined engine hut, looking down into Australia. I look at the tumble of blocks along the edge of the col.

'Oh,' I say, 'I wanted to ask. Where's the access bolt for *Great Bores of Today*?'

'Up here. One of these blocks. Hang on, I'm not sure which one.'

We step from stone to stone, me leading for a change. It doesn't feel hard any more, a fluid pace from ridge to ridge, flat sloping face to a nice foot-sized chip in the top of the rock.

'Somewhere round here,' he says. I look back towards him as I step over the side of one boulder. Below his feet is a bolt-hanger.

'Here it is. Oh, hold on, no,' he says. 'This is the one for *The Mu-mu*. Should be a bit further. There. That's it.'

I look at it and walk to the edge to plan how – one day but not today – I could rig up carabiners and abseil down. You finish the climb yarding up deep shot-holes to the top. There are too many of them for blasting to explain their existence, but maybe it was where the quarrymen had wanted to mount an access ladder. The shot-holes now fill with water and take a long time to dry, sopping and slimy as they are with green sludge. The guide book advice is to abseil down, dry them out finger deep with an old T-shirt, then fuck off and warm up on something else. The shotholes would be dry by the time you got around to it. Lee didn't bother. He climbed it, wiping his fingers on his trousers as he went, like a mechanic wiping grease gobs on his overalls.

'Cool. I fancy that, but not today.'

We look down again into Australia.

'*Dekophobia* block,' he says. 'Do you remember walking down there when it was wet? There's *My Secret Garden*, that's as far as we got.'

Looning the Tube, Gadaffi Duck. Across and above are *Clash of the Titans* and *Plastic Soldiers*. I can see the level where *The Beanstalk* is, and *Rock Yoga, Slatebite, Gorbals, See You Bruce, Slaboholics Anonymous*.

'Do you know,' he says. 'It's only now I'm standing here, I realise I have done some stuff.'

I look up too, at the few climbs I've done. Less than Lee, definitely. Some I did with him, some I did with other people. Others I know that he and Becky did, on one of their weekend trips out of Sheffield. We'd go up to a level and I'd ask about a line, and he'd tell me whether it was good or not, not too much detail so it wouldn't ruin it for me.

Further down the hill are all the climbs on the Rainbow Slab. I haven't done any of them yet. I still haven't done *The Take Over By Department C* yet. Last time I tried it, I fucked it on the last move and Lee said, 'I thought you had it that time,' just before it started to rain.

In Vivian Quarry are a load of climbs; I've never even walked to the bottom of *Comes the Dervish*. I read somewhere that you couldn't call yourself a slatehead until you'd done *Dervish*. Others say it's too polished to be fun. Or that the fingerlocks are bomber and it's soft for E3. Garry tried it and backed off a few metres up. Becky tried in muggy conditions and backed off; as she climbed down she fell, ripping out the gear she had placed. Supposedly it isn't worth placing, but that last piece of machined brass held her fall, just off the ground, saving her ankles or her pelvis.

'What are you going to do next?'

'*The Quarryman* is the next big thing,' he says. 'Might get back on it next year.'

I wonder if he'll tell me when he's going.

The wind still blows bitter through the col. I think I've had enough for today. It's hard to say when you've had enough.

* * *

I pull into the road I live on; it is a horseshoe shape breaking off from the main truck-heavy road that leads ultimately to King's Lynn. I curve around nice and slow, with respect for the families that live on the estate; there are more old people than kids. Some bought their places, some have had the council tenancy so long they may as well have bought them. Some inherited the houses when their parents died and rent them out privately.

I pull my van, with the lads, up onto the kerb. My son opens the door, walks out, wearing tracksuit bottoms and holding a wooden shield I made him out of some planks, and a Nerf gun. The dog runs around his legs and hunches in front of me, his whole body shaking from wagging his tail. Then he runs at Garry, then Ben. He has a lump of blue rope, one of his favourite toys, which he drops in front of us to be thrown so he can catch it. When we don't throw it, he picks it up again with his mouth and drops it again in case we didn't notice. The blue rope is soggy with slobber, and when he pushes it against my trouser leg I can feel its wetness.

Garry and Ben load their gear into Garry's pickup; Garry'll run Ben back up to Norwich. In the next few days, we'll discover all the bits and bobs that have found their way into each other's backpacks, or gear under the seats of my van, and meet up at Highball to swap it all over, ready for the next trip. I wave them goodbye as Garry peels out, then reverse my van into its normal spot, where it sits quietly.

I grab a couple of my bags and ferry them in – 'Out the way, Ned!' – and dump them on the sofa, a red leather one with its springs gone that one of my mother-in-law's best friends donated.

Tanya is in the garden, and I shout does she want a cup of tea? Fill the kettle and put it on the hob. The kettle was an old camping one. When we moved here, we didn't happen to have an electric kettle, so we just used this one, and there seems no point in replacing it.

Tanya walks in; her fingers are soil-covered from weeding in the garden.

'Is that it?' she asks. 'Are you home now?'

'Yes,' I say, and for the moment, I am. For the moment, there is nothing else I want to do, no ticklist of climbs or projects. Maybe the hunger for movement and slate will be back, but right now, there is nothing.

* * *

Sea cliffs? I've never thought about sea cliffs before....

Endnotes

[1] Stevie Haston, 'The World of Stevie Haston: The Way of the Dervish' (15 June, 2010). Accessed online at ukclimbing.com, http://www. ukclimbing.com/articles/page. php?id=2799, 21 January, 2019.

[2] Telephone interview with Paul Trower, from notes, August 2016.

[3] Haston, 'The Way of the Dervish'.

[4] Ibid.

[5] Ibid.

[6] Letter from E Penman, 9 August, 2016.

[7] Penman, letter.

[8] Simon Panton, route description, in Simon John Panton, Pete Robins, Mark Dicken and Martin Crook (eds), *Llanberis Slate* (Ground Up Productions, 2011), 304.

[9] Panton, *Llanberis Slate*.

[10] Letter from E Penman, 9 August, 2016.

[11] Email from John Cleare, 20 July, 2016.

[12] Telephone interview with Paul Trower, from notes, August 2016.

[13] Interview with Claude Davies, 13 April, 2016.

[14] CE Davies, 'Always a Little Further', *Climbers' Club Journal* 20 (1970–71). Accessed online at http://www.climbers-club.co.uk/journal/ original/1970-1%20Journal_nc.pdf.

[15] Davies, 'Always a Little Further'.

[16] Ibid.

[17] Jack Geldard, Mark Reeves and Mark Glaister, *North Wales Climbs: Rockfax Rock Climbing Guide Book* (Rockfax, 2013), 67.

[18] Email from Andy Newton, 14 July, 2016.

[19] Interview with Martin Crook, from recording, 1 July, 2016.

[20] Trevor Jones and Geoff Milburn, *Welsh Rock: One Hundred Years of Climbing in North Wales* (Pic Publications, 1986), 271–272.

[21] Interview with Martin Crook, from recording, 1 July, 2016.

[22] Interview with Andy Newton, from recording, 30 June, 2016.

[23] Potatohead not forbidden!

[24] Crook, interview.

[25] Crook, interview.

[26] Ibid.

[27] Ibid.

[28] Ibid.

[29] Ibid.

[30] Interview with Mike Raine, from notes, 9 May, 2016.

[31] Newton, interview.

[32] Newton, interview.

[33] John Redhead, *...and One for the Crow: Words and Images of Ascent* (Serious Clowning Publications, 1996), 9.

[34] Email from John Silvester, 10 June, 2016.

[35] Silvester, email.

[36] Redhead, *...and One for the Crow*, 122.

[37] Redhead, *...and One for the Crow*, 124.

[38] Newton, interview.

[39] Newton, Interview.

[40] Redhead, *...and One for the Crow*, 16.

[41] Redhead, *...and One for the Crow*, 20.

[42] Ibid, 20.

[43] Ibid, 32–35.

[44] Silvester, email.

[45] Martin Crook, 'Diary of a Slatehead', in *Llanberis Slate*, 199.

[46] Redhead, *...and One for the Crow*, 30.

[47] British Pathé, 'Slate Quarry' (1962). Accessed online at https://www.britishpathe.com/video/slate-quarry-beware-other-colour-pics-share-this-1/query/Slate+Quarry, 14 November, 2018.

[48] British Pathé, 'Workless on the March' (1958). Accessed online at https://www.britishpathe.com/video/workless-on-the-march/query/Workless+on+the+March, 15 November, 2018.

[49] Panton and others, *Llanberis Slate*, 363.

[50] Raine, interview.

[51] Panton and others, *Llanberis Slate*, 216.

[52] Email from Steven Haston, 21 March, 2016.

[53] Paul Pritchard, *Deep Play: A Climber's Odyssey from Llanberis to the Big Walls* (Vertebrate Publishing, 2012).

[54] Email from Nick Harms, 11 June, 2016.

[55] Harms, email.

[56] Ibid.

[57] British Pathé. 'Slate Quarry' (1962). Accessed online at https://www.britishpathe.com/video/slate-quarry-beware-other- colour-pics-share-this, 14 November, 2018.

[58] R Merfyn Jones, *The North Wales Quarrymen 1874–1922* (University of Wales Press, 1982), 57–58.

[59] Jones, *The North Wales Quarrymen*, 59.

[60] Jones, *The North Wales Quarrymen*, 59–60.

[61] Jones, *The North Wales Quarrymen*, 57.

[62] Nick Harms, email, 11 June, 2016.

[63] Harms, email.

[64] Ibid.

[65] Johnny Dawes, *Full of Myself* (Johnny Dawes Books, 2011), 33.

[66] Telephone interview with Andy Newton, from notes, 24 May, 2016.

[67] Dawes, *Full of Myself*, 104.

[68] Dawes, *Full of Myself*, 105.

[69] Telephone interview with Bobby Drury, from notes, on or around 22 October, 2016.

[70] Dawes, *Full of Myself*, 149. The ascent of *Indian Face* is one of UK climbing's most important stories. However, it doesn't take place on the slate, so you'll have to read up on it yourself.

[71] Dawes, *Full of Myself*, 149.

[72] Andy Cave, *Learning to Breathe* (Arrow, 2006), 101.

[73] Dawes, *Full of Myself*, 32.

[74] Dawes, *Full of Myself*, 139.

[75] Johnny Dawes speaking on Adam Hocking, 'Hardest Slate Rock Climb in the World', YouTube, 25 August, 2015. Accessed online at https://www.youtube.com/watch?v=4KQFQXrMmwM, 1 July, 2019.

[76] Hocking, 'Hardest Slate Rock Climb in the World'.

[77] Dawes, *Full of Myself*, 139–40.

[78] Drury, interview, 28 July, 2019.

[79] Drury, interview.

[80] Ibid.

[81] Ibid.

[82] Ibid.

[83] Joe Brown, *The Hard Years: His Autobiography* (Victor Gollancz, 1967).

[84] Paul Pritchard, 'Slateheads, Rubble Merchants and Others', in *Deep Play*, 37 This chapter is the perfect account of the Llanberis scene, with namechecks of anyone who was anyone, if you can work out the nicknames.

[85] Email from Nick Dixon, 11 January, 2017.

[86] Email from John Silvester, 5 June, 2016.

[87] Alun Hughes, 'Birdman of the Karakoram'. Accessed online at https://vimeo.com/7289196, 13 December, 2019.

[88] Interview with Andy Newton, 30 June, 2016.

[89] Harms, interview.

[90] Redhead, *...and One for the Crow*, 84.

[91] Redhead, *...and One for the Crow*, 84.

[92] Redhead, *...and One for the Crow*, 85.

[93] David BA Jones, *The Power of Climbing* (Vision Poster Co, 1991), 174.

[94] Interview with Pete Robins, from notes, 13 May, 2016.

[95] Interview with Pete Robins, from notes, 13 May, 2016.

[96] Ibid.

[97] Hocking, 'Hardest Slate Rock Climb in the World'.

[98] Phrase used in Redhead, *...and One for the Crow*.

[99] Interview with James McHaffie, 6 May, 2017.

[100] McHaffie, interview.

[101] Ibid.

[102] Panton and others, *Llanberis Slate*.

[103] Bob Drury, interview.

[104] Bob Drury, interview.

[105] Martin Crook, interview.

[106] Interview with Andy Newton, from notes, 24 April, 2016.

[107] Interview with Andy Newton, 30 June, 2016.

[108] Interview with Andy Newton, 30 June, 2016.

[109] Calum Muskett, 'North Wales Pioneer Colin Goodey Passes Away', UK Climbing, 6 March, 2018. Accessed online at www.ukclimbing.com/news/2018/03/north_wales_pioneer_colin_goodey_passes_away-71504, 8 August, 2019.

[110] Interview with Colin Goodey, 19 May, 2016.

[111] Goodey, interview.

[112] Ibid.

[113] Ibid.

[114] Ibid.

[115] Sue Goodey, interjection during Colin Goodey interview, 19 May, 2016.

[116] Colin Goodey, interview.

[117] Colin Goodey, interview.

[118] Interview with Ian Lloyd-Jones, from notes, 17 April, 2016..

[119] Lloyd-Jones, interview.

[120] Ibid.

[121] Ibid.

[122] Lloyd-Jones, interview.

Climbing Terms

Put up a climb
To make the first ascent of a climb and name it.

Hand-jamming
Technique of fitting your hand into a crack then clenching it so it wedges in place. Brutal and painful to learn.

Protection, Pro, Gear
Metalwork placed into cracks or fissures in the rock as you climb. A rope can then be clipped to it with a carabiner; if you should fall, this would catch the rope so you wouldn't fall all the way to the ground.

E-grade
A climbing grade used in trad climbing, 'E' standing for 'Extreme'. The number following, eg E1, E5 etc, indicates how extreme it actually is.

Stance
A place for a belayer to be able to stand while they belay. Halfway up a climb, this might mean using a ledge and simultaneously hanging from gear or protection wedged into the rock.

Chains
Permanently placed chains at the top of a climb, which climbers can use to thread and lower themselves ('lower off') to the ground.

Cleaning a line
Abseiling down a prospective route and removing loose and dangerous rock, vegetation, mud etc. Also may involve testing some of the holds or moves to see whether the climb is at all possible.

Bolt
Permanently placed bolt, drilled into the rock. Replaces hand-placed protection in sport climbing. In the slate quarries, augments hand-placed protection where none is available and still classed as trad climbing.

Bolt-hanger

Metal eye attached to a bolt through which a quickdraw can be placed to provide protection.

Trad, Trad Climbing

Climbing where protection, eg nuts, cams, are hand-placed by the leading climber and removed by the second climber. On slate, occasional bolts would still be acceptable on a trad route if there was no hand-placeable protection.

Sport, Sport Climbing

Climbing where protection is provided by regularly placed bolts. Much safer than trad.

Run out

Where the climber has to climb far above their protection before reaching the next protection. Can be more-or-less dangerous – is usually deeply frightening.

Quickdraw

Two carabiners linked by a short length of fabric sling, used to connect rope to protection.

Rope Access

Category of work where a technician uses abseiling and rope techniques to carry out work; everything from window cleaning to windmill repair.

GriGri

Specific model of mechanical device used to belay and abseil on.

HVS, Hard Very Severe

Climbing grade for trad climbing, one below the start of the E grades.

Redpointing

Repeatedly practising or trying a route before ultimately climbing it 'clean', ie in one go, without any falls or without hanging on to the rope.

Bibliography and Further Reading

Books and Texts in Print

Paul Pritchard, *Deep Play: A Climber's Odyssey from Llanberis to the Big Walls* (Baton Wicks Publications, 1997).
Paul suffered a serious brain injury in Tasmania. His story of that and his fight against it are told in *The Totem Pole* and *The Longest Climb*, both well worth tracking down.

John Redhead, *...and One for the Crow: Words and Images of Ascent* (Serious Clowning Publications, 1996).
Hard to find outside climbing shops; at the time of writing V12 in Llanberis still had a copy or two. Totally original, highly inspiring and not for the faint hearted.

Johnny Dawes, *Full of Myself* (Johnny Dawes Books, 2011).
Charming and beautiful book from the greatest movement technician of all time.

Simon John Panton, Pete Robins, Mark Dicken and Martin Crook (eds), *Llanberis Slate* (Ground Up Productions, 2011).
This guide book is currently out of print, but well worth tracking down for Martin Crook's 'Diary of a Slatehead' passages.

Paul Williams, *Llanberis* [Climbers' Club Guide to Wales series] (The Climbers' Club, 1987).
Out of date, out of print, but with a tremendous introduction to the vocabulary and culture of climbing on slate, from a much-missed giant of the scene.

John Cleare and Tony Smythe, *Rock Climbers in Action in Snowdonia* (Mountain Camera, 2016).
Recently reprinted classic, excellent descriptions of the sixties climbing scene, although, except for one picture, little about slate.

Joe Brown, *The Hard Years: His Autobiography* (Victor Gollancz, 1967).

Simon Thompson, *Unjustifiable Risk? The Story of British Climbing* (Cicerone, 2012).

Mark Reeves, Jack Geldard and Mark Glaister, *North Wales Climbs: Rockfax Rock Climbing Guidebook* (Rockfax, 2013).

R Merfyn Jones, *The North Wales Quarrymen 1874–1922* (University of Wales Press, 1982).

David BA Jones, *The Power of Climbing* (Vision Poster Co, 1991).

Jerry Moffatt and Niall Grimes, *Revelations* (Vertebrate, 2009).

Trevor Jones and Geoff Milburn, *Welsh Rock: One Hundred Years of Climbing in North Wales* (Pic Publications, 1986).

Andy Cave, *Learning to Breathe* (Arrow, 2006).

CE Davies, 'Always a Little Further', *Climbers' Club Journal,* 20 (1970–71).

M John Harrison, *Climbers* (Gollancz, 1989).
This novel does not have much about the slate in it. However, as a (fictionalised) account of climbers in the eighties, it is close to unbeatable, a true cult classic.

Films

Adam Hocking, 'Hardest Slate Rock Climb in the World', https://www.youtube.com/watch?v=4KQFQXrMmwM.

British Pathé, 'Slate Quarry' (1962) at https://www.britishpathe.com/video/slate-quarry-beware-other-colour-pics-share-this-1/query/Slate+Quarry.
Not to be confused with the similarly titled film from 1964 which features the workers in the Penrhyn quarry a few miles away.

British Pathé, 'Workless on the March' (1958) at https://www.britishpathe.com/video/workless-on-the-march/query/Workless+on+the+March.

Online Sources

steviehaston.blogspot.com is well worth a look. Stevie also published a series of articles about his life and climbing on the UKC site (ukclimbing/com). Particularly valuable for this book were 'The World of Stevie Haston: The Way of the Dervish' at https://www.ukclimbing.com/articles/features/stevie_haston_the_way_of_the_dervish-2799 and 'The World of Stevie Haston: The Education of a Mountaineer' at https://www.ukclimbing.com/articles/features/stevie_haston_the_education_of_a_mountaineer-2665.

Calum Muskett (2018), 'North Wales Pioneer Colin Goodey Passes Away' at https://www.ukclimbing.com/news/2018/03/north_wales_pioneer_colin_goodey_passes_away-71504.

Quarry Names

The quarrymen gave the original names to the various areas, sinks and walls that they worked on. There is a huge mismatch between the names given by those who came afterwards: the young – predominantly English – climbers. Often, the latter made up their own, relating areas to the physical features they found there, such as Rainbow Slab, or to the name of prominent climbs within those areas.

There follows a partial list of the original quarrymen's names and their climber-given equivalent, derived from the *Llanberis Slate* guide book referenced above and with rough translations of the Welsh-language terms. For example, 'ponc' refers to the levels or platforms the quarrymen worked from, and many of the original names for other areas are drawn from either geographical features or family members. The National Slate Museum, situated near Vivian Quarry, is a must for anyone interested in the history of the quarries when they were working.

Within the quarries, the original names of the areas given by the workers should not be lost. Equally, the names given by the climbers should not be forgotten. The two cultures are rich, humourful, poetic and, I hope, complementary:

Ponc Allt Ddu (black hill level) – Bus Stop Quarry (inspired by an obvious bus stop).

Sinc Harriet (Harriet's sink) – Dali's Hole (derives from the blue colour of the water and the shapes of the flooded, now-dead trees).

Sinc Galed (hard sink) – California (the name was misapplied to the wrong place by climbers).

Ponc Morgan (Morgan's level) – Serengeti (reminiscent of a large flat plain in Africa).

Dyffryn (valley) – Never Never Land (refers to an early climb in that area).

Adwy Califfornia (California gap) – Watford Gap.

Garret (boy's name) – Australia (the name was misapplied to a single small area within the Garret working).

Ponc Tophet (level named after 'tophet', the biblical name for hell) – Skyline Level (a prominent slab of rock silhouetted against the skyline).

Llwybr Llwynog (fox path) – Steps of Cirith Ungol.

Ponc Penrhydd – Looning the Tube Level (level named after a prominent climb).

Ponc Awstralia – Far Out Level (the Welsh name is the origin of the error of Australia for Garret).

Ponc Teiliwr (level named after a 'teiliwr': tailor) – G'day Arete Level.

Ponciau Califfornia – Rainbow Walls (the walls around Rainbow Slab, named for its prominent ripple feature).

Index

Acknowledgements

No book gets written by just one person.

I would like to thank anyone who I interviewed, who replied to an email, provided a contact or otherwise helped with research. Some interviews never happened but, nonetheless, thanks for any reply to my cheeky requests. Stevie Haston, John Redhead, Martin Crook, Andy Newton, Mike Raine, Ray Kay, Nick Harms, John Silvester, Nick Dixon, Bob Drury, Eric Penman and Martin Bennet, Ian Lloyd-Jones, Colin and Sue Goodey, Mark Dicken, Pete and Rachael Robins, James McHaffie, Johnny Dawes, Paul Pritchard, Claude Davies.

Thanks to the quarrymen and the people of Llanberis and surrounding villages. I always love it when I'm there.

Thanks to anyone who read, edited, workshopped or otherwise helped kick this into shape. Helen Smith, Kathryn Hughes, Ian Thomson and Jean MacNeil. Justus, Kinga, Aaron Deary, Suresh, Saloni, Peiyi, Judith, Ingrid, Romana, Freya, Susan, Ivan, Lorna. Particularly Jess Morgan, Aaron O'Farrell, Kate Romaine and Yin Lim. James Parry for advice. Anyone else who helped.

Thanks to anyone I've climbed with on the slate. Lee Mitchell and Becky Inch. Garry Smith, Ben Hiscoke. Sam Brown, James Boston, Rob Barker, Steve Gaines – sadly missed, Violeta Krakowska (sorry you aren't in this book more: you do deserve to be), Tom Jones, Darryl Hinchly. Adam Fearn, Alex Cutts. Hasier Otaduy, Santi Gonzalez, Alex Marin, John Ives, Magnus Silverwood. There are many more – I'm a promiscuous climbing partner and I've been on the end of a rope with loads of you – thanks for the good times; none of them were bad.

Thanks very much to Freya Dean and Andrew Kendrick at

Hinterland for first running and paying for 'Hogiau Pen Garret', allowing me to use it as the basis for one of the chapters of this book, and for the more personal level of encouragement and support. Thanks also to *Cardiff Review* for publishing another early section as 'Supermassive Black Hole', and to *New Welsh Reader* (121, autumn 2019) for publishing 'Never Never Land'.

Thanks to the Society of Authors, particularly Kate Pool, for essential advice.

Thanks to Ray Wood for cover and interior photos, and to John Cleare for his interior photo.

Thanks to all at *New Welsh Review*, especially Gwen Davies for co-judging the prize, editing, some translation and production, Harri Roberts for proofreading and indexing and an eagle-eye, Rebecca Ingleby Davies for the eighties-inspired cover design and colourscheme; also to Julia Forster at *New Welsh Review* for marketing and promotion, and to Cynan Jones and Richard Powell for co-judging and finance, respectively. Thanks to all at New Welsh Rarebyte for making this into an Actual Book. Also to Roz Dineen at the *Times Literary Supplement* for publishing a preview extract. And to Cathryn Summerhayes, Helen Mort and James (Caff) McHaffie for their enthusiasm and endorsements.

Thanks to my mum, Anna, Phil and Alison Hardy.

Lastly, thanks to Tanya and Ellis for constant support.

I hope I haven't missed anyone. If I have, thank you very much, even if you are not named here. Mistakes are my own.

Protect the rock, be honest about what you've done and how you've done it.

Author Biography

Peter Goulding is a climber and writer from the north of England. He was born in Liverpool in 1978, lived in County Durham for years, and currently lives with his partner and son in rural Norfolk. He works at Center Parcs as an instructor, and goes climbing to north Wales and the Peak District as often as he can.

In 2019, he won the New Welsh Writing Awards: Rheidol Prize for Writing with a Welsh Theme or Setting.

Praise for Slatehead

'Peter Goulding's witty, razor-sharp prose captures both the futility and the all-consuming nature of climbing: "No-one cares whether I get up these rock faces or not. It won't repair a relationship or bring the dead back to life." And yet each route remains utterly compelling. *Slatehead* is an absorbing, wide-ranging account of a love affair with rock, how it becomes a mirror for the self, how – in the end – we love this sport because "climbing forces honesty".'

> *Helen Mort*

'Good and clear and honest. Like the climbers it presents, the story is careful and risk-taking, ambitious and humble. These are the things of great writing.'

> *Cynan Jones*

'Peter Goulding gives a personal account of falling in love with the north Wales slate quarries, immersing himself in the climbs and the history... As well as the climbing scene, Peter has done a great job of looking into the life and hazards of the quarrymen themselves, their past times and some of the histories of the conflicts between the communities and the clueless aristocratic quarry owners who cared little for the health of employees... An intriguing read.'

> *James (Caff) McHaffie*

'Peter has introduced his readers to a cast of wonderful characters who immediately challenge the average person's misconception about young, unemployed, working-class men struggling in Thatcher's vision of Britain in the nineteen-eighties. Their addiction to ever more dangerous climbs was both thrilling and terrifying, and each challenge on rocks with higher heights and weirder names felt like another twist in a literary thriller.

The way these men viewed the slate with such reverence, as if they were about to climb the Crown Jewels was both humbling and exciting. Peter made me want to look at the rocks near my Welsh homeland with a new reverence.

These young men, often assumed to be trouble, would sit patiently in cafes, in cars, at the side of a rockface and just wait and wait, for the rain to pass, for the slate to dry, for the conditions to be just right. In a world of tech and instant gratification, their stoic acceptance – that some days they just wouldn't be able to take one step – was really emotional and almost romantic. These men, who could hardly scrape the money towards a hot breakfast at Pete's Eats, worshipped the slate so much and appreciated the skill of another climber so passionately that they would share pork pies, lend expensive new climbing shoes and belay for another climber for hours, when, really, they must have been desperate to be trying to find a new climb for themselves.

I laughed out loud at the in-jokes, the rebellious nature of the climbers – who ignored safety warnings, barriers, shouting security staff – in their quest for the new climb and the honour of naming it. And what names! Each new one pushing the boundaries of language and decency... with so many secrets beneath the words, showing the intelligence and poetic nature of these men, thrown on the scrapheap of unemployment but seeking a release for their creativity in the rocks.

[This is] not just a tale of men climbing, it [is] a critique of the eighties that [feels] almost like a group rock and roll music autobiography. In their own small world of slate, these men were heroes – and this heroism, however unacknowledged in the wider world, stopped them from becoming layabouts, drunks, no hopers. Of all the men Peter writes about, the majority went on to have successful careers because of the rocks: in climbing, teaching, art. The slate saved them, and Peter illustrates just how important a thing that is, by allowing the slate to be a character in the boys' story. No slate, no climbs, no life.

If only [contemporary] recordings [had been] made… of these young men on their climbs. [This story is] ripe for a documentary, perhaps a 'Where are They Now' [format]. I would certainly want to watch it. And I definitely want to slip up the back streets near Snowdon and take a look at those rocks for myself – see the bolts, see the shadows of those men whose lives were changed by the simplicity of a sheer rockface.'

Cathryn Summerhayes (Curtis Brown literary agency), writing about 'On Slate', the sections of this book that won the New Welsh Writing Awards 2019: Rheidol Prize for Writing with a Welsh Theme or Setting.

Thank You to our
#SecureNewWelshReview Supporters